NUCLEAR IMPACT

Broken Atoms in Our Hands

An Anthology of Poetry

Edited by Teresa Mei Chuc

Nuclear Impact: Broken Atoms in Our Hands

Library of Congress Control Number: 2016944000

ISBN: 978-0-9915772-4-8

Front cover art: "On the Road to Perilous" by John Sokol
Back cover art: "Boreas" by John Sokol
Interior layout/design by Jason Orr

Published by Shabda Press
Pasadena, CA 91107
www.shabdapress.com

dedicated to the victims
of nuclear disasters and warfare
and to Mother Earth
and all of her creatures we must protect

Table of Contents

Introduction

In *Nuclear Impact: Broken Atoms in Our Hands* is the symphonic voices of 163 poets living throughout the United States and world, in places such as India, Britain, Ireland, Canada, Philippines, Japan, South Africa, Guam, Singapore, Poland, Australia, France, Vietnam, Dubai in the United Arab Emirates, Germany, China and Pakistan, on the impact of nuclear power and warfare on human life and the planet. Navajo poet Hershman R. John's poem, "Theory of Light," opens the anthology. Towards the end of Hershman's beautiful and heart-breaking poem, he writes "The sun's core/ is made from turquoise and the moon's mass is made from radiant white shell/lighting the metallic half-life in susurrations across/the Navajo-Hopi reservations." The poems in the anthology take us through Navajo-Hopi reservations, the Nevada desert, Los Alamos, Hiroshima & Nagasaki, Three Mile Island, Trinity, air raid drills, Chernobyl, Pripyat, Ogoturuk Valley, Alaska, Fukushima, nuclear testing in India and Pakistan, and more. In the poems, we experience the legacy of nuclear power created by human hands and its effects on human life and all life on Mother Earth. In the second to the last poem in the anthology, Vivian Faith Prescott, a fifth generation Alaskan of Sámi heritage, reveals nuclear impact in the tundra, the Chuckchi Sea and villages, in her brilliant and chilling poems, "Project Chariot" and "Recipe for Disaster at Ogotoruk Valley." Through the words and clarity of these poets, we see the reach of nuclear impact from the desert to the far reaches of the Artic.

Pablo Neruda's poem, "Ode to the Atom," in William Pitt Root's translation, begins, "Infinitesimal/star within/uranium,/you appeared/to be interred/ forever: concealed,/your diabolical/fire./Then one day/loud knocking/at the tiny/door:/it was man." The poems in the anthology remind us of what we have unleashed in the atom and our responsibility to all life on this planet.

Teresa Mei Chuc, editor

1

HERSHMAN R. JOHN

Theory of Light

OFF – ON

A switch
illuminates Einstein's
three pages of thoughts
like a camera bulb flash-blink
capturing silhouettes,
and ignites God
as pure

Energy.

Tiny flecks of waves
speed across time, across
the night sky like a lovers' meteor shower,
across the desert, over our
hogan, across my
cornea.

Christ's star: a super nova
sings, burning bright for days like rays
from a candle enticing bats or wise men. Navajos saw
this too when the flames in the sky began—
it was Coyote placing *his*

last star, a reminder known as *Mą'ii bi so'*.

3

Mass can become energy:
for a second faster than time,
in front of an old trading post, Einstein's
soul becomes a frozen static charge, the sparks
seen in an eye-dazzler rug. The photograph's soft colors
show him wearing a warbonnet slick with feathers,
pure and thick, thick as an angel's
wing. The outline of his teeth's bright magnitude reaches
out across history as a laugh or a quasar. Smiles
all around him, a group from Moenkopi's
cliffs. The Hopi corn maidens
are dressed in woven rug

dresses,
their hair tightly wound
spiral galaxies on each side of their heads,
a sign of fertility. Einstein admires the green cornfields
and the maiden's pacifist and pure ways of grinding blue corn into fine meal,
all day long, then into paper-thin piki bread. *Untouched,*
war can't ever be made from good food.
His white mustache moves and looks
Like a fish's
skeleton.

Behind the trading post, unseen on
the dirt, in the umbra cover of the sun, is a Navajo man
drunk, grasping an empty whisky bottle.

One Hopi grandmother knows Albert
Einstein as a famous man, rather than just another white
tourist as the other corn maidens see.
As a mother of twelve, she shares his vision.
He knows something about a star's souls and its hopes
and she thinks of the coming

Equinox tonight—"The Moon Kachina comes, big as a ripe watermelon."

Moonlight
comes from the piece of white shell
First Woman placed in the sky one winter night.
Even Navajos knew then that the energy and mass of stones
could power the whole sky—a long time ago,
First Man placed a piece of turquoise
in the sky; its small mass became
our sun.

A burning, burning ball of hydrogen-helium.

It burns to grow corn, melons,
beans, and squash. It burns to grow fusion
and nuclear reactors. The Navajos mined raw uranium
for the White man for years and years, with bare hands. They ate
their cold frybread and greasy mutton salted with shiny tailings. They went
home like bees covered in a thin pollen. Their sheep drank from
radiated mine wells. The grandmothers butchered and
roasted more mutton for their working men and
hungry grandchildren. In Los
Alamos, a Zuni family

grinds winter corn for tortillas
and watches the volcanic smoke rise thick in the horizon—
deadly fumes hot from Nagasaki. They see the Hopi Butterfly Maidens
on Bikini Island; a drunk Navajo who, once a miner,
is now dying from radiation

poisoning. Coughing up blood, pain
in the joints, losing vision, an eclipse. The sun's core
is made from turquoise and the moon's mass is made from radiant white shell
lighting the metallic half-life in susurrations across
the Navajo-Hopi reservations.

It all ends—

In one pryroclastic flower engulfing clouds and light.

* Translation of Navajo words: Mą'ii (Coyote), bí so' (his star); so the
Coyote's star

KAREN WARINSKY

History Lesson

Grey rocks like so many igneous prairie dogs
interfered with good skiing,
obstacles on the hoary ground.

Trudging sideways up the Japanese mountain
I hoped for another run, falling, falling,
hurting each time, hefting up on metal poles,
phoenix in a nylon jacket.

Through damp mist he saw me; offered help,
a middle-aged man in simple clothes,
puzzled at an American girl in his country.

Patient guardian, this Kendatsuba tried to teach,
shook his head and laughed,
amused by our unlikely companionship.
Later, standing close as the clouded sun dissolved into dusk
he pulled off his gloves.
Matchstick scars revealed—dozens—
raised on the backs of both hands,
a crisscrossed affliction.

The Blast.
The Cloud.
Ten miles from his home.
He was five, standing at the window as glass shattered,
and smattered over his body.
And it was many years past Hiroshima,
but I had no words, only my hand
touching his for a moment.

KAREN WARINSKY

Hiroshima Shadow

We will not "repeat the error"
the cenotaph says,
but it seems we only repeat the errors of war
unable to find our way to another path.

Decade upon decade, demand upon demand,
no one backs down, no one finds a new way,
and even the shadow of the man from Hiroshima
blazed into cement steps
is not enough
to move all hearts to peace.

ELIZABYTH HISCOX

The Pedestal

In hindsight this could be when it started
Stumbling: smile. Embarrassed late October jog.

Patient has no family history of this kind of problem
She is a rebel in this illness business.

MRIs done in 96 and 97 and the doctors found no lesions did not think
Remember? Whirl of light there just beyond your face.

Bowels are also wrapped in muscle that can become weak
A shitting-yourself, shitting-others future.

Some relief can be achieved with tilting of the chair or bed
The mind is working, skin is trying-on slow sores.

The purpose of the transfer board is to take the weight off the caregivers
The heart's real purpose: pump the weight of life. Of

A therapist must come to the home for an appropriate assessment
A stranger walks past nodding Iris planted deep
those purple blooms, from Kim's third birthday, underfoot.
A stranger walks where you have kneeled and felt the earth.

This ankle is more frozen than the other side
That ice that took the legs is sheltering still, here.

One could be pushed into low levels of oxygen in the blood
Already one's been pushed past all of it, come back.

Some is genetics, some isn't, some is genetic predisposition
So there is daughter one. There's two. Say promise, time.

Patient born at White Sands New Mexico
They said to finish families up before arrival.
On base, in that New Mexico you cried your birth.

Is this your daughter? It's good in times like these to have had kids.
This eggshell-puncture sickness thickens blood to blood.

HOWIE GOOD

Reality Anxiety Disorder

1

Given how much else is going on, there's barely time left for the spectacular dreams of the dying. This, fortunately, doesn't count among disasters of the Jewish people. I'm in such a good mood that I wave to the plainclothesmen stationed in the crowd. "If you wish to study the disease," one of them tells me, "you must live in the swamp." It's only then that I notice he's coated with sand. The bigger question never gets asked: swimsuits that slim? Meanwhile, incensed at your driving, the man in the car behind you is groping under his seat for a five-shot Mexican revolver.

2

Words sail off the edge of the sky like hijacked flights, but you still get letters, ridiculous letters, from grateful former students. It's all about yearning, about what happens when the doomsday clock advances to three minutes to midnight. You pull the cushions off the couch, the books off the shelves, try to pull up the floorboards with your bare hands. Sweating or chills aren't uncommon. A woman with a backside like a pear trembles watching you. And though it's already old news, you have yet to hear the worst, that America's greatest chess player killed himself in a tub surrounded by 12 pairs of children's shoes.

3

Generalized weeping wheels into position, nothing I haven't seen before, flames erupting from windows, dead flowers in a vase, flesh and fur being scrapped away with elk-bone scrappers and the hide made pliable with the buffalo's mashed brains. Subjective reality sucks. "Time to electrocute your thinking," a frilly little voice says. And, in fact, I carry my relationships on the iPhone in my pocket. It's a good thing there are no children around, because if there were, a woman with a cruel mouth but a motherly manner would be leading them back into the burning building.

4

A torn and burnt napkin subs for the head of a small brown dog. "The whole point of flowers," a woman kneeling in the garden begins shouting, "is that they die." By the time the police descend on the scene, a series of gaily decorated signs have lost their original meaning. Only an eye and a hand remain and the unpronounceable names of hidden things.

5

Siri refuses to speak certain words above a whisper (measure, cleave, silver). I'm reminded, oddly, of Dali's love child teetering on the edge of a precipice. Getting to work has come to seem more and more like work itself. There are no clocks anywhere, though there are carcasses in various stages of decay, and I very well might encounter a man who has worn the black uniform with the skull-and-crossbones insignia. You should be able to guess what happens next – the permanently forgotten people in old photos open their mouths to scream.

JULEIGH HOWARD-HOBSON

The Ashes

They sent forth men to battle,
But no such men return;
And home, to claim their welcome,
Come ashes in an urn.
–Aeschylus

Oh so slowly —the first dying embers take
Their time to fade, from red to powdery
Grey, crumbling from their glowing source to make
Ash. Ash which smothers, covering every
Thing no longer engulfed in brilliant flame,
Ash which drifts with no direction but out
Away from the heat which is growing tame
And dull, ash which grows higher all about
The perimeter and threatens to fall
But does not, sifting itself down here and
There waiting patiently for when it's all
Over, the fire's out, the blackened stand
Of wood and men no more than chalky dust
That blows around with any wayward gust.

JULEIGH HOWARD-HOBSON

A Year After

Now the clouds come low, choking sky and sun
Until the grey day ends and the clouds blot
Out the stars. No twinkling horizon,
No moonlight, no unencumbered dawn. Not
A speck of the heavens exists in this
Sky. Just cloud. Cloud piled on cloud, in lines of
Clouds, ranging across the world. It's useless
To hope for clear skies now where all above
Is shaded white, shaded grey. Nothing shifts
The clouds, no wind, no gale, no storm will blow
Them away. And none is expected, if
Something did drive them away, all below
Would shrivel and die in the sudden light
Of a naked sky, burning and too bright.

MICHAEL C. FORD

Memorial Day

what is there now of
the flames the bomb
left doing it and where
is what may be left of
the fire in the survivor
flyers who did it or how
does the invisible fire
behind bomb bay doors
seem to the rest of us so
seriously open to viewing
as a turret gunner who is
mindful of human targets
which are competitive as
warheads absolutely mad
with munitions contracts
and willing to reduce
what has been already
reduced by the decision
of government geniuses
who just wanted to see if
the bomb works as good
on the 2nd bombardment
just to see what the bomb
takes in a wake of embers
oh Nagasaki

MICHAEL C. FORD

State of the Union

*Man has no right to kill his brother. It is no excuse
that he does so in uniform; he only adds the infamy
of servitude to the crime of murder.*
                              - Percy Shelly (19ᵗʰ Century)

Innocent victims whose weapons are seduced
By grease of ignorant contraband have become
smugglers in the night. Rages of avarice pay
wages for the art of war. Proud assassins
assemble around graves profaned by military
loons and cougars. Look at that invading

sparrow! Its toes tighten on tethered twigs, as
National Endowment spies tell lies that make
us die for prizes: blood money, war money:
all honored in the enemy camp. Literary
bureaucrats embalm our integrity. We are frozen
in library morgues of corporate bribery. They are

railroading writers in genocide of a weapons contest.
Soon, we will not have any more prayers, adventures,
values, morals, ideals, dreams to determine what a
living Hell it is: and Heaven is crowded with the
academic clouds of discontent. When will the 1,000
years cumulous feast begin? Sinister schemes to turn

nuclear war into a video game: to dynamite and dam the rapture. Whether it was to defoliate Southeast Asian villages or Middle Eastern desert sands these war-mongering goons are plundering with industrial guns: and too many idiot fingers squeezing like that sparrow's bivouac with insensitive toes on triggers.

MICHAEL C. FORD

Nuclear Summer

It isn't anger anymore: it is a disillusionment that your government uses you in a way that destroys you!
Resident of St. George, Utah

Picking up the Utah opalescence...it is
WHITE memory...it's white
memory: PURE as a pearl
                under a street lamp.
And white memory
turns around what's back
there... a California set of
                suburban cement
wickieups between
Claremont and San Berdoo.

It's a WHITE motel.... the sign
                out front
is inviting refugee victims of
atomic cancer from Cedar City to

SLEEP IN A WIGWAM

Now all the way from Utah border…all
the way from
> IRON COUNTY
> HURRICANCE
> SNOWFIELD
> NEW HARMONY

Nuclear America
makes me WHITER than a terminal sick room

1945 8.9 11:02

I

Before the sky rains black tears
children sing in the classroom, citizens prepare
tea, cakes, it's a weekday—
shops are open
traffic moves slowly through the streets

    It hits so fast
skin, eyes sear in the light

Forty thousand silent voices
        Forty thousand more
with broken notes pluck the air—
      "Water" "water"

II

Baku pours tea, motions to the cakes—
plump, round, a perfect fit
in the palm of a hand

      Five fingers spread
in a circle below his heart
covering the space
where the tumor grew

Eyes veiled as a lizard's view

ALWYN MARRIAGE

Across the Mountain

Trawsfynydd and Llandecwyn

An optimistic age of free love, promises of power
freed from the need for fossil fuels, joined the grid
to blocks of magnox, castles built in air.

These, multiplying, spawned another crop
of nuclear plants to process and provide
an infinite supply of energy on tap.

Now decommissioned, Trawsfynydd hunches,
hides its history, glowers in cubic impotence,
power a memory encased in concrete.

On the other side of the mountain
a pilgrim chapel also muses
on former power, taking a long view,

gathering in the prayers across the ages:
*Save us from pestilence and plague,
from AIDS and SARS and terrorist attack.*

A far horizon of ruffled mountains strokes
starched clouds, the Llyn peninsula points
westward, stretching sleepily to greet the off-shore saints.

Silence beneath silence, stillness of ancient stone,
peace of prayers by candlelight at night's approaching
followed inevitably by breaking dawn;

the mew of buzzard, slowly passing cloud,
sheep's ancient ruminating cry of *kyrie, christe, kyrie,*
answered meekly by lambs' *elei, elei, eleison.*

ALWYN MARRIAGE

the price of nuclear energy

Environmentalists, it seems, like atoms
are split in their response to nuclear power,
each side seething in its certainty.

In our search for clean, green electricity,
this ticking time-bomb seems to hold the key
to inexhaustible resources that might still provide

power as renewable as wind or tide –
but possibly created at the cost
of human life and future world security.

For few deny the risk of a catastrophe,
potentially poisoning water, land and air,
disturbing the delicate balance of cosmic stability,

and leaving dangerous indestructible detritus
hanging round indefinitely to mock us
with our own destructibility.

ESTEBAN COLON

After Us

Forgotten alarms and sirens wail
smoothly shattering sky
in
small pockets
animals avoid,
till
batteries die
in jagged
metal
glass

ESTEBAN COLON

Standing on this Flat Earth

the edges aren't always as far as you think
nostalgia display screens grind hope from strangers who have powdered
the things of dreams
scream on street corners of a track mark Jesus Christ hotel room obituary
the edges aren't always as far as you think

we are prodigal in our existence

Nephilim walk past downcast eyes like a dark brilliance too large for
irises and
every day we try to capture light like pictures held between thumb and
forefinger, pray for rain like
dollops of liquid infinity, sniffing lines of reality so hard our noses bleed, I'm
sniffing lines of reality so hard my nose bleeds, the edges aren't always as far
as you think – spirals of coils never seen, like artificial intestines hugging.
gears of war wrap arms around me, veins grind rust pushing orange dust
out every cut, till
spotted grease black hands builds skin
the size of wills and egos
skin chapped leather on human bones
and
the edges aren't always as far as you think
the edges aren't always as far as you think

MICHAEL SKAU

After the Bomb

AFTER THE BOMB
I

Over the lakes and rivers, the swamps
surrounding them, miasmal mists rise
like fur, putrid hackles on the few
trees and scant brush. Standing and flowing
waters glare phosphorescent, garish
lights leaping at night in smothering
spread, feeble searchlights in fog, alarms
transmitted from no one to no one.
Apprehensive, we try to avoid
the waters, but thirst and stench seduce
us. After reluctant plunges, we
notice that our toenails, fingernails,
eyes, hair (if it grew back), and exposed
bones glow at night like crucifixes.

AFTER THE BOMB
XIV

With no communication systems
working, nobody knows what happened
or who was at fault, our side or theirs.
We all feel we should have known: weapons
always get used sooner or later,
especially when offered as gifts
to those with appetites for power,

the only ones who run for office.
All politicians, eager to make
the infinite mistake, are targets
of our snarling curses. In the camps
chaos thrives because, distrustful of
leaders, as though by secret vote, we
shy away from any government.

AFTER THE BOMB
XXIV

Imagination remains fertile
about our health. We just need to hear
of new maladies to begin to
mimic their symptoms. Sympathetic
ailments are rife: unwounded persons
erupt in gruesome suppurations,
raise keloids, develop limps, double
vision, bleeding gums, and high fevers.
Emotional traumas also sweep
like colds throughout the camp: sometimes I
wake in nightmare screaming from the loud
blasts, tremors that shake the earth, flashes
that light the sky, blind the eye; across
the dark camp others are screaming too.

LIZ DOLAN

Air Raid Drills

As a child, I was drawn to air raid drills
which wimpled, rat-faced Sister Reparata
orchestrated from her desk,
a break in the routine
of folded hands and numbing notes.
We scrambled under our desks
heads tucked, knees bent
like blue and white turtles
retreating into our shells.

Who would drop a bomb on us?

My terrified classmate, Joyce Ostraticky,
wept into her navy blue taffeta tie.
She longed for the Holy Father to open
the letter—Russia converted—
through prayers to Mary.
She smiled down on us,
the yellow daisies we brought
strewn at her foot
crushing the head of the serpent.

MARC HUDSON

An Anniversary Noted

Honeybees in the blue
Spirea, the flawless light
of Santa Fe, seventy years later—
the span of a given life—

hens clucking in the little chicken yard,
occasional hammering of the roofers at work
on the adobe next door
and the emeritus professor of English
not quite yet born then, musing
over his coffee—

the world can be remarkably kind
and relatively generous
with time, to some,
but for those slightly older children,
the arrival of Little Boy
and Fat Man meant oblivion,
or worse. They would never have
the leisure of such a morning,
the chance to glance over seventy years,
much less read the *Gita*.

That August morning, their play
concluded, their future
gone in a flash—indeed, as if Shiva
had taken his trident
and shattered the worlds.

LOWELL JAEGER

Ants

Ants do what ants do: hive
in crumbling rocks and cracks, build
villages in my garden wall, frenzy
through daily routine in what looks to me
as rushing to and fro for no discernible cause.

Instinct bugles its alarm, calls me
to select from the garden shed
an array of powders, sprays, bombs.

In the blast of afternoon heat, the ants
zigzag, lofting bits of leaf and bark,
workers' orders relayed — we think —
in chemical codes of one's antennae wiped
across another's. Do they suspect me?
Do they see me? How can they comprehend
the impending doom
                    raining down
from my shaker of Bug-B-Gone,
napalm searing
their polished uniform hides.
Some run, some collapse, some writhe.
I bulldoze their bunker with my shoe,
upending stones beneath which lie

nurseries of the unborn, a next generation
assigned to care and feed tomorrow's queen . . . till
my shadow looms overhead,
and I've put an end to all of that. Which is natural,
isn't it? Ants do what ants do.
My species too.

LOWELL JAEGER

Ernesto de Fiori's "Soldier"

"So it's not just staying alive;
it's staying human that's important."
– George Orwell

This bronze man stands hairless as a worm
on his little pad of stone with no place
left to go. Earlier he woke with his face
in his hands and his hands in the faceless warm
remains of the not-so-lucky all around. Their sap
he wiped on his sleeves and scraped it beneath his nail.
Then he picked his way up this knoll, leaving a trail
of first his khaki shirt, his dog tags, his steel cap,
then his right boot, left boot, underpants and all
until in the grey break of day he stands
the last man left when war is done. His hands
don't want to touch a thing. His bare feet forever stall.

Some days his swollen sockets ask, *What have we done?*
Some days his lips half sneer, *We won.*

LOWELL JAEGER

Most Influential Man of His Age

This faraway glint in Einstein's glare,
famous photo with frizzy hair,
pauses me to stop and stare.

This portrait printed on the page,
neither king nor soldier nor sage.
"Most influential man of his age,"

says the plain-spoken text.
He looks a bit perplexed,
worried what might come next

once the phantom atom has been split,
explosive as holy writ
once we get ahold of it.

LOWELL JAEGER

Nothing Lasts Forever

Toothaches.
Diarrhea. Bee stings. Heat waves.
Cold snaps. That stupid tune stuck in your head.
Hiccoughs. Drippy faucets. Traffic jams.

A good buzz.
Bad trip.

Regimes, left and right.
Pacts between regimes.
Prudence enough
not to pull the switch.

Rocket fire.
Sirens.
Panic.
The planet in bloom.

Then nothing.
And nothing

lasts forever.

LOWELL JAEGER

Place of Discoveries

Place of Discoveries
the sign says
at the threshold
of Atomic City. Where Oppenheimer
fathered a bomb.

A brilliant man, says the twenty minute visitor center video
— and humanist —
Oppenheimer nicknamed the first explosion
Trinity, alluding
to the Holy Sonnets of John Donne.

Oppenheimer's research mushroomed
into nuclear energy, space exploration,
medical advancements.
A chain reaction, the video says,
one discovery leads to the next.

Some worried the blast might radiate
heat enough to ignite
the atmosphere.

From his vantage point
at a distance behind cottonwoods,
— as Oppenheimer witnessed White Sands —
a voice in his head recalled
the Bhagavad Gita:
Now I am become Death,
the destroyer of worlds.

One discovery leads to the next.

LOWELL JAEGER

Remainders

Newsreel clips of nightmare
H-bomb tests blasting whole
islands whooshed off the map.
We ducked under school desks
and cowered, covered our heads.

Civil Defense sirens bugled,
and panic drilled us with alarm.
Precious little remained of playtime
no matter how much we wished it back.

We shaped towers and houses of sand,
peopling our cities with sticks.
And wrecked them like Nagasaki,
like Hiroshima, like footage from newsreels
of nothing left over
but orphans
and ashes and bricks.

LOWELL JAEGER

the drill

high on the power-pole
centered in our playground
yellow trumpets
civil defense horns
to worry us
nuclear warheads
headed our way

when in the midst of play
the alarm sounded
we scurried
like ants
into steam tunnels
beneath our school

where we huddled mute
shut from sunlight
cross-legged on concrete
our spines numbed
blind against the cinderblock

our teachers tussling our hair
cooing to calm us
their eyes blinking twilight black
their smiling lashes panicked wide
waiting for our walls to tremble
and echo in the blast

LOWELL JAEGER

On Facing Miro's "Tete"

Once I scrambled in my sleep half way up the cellar stairs
and woke in my nightmare
sure the door to the floor above loomed
like a green moon I could run to and close behind me.

I'd dreamed again that night the light
of lights in the atomic darkness. *Look away,*
Mother warned, her last words
blaring like the yellow trumpet of civil defense
from the power pole in the yard outside my school.
That's what I heard as they marched us single file
to the underground: Mother's alarm.

Such a nervous boy. *Very imaginative,* teachers reported.
So once a month they shut us from daylight, cross-legged
on concrete, my spine erect against the cinderblock
—as the siren screamed — and I sat smiling
with eyes wide, blinded in contemplation of doom.

I wasn't old enough not to look
at what others more snug in themselves
couldn't see. In the era of the bomb
shelter, on weekends fathers dug the family tomb
while neighbors sputtered over Geiger counters,
stores of drinking water, blankets, dried beans,
new-built basement shelves. Debated how long
do tins of crackers last.

I've never lived with this danger passed.
In the dream, I've filed again downstairs, waiting
for the walls to tremble and echo at the last. A nerve explodes
in me and I'm leaping three, four rungs
up the ladder to the exit, so absolutely sick
of it all not even nuclear never-after
can hold me. Then I'm on all fours

climbing, bound toward that door, the moon,
when below mushrooms a cold white blast.
Look away, I tell myself. But I turn . . . .
Mother remembers only finding me naked,
half way up the cellar stairs, groping in the dark,
my face twisting, wincing, drawn. In my hand,
her double bell Wesclock pounding out another dawn.

LISA STICE

At the Atomic Museum

In the 1950s, Nevada test-site engineers were told
there would be no long-term effects from
the experiments. The government praised them
for their patriotism in Christmas cards to each family.
The men collected and carried home souvenir
uranium rods to show their kids and wives.
At the Atomic Museum, I read copies of denial letters —
        "Dear Mrs. S—,
        We are sorry for your loss.
        To help put your mind at ease,
        our research finds no correlation
        between your husband's work
        environment and his lymphoma."
        and once confidential files –
        "S— received 891 rads of neutron radiation,
nearly a lethal dose. His badge will be kept
in a lead box in the case further tests are warranted."

My brother gave me a Vaseline Glass candy dish
last year for Christmas. It glows
under black light. Who owned it
when it was just a lovely novelty?
Maybe a woman with a courted daughter.
The girl might have sat on the couch with her sweet
as they ate sugary treats out of the dish.
Would the candy glow under black light, too?
Maybe the mother gave the girl the yellow glass
as a wedding gift, each lemon drop and ribbon candy
dissolving into syrupy malignance.

The museum's display of vintage TVs loop,
duck-and-cover commercials: *If you see a flash,*
lie face down on the ground and throw dirt over yourself.
Just in case no one would be left behind to dig a grave?
If you see a flash, hide behind something like a tree.
Photographs behind show refrigerators used as shields,
like tombstones, sitting in the desert sand.

Kids in southern Utah ran outside, excited
to see snow fall in July. They held up their hands
and stuck out their tongues to catch
the falling ash, rolled in mounds on the ground,
threw handfuls at each other. Frolicking in the wonder
of it all, they never hid from the flash they didn't see.

I read about the uses of mill tailings and watch newsreels
of construction workers pouring radioactive cement
for the foundation of a school,
such an industrious solution for all that waste.

My hometown was built on mill tailings. Before I was born,
crews broke up and removed old foundations
and replaced them with less tainted cement, but
contaminated water still ran through irrigation ditches
to water cornfields and asparagus patches, and
contaminated water ran through our kitchen pipes.
Five members from little St. Ann's Church were diagnosed
with brain tumors in 2007. My uncle's neighbor had a tumor
on his spine, tangled around nerves.

I browse through the gift shop at toy Geiger counters,
Glo Sticks, DVDs of the duck-and-cover
tutorials. I spin the postcard rack and carry home a souvenir
picture of sunglassed men posing in front of a mushroom cloud,
safe and still smiling.

STEVEN STAM

Seconds After Impact

Dust hovered. Floated. Incinerated.
But I waited, waiting was all one could do,
In the heat, my heart slapping my ribcage,
The sweet stink of singed hair floated into my nostrils.
The scent pungent and catalytic, hot enough singe my hair,
To melt the contents of my nose, the salted beard on my face.
A blast takes a handful of seconds—can one hold time?
A death takes more. Here time absolutes collided.
As I burned and my skin began to melt,
I thought about my morning routine: how I still needed to
Use the toilet. I had always expected to die at peace, yet
As the concussion force lifted me off my feet severing my spine,
I only desired to scrape my teeth clean and take a pee.

ALEX DREPPEC

Atomic Agatha

Atomic Agatha annunciates:
"Atom adulators, agglomerate,
accepting atomic absurdities,
acne acme's apt, adamant apogees.
Atomic adventurers, analyse:
aberrant accidents amortise.
Accept anatomical amputation,
accept anatomical atomisation,
adenoid's aggrandisement!
Accept Agatha's advisement!
Aspirin, alcohol, apathy
ameliorate accidents abruptly.
Amusing, adolescent Abilene:
accept an atomised Aberdeen!"

ANJANA BASU

Atoms

thunder destroys and the rain in a deluge
this was different
brahma spoke
from the heart of silence
splitting wide the worlds
 light destroyed
taking the clothes from skin
the skin from bones
the bones from each other
perhaps
Every atom in your body
came from a star that exploded
and you are now stardust
in the galaxy one tear can kill

Three color city
Red, black and brown
Dead fingertips catch fire

don't cry for me
destroyer of worlds
your weep blood rain

blossom time by the river
banks implode
time turns inward, stops

 an imploding star
dancing by the glitter dust fire
in this galaxy a tear can kill

RAE WICK

Back From

He's home.
In pieces.
A human Ikea side table
bought on early-morning impulse
at a garage sale across town
for 2 dollars.
The instruction manual is missing
and it's half-split on top.
Assembled, used,
Reassembled, used
Disassembled.
The particle board has swelled
and stiffened under the conditions
of an unfamiliar climate
so that even if all parts are inventoried
and squared away
there is no telling
if they will fit back together,
and there might be a screw gone now.
                    –You never can know.

So it remains in the basement
leaning against the tv
for support
on one wobbly leg,

no use left
to serve
the few
and the proud
people who know
they didn't get what they paid for.

ALEX DUENSING

Blank World

For millennia, the earth
like any other planet
had a double:
its other possible reality.

In that other place, our families knew
one another...
celebrated special occasions together.

If you were quiet
you'd be able to sense that
earth from earth—
the way my family sings
our own version of "Happy Birthday"
adding
"may you live a hundred years"
and
"we love you, we do"
to its verses.

Now, after that moment
when the doomsday clock
came so close to midnight
that it could have been
one day or the next,

if you try to sense
that other earth,
our families will not be there.

Instead, you'll become accustomed
to the emptiness of space.

LANA BELLA

Hiroshima, Winter '97

One morning in winter of '97,
long after the atomic bomb,
as our train lumbered
on the Sanyo line snaking
past Hiroshima station,
my grandfather raised gnarled
hands over the glass pane,
fingers brushed away cold veil
of the dawn as if a troublesome
fly, his rheumatic eyes,
ghostlike to the flicks of old
memories with black rain and
churning flames which had
felled and felt as far away
as thirty seven miles radius,
leaving his city barren
with dust and its remains
luminous in crimson inferno.
Moving my mind's eyes
into a tomorrow, I studied
the sun-ridden web of scars
on his neck, where I knew
the flesh lay rotted into bones,
leaving his seared skin
below a bag of loose rags
hanging from his spine. As
suddenly begun, the sun rose,

his fog lifted like an eiderdown
shaking free from a long
stretch of yawns; I watched
him stirred his thoughts
towards the honeyed spots that
clung over the Ōta River
and sown commercial buildings,
because he knew he had
wept and died here, now his
hollowness just glistened
like a mantra in the light, only

in the empty dark can
he feel yesterdays with soot
and relics under his fingertips.

LANA BELLA

As My Tears Are But Water

Please, darling,
do not remember me
as casualty nor the bearer of
woes, lest I go into
time like bog yearns over
watery floorboards.
For my tears are but water
when the dawn once
more raises the curtains
of inhumanity, with I,
the lost son of Nagasaki.
I often think of that red river
that moved with blood,
in the morning of August '45,
as it pulled me into my
half-burnt coughs, where I
tasted sharply the searing
phlegm. My skin pricked with
so much ruins all the fat
turned inside out;
there, by the edge on the far
side of screams
and macabre glow of sunset,
I waited on the leaf of time
like a footnote,
until twilight sagged upon
an arsenic-ingot gray of

the surrendering sky.
Later I will have walked
a thousand miles on America's
warplane's skin;
my whole absorbed into
the air, ground, and water,
sucked towards the dying sun.

LANA BELLA

The Thing About Dying

Is it possible to line a defense
when the heart is pulled
out from one body
and placed into another
who needs it to live?
The small girl turns her face
to the gun-metal clouds,
disciplines her twined stump-
hands from reaching down,
picking through
the rubble for strewn corpses,
that are bathing in
the red hurling fist of
the smoking pyre.
In her dreams, the angels
come home to die, the heavens
fling stars in straight rows
so the supreme pilots from the
sky can see her city already
is clutching to rocks,
emptying all shimmer into
the oxygen diet that is being
hauled away, gnats clinging to
entrails exposed the slick
kernels of the dead.
And because she knows
she will die here like a billowing

visible before another storm,
she will let her dimming
body float there like an asterisk,
hovering above this hollow
in the granite heart of Hiroshima.

SHAHÉ MANKERIAN

Where I Was Born

Twenty years later, we went back to Beirut
and stood in front of CMC Hospital
for a photograph. We couldn't go inside.

During the war, it burned down,
not because of misguided bombs,
but because a doctor set himself on fire

after they wheeled his dead wife
into the Emergency. Years later, hollyhock
bushes and wild fig trees covered the pink

and black walls of the entrance.
Militiamen had posted pictures of martyrs
on the crooked wall that separated

the sidewalk from the front lawn.
The statue of Virgin Mary with broken
hands cried near a dehydrated water fountain.

SHAHÉ MANKERIAN

Hussien Lost a Leg and Twenty Bleating Sheep

When the bomb exploded,
the imam found the shepherd staff
near the broken window of the mosque.

Lucky, the sheepdog, licked
a left foot by the well. She recognized
the thick wool stocking, the black shoe

without lace, the twisted ankle.
Before he wrapped the jagged wound
with fallen mulberry leaves, the imam

unbuttoned Hussien's one-legged
trouser and removed it. Blood soaked
his jaundice white underwear.

A wayward lamb chewed
on a cartilage of a nose as Lucky
began to howl. The shepherd boy

didn't wake up even to the deafening
sound of the sirens or the second
prodigal explosion.

SHAHÉ MANKERIAN

Snapshots of Summer Captured by Children

Through a broken kaleidoscope,
even the bronze body of Christ
sweats on the cross. Two bees

drown in a pool; a boy completes
a somersault from a diving board.
A forgotten banana turns brown

in a grease-stained paper bag.
On a hilltop a girl with freckles
watches the bombardment of Burj

and cheers from a plastic chair
while eating popcorn. Heavy
boots erase chalk drawings

of sunrise on a sidewalk. No one
chases the ice cream truck except
for the cripple. A dervish

pressure washes a new graffiti
on the western wall: Where did
you hide your son's timid heart?

Published in the anthology Nuclear Impact: Broken Atoms in Our Hands

PAUL LOBO PORTUGÉS

Sorrowful Months of Unusual Rain

Sorrowful months of unusual rain stunt fluffy rainbow asters sowed under last cool March's invisible sadness. Spittle bug suck at delicate stems of dainty wallflowers companion planted with hoped for pearly tuberoses. Streamside our borrowed flower field, common crow watch us plant Aztec zinnias just before the red Toltec sun comes down. The talking windbreak eucalyptus sway in the lazy breeze-scattered radioactive air from Fukushima's cancer and regret.

I wander down rows of baby's breath avoiding husks of dead caterpillars. Yesterday spread the last volunteered ranunculus on my surrendered good friend Rexroth's beat grave remembering a rainy Buddhist Xmas he was gladly writing pious poems about Hiroshima's nuke shadows of children etched forever by black rain on the schoolyard wall.

BRITT MELEWSKI

Clear of the Ruins

It is a harnessing of the basic power of the universe. The force from which the sun draws its power has been loosed . . .
—Harry S. Truman regarding the hydrogen bomb

I

While you rest,
I claw at the shirttails of the light.
You're finally away
from the crashing bells
and steel wishes
of monsters, away from
the concrete room.

It is a perfect orange light
that keeps you, stalls
my standing, my age,
the decaying busts of marble
kings—everything
slowed to a gaze.

I can almost feel
the particles you run with,
the particles that run
through you. I can almost

name them.

II

There are spaces of the mind
untold, formless,
evil, joyous,
spots of copper veining
soundlessly through our blood,
unbeknownst. A teardrop
of glass that takes on light,
presses it into the crooked rainbow
splayed across your gray pillow.

Call it memory's siege,
my heart railing
for you at your worst.

III

Remember when—

can you remember
how awful I was
at handling the garbage,
the taxes— my fat
fingers— when I almost
dropped the baby,
our son?

IV

The foundation of this blue
planet is a composition
of unmanned blue guitars
bleeding. There you are
again, staring at me
through your disabled
eyelids—my faulty meditation,

a game of backgammon
with one missing rock.

V

I want to net it
and stuff it
underneath my tongue.
The little you.
What's left of you—
the little you
that fades.

VI

You smile like nothing
happened, the smell is
unbearable.

Our human city will not last
the year. It will stop
growing like a weed.

I too will drop away
into the chasm,
into the light's wake.

Your memory will finally leave me
when the child who spun
the wheel of a pink bicycle
to the tune of no tune
too is gone.

VII

Workmen in your body
build an invisible levee
with cotton stones.
An aftermath forms within
you: bridges' suspension cables
from your eyes—

a forest grows underneath
your feet as if you were
to run down a stairwell

in my dark
clunky dream.

Fuck heaven.

VIII

I'll never be able to confirm
the replenishment—
that glowing promise,
whether it's a brilliance
or bore.

I'll be damned.

I want to bet against myth,
against you,
just to say I bet you.

My faith has always cowered
in the windy cool of a massive shadow,
it's fickle valence
and restless wavering.

Will the stars
remain after they're dead—
night lifted in thine arms—
at least for a moment,
their sockets nestled
all in a row, sucking away,
ever-hungry,
every wave,
every slipped and falling
girder, everything you?

BRITT MELEWSKI

Candy Crush Dream

Years before the disaster,
I sat next to you in Spanish
class and thought about your body
growing— how it would blink
in the lamplight at night
while we played hooky
from the nuclear McDonald
world, everything fuzz
and lip.

I thought about the family
we wouldn't be able to create
because the ocean
has been sentenced to death.

The bird of light
breaks right and lands
on a mindless bluff.

This is totally unorthodox.

Why did I exist, anyway?
To watch a ball game
and clean my thick teeth?

I volunteer myself instead
of my squirming daughter
who, if she had been born,
might have smiled
from the auditorium
of her polka dot dress.
Instead, she is a pile
of feces on the ocean floor,
a humpback whale popped
and unplugged with sores.
The beaches and trees
goo-stained, miles
of algae and jellyfish fried
and unstuck
from their ancient biology.

On a Wednesday, I think,
what, then, will we eat?

Take it all away from me.

Slightly more silent
now are the deadened
waves. My wallet is missing
the picture of you
because you can't be
the healthy plume
you might have been—
a gentle speaker whispers,
in place of somebody
that somebody else
desperately needed.

I am sorry
I didn't do anything
about anything,
but you were always
my love, my partner
in adolescent crime.

Wasn't it always the case
that the core would sink
below the concrete in Fukashima?
If not now, then then.
If not there, then there,
or anywhere else
in a low place,
seeping into Earth's
bloodstream.

I will die without you,
in the bent spoon
of the street.

Slowly and painfully
the sun rises
and I say *hey I think I see
the sun.*

This is important
because every moment
before this one
has been a step toward you,
grabbing at doorknobs
in the dark.

Now, as the disaster
crosses the Pacific,
the mountains, the plains—
the leaky, expanding ground
zero— every moment is a step
away from you, another inch
dug into the cool of the ground.

The antelope in the flatland
moves like thick soup,
absolutely confused,
more than slow, sick.

I would lend you
my skeleton
if I could tear it out.

Why can't you see me
trying to make you feel good?

The scar on the inside
of my arm takes the shape of you.

I want you, a windfall of you.

After drinking a few, the only
survival methods I can handle
are four-letter words,
a candy crush
video game— its holographic
touch—coal burning away
all of our distances,
the image of people,
many people breathing,
breathing nice.

DEBORAH P KOLODJI

haiku/senryu/tanka

Hiroshima Day
in the friendship garden
flashes of koi

orange dragonfly
over the koi pond
Hiroshima Day

darkening clouds
a red light blinks
on the nuclear power plant

nuclear winter
settles over the wasteland
left behind—
can we survive
the chill in our hearts?

DES MANNAY

My Last Journey

"Two feet of a victim whose body vanished in a single puff; they stood upright, stuck to the concrete road", Kenzaburo Oe, Hiroshima Notes

Two feet.
Tall
Erect
They stand there
awaiting
The return of my body
Where am I?
Did I really breathe
In the white heat?
Was I blinded
By the light,
As the radiation
Ripped through me?
Did I get the chance
To cry out in pain?
Beg mercy for my
Mother, father, sister,
Brother, lover, daughter?
Or did I just Vaporize?
Disappear
Into the ether?
Were these
My last thoughts?

Or the imaginings
Of another -
Looking at
Remains
At the epicentre:
Hiroshima?

DES MANNAY

Dead Dolphins

Their lungs were white
Ischemia
Indicating
Loss of blood
To the organs
This is radiation
Poisoning
No other symptoms
Of disease
There were 17 of them
Lying there
On the beach
Near Fukushima
Nobody
Has Ever Seen
Such a thing
Before

DES MANNAY

The Ruination

Ponderous, ornate and shattered by fate,
A world built by monsters is rotting away
Where other parts and other places lay molten,
still this structure stands...
Natures revenge holds these unnatural innovators
back into the earths grasp.
All generations of this species have passed away,
Survived by the world they all but destroyed

There were cities of a thousand souls
imagining themselves immortal - like Gods;
over whom science had triumphed.
Drunkenly they staggered onward,
intoxicated by 'success'; whatever that is.
Until the radiation changed that.
The sickness came and death destroyed the masses.
And nature, once bound like Prometheus,
was once again free to reclaim this abandoned space -
A ruin reduced to heaps.
Where once humanity heaped - gold and silver,
gems and precious stone, wealth and property.
The spoils of war, and called this 'civilization'.
Until they let slip the missiles once again.....

DARREN MORRIS

Variations on a Theme by Shinoe Shōda

Poems Written after Shinoe Shōda's *Sange*

Witness

Our omega burst
upon us, and now
for you, the living,
an elegy of grief
that transcends event.

DARREN MORRIS

Variations on a Theme by Shinoe Shōda

Poems Written after Shinoe Shōda's *Sange*

Moment of Impact

Godless light and quake.
Then, a wink of serenity
and nothingness, which were
the last particles of beauty
succumbing to atrocity.

Before me, an insane
and hopeless chaos.
Cyclones of molten air
ascended in golden
spires and skipped away.

A pale, blinded,
blood-smeared child
appeared, screaming,
Mother. Her voice
sharp as a sickle.

Yet, terror cloaked
my obligation to her,
so I could search among
the ruins and find
my father's blue body.

DARREN MORRIS

Variations on a Theme by Shinoe Shōda

Poems Written after Shinoe Shōda's *Sange*

The Unspeakable

A girl lay beneath
a burning beam. She
reached out her possession
and screamed, "Take it,
leave me." We left.

The whole sky was fire,
emptiness flooded the dead
and we rode them down
river. We waited for dawn
though we knew it would not come.

Soldiers fished us out and piled
us on a sandbar of bodies.
I tried to speak to her,
but she was distant as her
daughter's hand, and ashen.

A doctor appeared and tried
in vain to sew the skin
where the flesh had sloughed.
Such agony under the doctor's
stitches, until the thread ran out.

DARREN MORRIS

Variations on a Theme by Shinoe Shōda

Poems Written after Shinoe Shōda's *Sange*

The Objective of War

Most of the dead smolder
like embers. *Human beings.*
They are piled on the bed
of a transport. To where
does such futility travel?

There, pale fingers of child
and mother intertwine,
bounce away, fused together.
They had been discovered,
just that way in a water tank.

DARREN MORRIS

Variations on a Theme by Shinoe Shōda

Poems Written after Shinoe Shōda's *Sange*

By Their Suffering, They Are Stripped Bare

Burned corpses fat
on the black belt of river.
Indiscriminately, a boy
soldier pulled one out
by its fleshy rags.

His sorrow was
the only involuntary
and rational act. Hauling
each to the fire, he
demanded Sake, Sake

from those with no hands.
Those traitorous eyes
shone and conspired
against him. He swallowed
his tears like strong drink.

DARREN MORRIS

Variations on a Theme by Shinoe Shōda

Poems Written after Shinoe Shōda's *Sange*

Student Work Detail

The larger bones
must be the teacher's.
Look how the small
skulls are huddled
by the long thin arms.

The living ones carry
their dead classmates.
"We must, Madam," they tell me.
The futureless young
glisten with such naïve respect.

Yet, when they tire,
no one will tell them
when it is time to go home,
or where to sleep among
the wreckage, or to die.

DARREN MORRIS

Variations on a Theme by Shinoe Shōda

Poems Written after Shinoe Shōda's *Sange*

Mothers Implore Their Dead

A mother bowed and
wailed over a photograph
of her incinerated children.
She offered the image
her only food and begged
of memory: "Eat, eat."

DARREN MORRIS

Variations on a Theme
by Shinoe Shōda

Poems Written after Shinoe Shōda's *Sange*

Holding Area

Mail call returned
her daughter's brooch
and she spent all evening,
polishing it
with her breath.

She could sleep now
on her human side.
But the other
was sprinkled with
white-hot constellations.

DARREN MORRIS

Variations on a Theme by Shinoe Shōda

Poems Written after Shinoe Shōda's *Sange*

Repatriate

Before the glow of the city,
on his front path,
the repatriated soldier sat.
It was all that remained
of his home.

I offered him a melon.
He forced himself to eat.
He did not want to be
grateful or to need
this terrible life.

"Variations on a Theme by Shinoe Shōda" by Darren Morris: Collaborators and co-translators - Ami Hagiwara, Department of Global and International Studies, University of Northern British Columbia and Jeremy D. Schmidt. Darren Morris: "The poems included here are not pure translations of Shinoe Shōda's work, with which I take great liberties. They are interpretations, or response poems written "after" the original subject, setting, and sense. In rewriting them, I wanted to call attention to her self-published book of tanka form, Sange, from which they were taken, written and distributed in 1947, secretly, under U.S. occupation and strict censorship after the war. Shōda lived through the atomic bombing of Hiroshima, which the poems describe. A second remaining copy of Sange was recently discovered and donated to the Hiroshima Peace Memorial Museum."

DARREN MORRIS

Hiroshima,
August 6, 1945, 8:15 a.m.

Schoolchildren in bright white
shirts are holding hands
up the hillside fire road.
Soldiers adjust the battery
in the ditch and share
cigarettes and black tea
and watch the sky.
The regular business
of a bustling city awakens
into the fine, clear morning.
As the fisherman pushes his boat
into the water, so there are
hollows like soft eddies
above his lover's collarbones.
She is back at the house,
and her sleep is thinning.

DARREN MORRIS

Letter to What Shall Not Be

The people who have made it through
are generous with the little they have.
Can you grieve for what you will not know?
I learn from what they will not say
and this is how I discovered your name.
All war long I worried about you, alone,
swimming the rivers of my amniotic
fear, and though sirens nightly cried,
we stayed safe till dawn. I remain unconvinced
that man could make such a fire of the sky,
nor be blamed for leaving constellations
across my body. They must seem
the scintillant dome above the field
where you shall never lie. It is better
you went still and will never know
to question the wondrous agonies of space.
How small it can make one feel,
the way they cluster like hives of bees.
But they are not stars, only apologies.

DARREN MORRIS

Upon Further Examination

During occupation, U.S. medical corps
under the portents of administering care
probed the hibakusha for meaningful data.
Imagine a stage and spotlight identifying
a girl naked but for her body's mutations
holding her wings out in the nightmare silence
and invisible men in the dark theater thinking,
We could do better next time. We could kill more.

DARREN MORRIS

Cocktails with the Rat Pack

For frame of reference, before
shows, we hit Atomic Liquors,
a joint at the edge of old Las Vegas
when it wasn't built up and you could
take drinks to the roof, dangle
your legs over the façade, and watch,
not so far off, nuclear tests in the desert.

DARREN MORRIS

Sedatephobia

As a child, I woke some nights
in the middle of time.
And though it was dark
I could feel a shadow
under a great black wing
releasing the single egg
into its noiseless fall
through the clouds.
For that is how it would come,
without reason, the errorless
erasure of all. A payload
of nothingness in
the final triumph of science.
Obliteration swallowed
whole by those who slept
and those who could not.

DARREN MORRIS

Tōrō Nagashi—Motoyasu River

We have painted our prayers
on the rice paper walls of the boxes.
We roll up our pant legs and descend
the banks to set them on the water
and light the candle therein.
The current will collect the lanterns
like souls. The fire they hold
will fill them as they sail downstream
and turn them to ash, as they
once were themselves. They who
may not know that they are gone.

JONATHAN TRAVELSTEAD

Approach

An hour North of Kiev the hardtack road frays to potholes
and slush before the checkpoint designating the Russian-controlled
Exclusion Zone- a thirty-kilometer perimeter Oksana calls the *Zone of Alienation*.
Ukrainian flag patched on his cossack, a guard with a german shepherd
stops us at the candy-striped drop gate. Black gloves, kalashnikov
on a leather sling he waves us out so he can search the van, check my passport
against a xeroxed copy and the proof that I paid the two hundred dollar
tour fee, none of which he will ever see. Cleared as harmless, Oksana
arrows the white, unmarked van through forests of new growth
towards Chernobyl Reactor Number Four. Swerves, narrowly dodges
the wild boar which dart out from the snowy windrows of trees
planted above burial mounds where workers in 1986
dug trenches wide enough to consume the contaminated forest
they bulldozed and covered with sand. I can't help that it looks like
Christmas tree farms line the countryside, or that I want to see
with my own eyes when she says some of them glow,
giving off a hazy blue at night. Many things she should not show me,
but as I see the lip of a cooling tower's wide rim emerge from the treeline
like a milk bottle dusted in lead, I know that she will.

JONATHAN TRAVELSTEAD

Schoolhouse

Pripyat

See the door, torn mathematically from its jamb. Where hinges were
raw splinters and gouged wood bare signs of recent trama. A teardrop wreath
propped on a tripod just inside: fake roses and white carnations,
faded spruce boughs bent around. See the apothecary's cabinet flung open,

how it salts the hallway's lathe floor with shattered glass of decanters,
and the dwarven, elephant faces of gas masks. I enter where the hallway
branches into the nursery, see wire frames of double bunks crammed
in the corner like Wal-Mart shopping carts. The plank floor burnt through

in two places calculates sentiment perfectly- a campfire of cardboard
interlopers kindled to charred studs. Nothing is as it seems. Anagrams drip
spraypaint, and the graffiti overlaying the mural in the kindergarten room
seems overdone. It feels like a con, or a funhouse's illusion of horror

muddling the simple truth of a burial ground beneath it. The original wall
I can just see: a schoolboy in a blue uniform cap. Sheaves of lead paint
fall away, and I see a Soviet rocket rising behind him. As if from a vandal
with artistic aspirations, I see the desks have been posed in neat rows

to support the black effigies of children painted side-view on the wall
behind them. In an orange, pastel chair at the front of the class a rag doll
is propped and masked. White hair. Only the children's cubbies I think
may be authentic. Oil paints by brush, the yellows just dimming.

The dump truck has inflated, knobby tires, and a duck on wheels.
Hummingbirds with human eyes, circling a single sunflower. Names carved
beneath them, a tryst. Cyrillic characters over a heart, cyrillic beneath.
I turn from this ruin layered like dust over this schoolhouse, step carefully

towards the door so I contaminate nothing, then exit outside for the sure
honesty of trees.

JONATHAN TRAVELSTEAD

Forest Wormwood

From the van's window Oksana points the yellow detector
at the collection of skeletal scotch pines and acacias called the Black Forest
or Red Forest. Ticking at first, the device ratchets up to a chitter
and the digital readout shows forty sieverts, meaning we can't go there.

I see what needles haven't fallen from the whispy trees are brown,
that the snow doesn't accumulate at their base despite the bare branch.
She says the thickest limbs blush, choked with plutonium,
that strontium-90 is responsible for the color gingering the papery bark,

and curling it like wet paper, dried. That iodine, and cesium-127
rust the conifers' xylem and phloem with rosin hard as unlidded cans
of red paint. I think of cadavers in the Body Worlds exhibit in Chicago.
Muscles and veins, deflated of blood. How they injected them

with plastic so we could see statues made from the living.
An article I saw somewhere about The Atomic Man- Harold McCluskey-
read that an explosion blasted his face with americium and bits of metal,
irradiating his body with five hundred times the maximum allowable dose

and though he shouldn't have survived a day, he died years later
of an unrelated heart disease. Once more she waves the detector's reedy
faxing noise toward the wraithlike pines, can't explain how is is
they still stand. The sluggish diesel whines beneath us as she drives

into the land of comic book origins. Hometown of giant lizards.
Waxhouse mannequins for the carnival.

JENNIFER HIGHLAND

Critical Mass

Invisible, unstable glow

restless as a stack
of marbles:

See what a vigorous treasure
our gloved machines have amassed.

We have boxed it in concrete
five feet thick.

We have wired it with sirens
and blinking buttons.

We have hemmed it in with equations.
We have quantified and qualified it.

We have submitted the paperwork.
We have filed the reports.

And when all the systems
suddenly go dead

we are all equally surprised

at the way fever rises
in fervent metal

atoms ricocheting
through impotent water

all the backups
neatly bypassed.

The sirens do not sound.
The red buttons do not blink.

Equations somersault
down the page

propagating fast-forward
alpha to omega—
beta particle hurled
against cracking concrete—
gamma ray spawning
in river delta—
marbles spill
in every direction
no walls can contain
their prolific
exuberant
course

JENNIFER HIGHLAND

Honor

for the "Fukushima Fifty"

Daily I wade through air shimmering
with neutrons—
a sparkle the eyes are not attuned
to see; a dog-whistle hum just out of range.
The body has no sense
that can detect radiation,
and if I focus my mind
on the movement of my feet,
the tasks of my hands,
I do not even think
of the beta particles bludgeoning my skin,
the sleek gamma rays
stilettoing into organs
to whittle silently at the DNA.

These old bones were born
at the dawn of the nuclear age.
They have carried me through grim times
and boom times,
through national humiliation
and technological triumph.
They have been infiltrated quietly,
year after year, with strontium-ninety:
fallout from a war
into which I was born.
Cesium ripples in my muscles,
half-life slowly ticking.

I have come by train and bus to Fukushima
bearing my bright, invisible burdens
and an engineering degree four decades old.
Each morning I wake on my small patch of floor,
swallow dry biscuits and vegetable juice
and gather with my colleagues to review
the diagrams, the progress, the newest measurements.
Then I thrust my stiff limbs into a hazmat suit
and continue our desperate work.

For you, my countrymen, and most of all
for those being born on this new spring day
into a different kind of war,
I lay down my body,
muscle, bone, memory
and two skilled hands,
a barrier stronger than lead,
a shield against a danger
your eyes cannot see.
I give you my flesh, heavy with years,
while my heart, light as paper,
unfolds its wings
like a crane preparing to fly.

DAVE BURACKER

Five

At five, the fallout shelter
meant nothing, five miles
from Pentagon ground zero.

Five sides to a graveyard,
five emergency broadcast
beeps, squelching forth;

the large yellow iron siren
outside the playground was
not a tornado siren – it bellows
before missiles fall.

Five places to hide:

Five
Under the basement stairs
coiled under carpenter nails,
a splintered coffin for plastic
action figures, melts a mold
for toy guns, discharge sparks.
Four
Deep into the storm drains
until fire passed flesh, expels
family from concrete canals
        - a radiation birth.

Three
In dreams I cannot wake
to burn, a human candle
of fat and hair smoldering;
it is never better to
duck and cover.
Two
If Father could drive past
mountains as survivors in
a Monday night mini-series,
mothers embrace children
turn to nature in ashes
- in ashes.
One
The sky will fall – there is no
fifth horse to flee from fire –
we all hide in Mother's arms
- we all fall down.

DAVE BURACKER

Rewind

No one is ever from here.
Yet, I was spawned from
cicada husks on bark,
sparkler smoke,
yoke of wet asphalt,
fear of fallout.

I am native to sidewalks,
with a fear of slashers;
where stars disappear,
where marching band
drums carry a dirge
caught in cul-de-sacs.

We hid in storm drains,
dreamed of the bomb,
a Friday night film
retracted, on fire.

K.D. ROSE

Descent

On the other side of Ecotone,
Autumn Crocus, Larkspur, Foxglove and Oleander,
bored boys of summertime wish for war
to give life meaning as they suppose it did their forefathers;

make do with plastic playthings, shooting balls and sticky guns;
pick off children in virtual movies that sting;
express a rage under carpet carefully vacuumed every Sunday;
soaked to the brain in corporate dialogue, billboard speech and T.V. themes;
fur fed with poisoned milk by cabbage on the vine;

little cozy ants running through a picnic palace;
burst with freneticism that feels like charcoal embers;
lifelike all the same until the smell of fish and wafers
and contagious echolalia goad them into line.

Animal of their innards
the only way to god
who bars his own trough.

Computer carrion,
beast mechanics,
human husbandry,
divine excretion;

time is a midget on anthills of eclipsed radiation.

DAVID MORGAN O'CONNOR

Difficult to Speak

In Japanese there is a word
we can't pronounce Nijyuu
Hibakusha means twice atomic
bomb survivor yes lucky once
missed a train got cart-wheel
stuck in the mud
the second explosion found him
descending a steel stairwell both
less than two miles from epicenter
rising from ash his phoenix
of forgiveness crosses generations
baton handed from father to son
a silent garden of hope that generals
pilots scientists street sweepers
will not burden the schoolboy
bully push the button blameless
But you did it first!
skin peeled off like gloves
magnesium parachutes
tongue dangling to eyebrow
bone torched
halos roosting
without tears we are all beasts
eye-scratch
If History is our teacher
we have all been lazy students.

Across The Pacific the cronies
                              in charge play golf slightly
                                             under par buddies inebriated
                              make decisions like martinis
to drone   pummel   invade   sanction
                              anything on a map anywhere
                                             just an obstacle to business
Nijyuu Hibakusha
                    whispers without irony or hate
                                             I just want my wife back

MANTZ YORKE

Disintegrations

Haphazardly the pinpoint suns
convulse and burst,
their potency unrealised
till blast turns matter into blast,
metal disappears as gas,
and beneath a death cap
desert sand melts into glass.

Dull distillate of earth
descends upon the city:
a trumpet heralds thunder,
lightning, earthquake, fire,
bodies seared to shadows.
Spared, a tattered crow
lurches through silent ash.

Now malignant spirits fume
deep within their concrete tombs
whilst high priests muttering,
uttering cantations,
fingering their rosaries,
strive towards redemption
and the slavery of power,

to no avail. Foul vapours
leak through unseen cracks,
imprinting latent contours
in the soil. Awake too late,
we see the altar wine turn pale
and crabs pick flesh
from pain-tormented bones.

MANTZ YORKE

Ascension Day

Feral shadows prowl beyond
the flickering fire:
fear-filled eyes gleam back
a power unrealised.

I sense fulfilment as I watch
candescent prophets turn to ash,
whirlwinds sear the city streets,
sucking air from screaming lungs
while tongues caress
the buildings' wounds.

I am
Lord of the Earth
ascended from the algal slime
to claim the throne that's rightly mine.

I ride my red horse,
nostrils aflame,
breathing life to the pyre
built on the dark plain,
cremating the water,
the earth and the air:
in the embers of dawn,
pale is his hair.

Ant-hills now shiver
at the shock of his feet;
frantic, the living
flee from the light,
burying their futures
in collapsing sand
as the Second Law clutches
the shuddering land.

No sanctuary in the crumbling church
where peeling icons hear no prayers.
The King is dead! Long live the King!
Unbelievers, kiss my ring!
The present and the past are dead:
only chaos lies ahead.

These feet can't tread out the nitred line
drawn to the coronation feast
unwitting souls prepared to toast
the dawning of a radiant reign.

DOREN DAMICO

Earthwork Humanity

Under the pyramids
Dry remains
Ochre eyed queens
A weight of death
Mirrors and sunlight
Beams the spirit

Within Fresh Kills
Rubble and bones
Sudden graveyard masses
A transport of terror
Footprints and fountain
Memorials of fallen

Through Grand Canyons
Geographical strata
Millions of years
A split view
Time and river
Flows a story

Of Angor Wat
Street grid ruins
Temple surroundings
A last relic
Stand and aerial
Views of people

Now Permian Sea
Continental mountains
Fossil records
A desert ocean
Once and great
Waves of life

Within Hiroshima Dome
Atomic wasteland
Echoing laughter
A skeleton monument
Etch and somber
Shadow for peace

Over United Nations
Community gate
Purposed speeches
A hope eternal
Rise and glimmer
Earthwork humanity

DOREN DAMICO

Walking Peace Boulevard

Head tipped down to read a city's promises
Metal rimmed ovals filled with messages
Work Peace, Teach Peace, Live Peace
Wandering, Hiroshima Peace Park
Trees, children, statues, ravaged buildings
Heart frozen footfall crossings
Delicate offerings, colored paper hope
The Bomb was here, the toxic cloud
Black ash, deadly, radioactively loud
Dream Peace, Breathe peace, Speak peace
There is the memorial
Hailing students and tourists
Stopped watches, Buddhas melted, ignoble relics
Photographs that capture so hot, so quick
Intricate lives, tragically undone
Silhouette carcass scarring stone
Weapons today, 3000 times worse
The handy taped guide explains the science
The life in me defies compliance
Create Peace, Donate Peace, Vibrate Peace
Here is the legacy
Vow to fold 1000 origami cranes
Disarmament dedicated refrains
The flame at the fountain in the center
Its illumined promise burning
Even in sleep, my hands are folding

Consoled Peace, Mold Peace, Centerfold Peace
Walking, Peace Boulevard
Footsteps pounding unceasing rhythms
Heartbeats singing auspicious hymns
Walk Peace, Talk Peace, Love Peace

MARGARET S. MULLINS

Edamame Seeds

Following the 2011 Fukushima earthquake, tsunami and nuclear disaster

Two short bent women, sisters, each
with walking stick in right hand,
heavy carpet bag in left
stump single file uphill away
from water and destruction,
eyes ahead, pace steady;
each shepherds one small child.

In their late seventies now,
they remember skipping along
with their own grandmother who
led them up a different hill in 1945,
fleeing fires and destruction of their city below,
delivered from high above by a screaming silver
B26 war hawk.

Tomorrow they will hear from local officials
about the risk of radiation, remember
tales passed down from elders
of burning flesh, illness, death, persistent fear
in those who survived the initial blast.
Tomorrow they will figure a way
to help the small children begin to cry.

Tonight they take shelter from snow
in a schoolroom high up the hill,
draw their grandchildren close, whisper to them
that they'll be okay, feed them edamame seeds
and ration sips of water, try not to envision
the fate of their own grown children in the city below
or that of their parents so long ago.

BONNIE SHIFFLER-OLSEN

Elegy to a Shrine

I.

Sannō torii stands
like a single crane caught
in late morning,
reflected on the water—
one leg firm in good fortune,
the other holding longevity
like the smooth edge of an *obi*
folded under against its soft feathered belly.

II.

In the last breath of summer
and the ascending light of fall,
the sun reposes mid-path,
suspended in its journey.
Like steam rising over pots of *miso* and rice,
the gravity of early shadow cuts scattered shapes
from the camphor-scented leaves
still crisp in the throat.
The sky tangles itself in something sacred,
something profane—
an orb paused on the warpath
before plummeting from the high plain of heaven.

III.

In these moments of perfect grace—
deep knee bends
and bicycle tires on some spiritual pavement
—the great bird soars like a pillar
as if over an Earth not yet hot to the touch.
Something like a god.
Something like a reed cut at the root.
And this day sinks into silence,
into the heavy camphor in the heat that is not air,
into so many accumulations of ringing bells:
the beating of wings,
the burning paper in broad autumn light,
a punctuated morning.

PHIL SAINTDENISSANCHEZ

the reign of the smirkers
& snickerers is over

i.

i know you talk about me behind my back
        Shannon told me
                it was either foolish or careless
                        because it's obvious we tell each other everything
i wish you would at least tell true tales about me
        i have so many failed moments to choose from
                you don't need to invent stories about me, too
it's okay
        i understand
                you like to control your environment
                  & i'm more animal
                i would probably devour your environment
                until i was it
                            je suis un autre
                        always
                                not until death
                                      but especially in it
i am it
        before
                your ability to ignore is profound
                    i was lost in its prominence
                        placed at the forefront

for everything unknown is a threat
    &we must deflect & decry
        name before the birth
           if we want it to die
                i will be less honest in the future
                      at the forefront of the future
                        i will place my patience
                          for your benefit
(i'm trying to remember all the lines before i begin again to write)
the lovely angle of the cocaine mirror,
    as a professor,
        you can pause to admire yourself within it
           &

           what a white world you've woven!
                it is like all the white worlds
                that seem singular from within
                they are threatened by hunger
            they fade to stains on my sheets
              tossed in wastepaper baskets
                  to die

       in latex
         spider webs
           catch light
     beside my bed in rapturous ways
       divide waves
         & refract
     the rainbow awoke
       & spoke,
it's time to get out there & let them eat cake!
yes,
    you are right.
        i am late for the beheadings

ii.

aside from a number of very notable exceptions,
        Generation X was mainly just a bunch of bored cowards
                with lame excuses for their impotence
they are not alone in the blame
           being born in the still-warm, still-splintering, still-radioactive
bath of Hiroshima
                suffering daily, nightly from *Future Shock*
in its wake
                enduring the most fractured wave of ideas &
corresponding events & facts yet
             rushing back up into their brains,
                our brain
but if I ever allow CULTURE, Reagan idolizers, the ZEITGEIST,
the UNIVERSE,
          the infinite pull of a black hole of stellar mass, Hulk Hogan's
22-inch pythons,
          GOD
          to keep me from becoming the
          American superherosonofgod
please place my neck in the guillotine
       let it slowly split
          while lost, unfulfilled maids
             sing me French lullabyes
THIS IS AMERICA
where the baby butt 38-year old baby brothers of that baby-booming
atomic wave say
       things like,
           i'm getting kinda old, ya know?
son, your great grandpop ain't a twinkle in the first wrinkle of old
       we just burst from stardust damn near yesterday
& this fool is wearing neon sunglasses

& smirking
at other fools wearing neon sunglasses
& feeling
SOMEHOW
faintly superior
& bathing nightly in nostalgia
PUBLICLY
like he has the unfortunate honor & high distinction
of being
THE END OF IT ALL
shut your MacIntosh apple pie hole,
stop popping bubbles with the self-pity of pop,
throw some Xanax in your murse,
tighten the straps on your mandles,
&
TAKE THE INFINITE AMERICAN JOURNEY

iii.

ecstasy has waited long enough
& it is stasis that is
by nature
the patient one
i'm here to restore the natural order
NOW is the time to just LET A DOG LIVE
proclaimeth every DOG & DOG SYMPATHIZER
in the land
we were ruled by sneering, snarking whiskers shameful seconds ago
they are not so important now though
mainly I just want you all to know:
THE REIGN OF THE SMIRKERS & SNICKERERS IS OVER

breathe a sigh of relief
they are all transparent & pale
      we have never touched
we have ghosts on record now
      their blood is on my canines
            HAIL

R.G. EVANS

Fallout

Beside the crucifix in the Catholic school lunchroom
hung a black and yellow fallout shelter sign.
We'd cross ourselves for Grace, but instead of praying

I'd think of fallout, imagine it as snow-like flakes,
gray and silent, floating down to cover and burn
everything they touched. Born too late for air raid drills,

we had no rituals to teach us how to fear the atom
like the ones that showed us how to fear our Lord.
Nuns taught us geometry and about the triune God,

but I studied the yellow trinity of triangles
inside that priestblack disk. One for the Father,
one for the Son, and one for the Holy Ghost

who moved across creation as a dove, a breath—
or as tongues of flame that descended upon the Apostles
at Pentecost. Christ's isosceles wounds watched over us

as we ate lunch amid the mysteries of our faith,
sheltered from any fire that might fall out of the sky.

ANDREW MERTON

Fifth Grade Air Raid Drill, 1955

I tell Mr. Carter there's a crack in the ant farm,
but he has more important things to talk about today.

After the bomb, trees will wither, milk will glow.
You might live a year before the insects get you

but first you must survive the blast.
Duck under your desks

and stick your heads between your knees.
I pretend to do as I'm told.

When he turns his back I crawl away
on six legs, triumphant.

MIRIAM WEINSTEIN

Here — for a moment

Haunted by images of atomic warfare, dark clouds hovered like helicopters
in my imagination as I ran, ran with a pack of friends across

clipped lawns playing hide-and-seek. Late afternoons, and I followed
my darkening shadow home where arms waited to enfold me.

Hands folded politely in the '50s formed into fists in the '60s, protests
burned along the streets of America, boys broken

or burned in Vietnam and, for the first time, we witnessed war
while sitting on living room couches,

witnessed bodies lifted from war zones, piled on gurneys, flown home.
The dead — a number at the end of the newscast.

Leaving my childhood home, I found temporary dwellings
dotting the map of North America; I studied

the art of evasion, and learned to avoid the terror beating
in my heart by studying the steady beat of wings

by the shore of Lake Harriet, heartened
to see the fanned formation of geese flying overhead.

Hugging the Baltic Sea — Estonia, Latvia, Lithuania; fanning out to touch
Russia — Belarus, Ukraine, Kazakhstan. One after the other: Moldova,

Georgia, Armenia, Azerbaijan; the Cold War ended as new countries
formed along river beds and hillsides, one after the other,

Uzbekistan and Turkmenistan; new boundary lines
embraced farm land and forest.

Now, I use the lines of poetry. I write about lines,
and their unlikely intersections. Regardless,

the sun rises at dawn and sets at dusk. Regardless
of what happens between those moments.

Here — for a moment.

Moments — more than minutes, or hours, more than days
or weeks or months — matter. Moments turn into years as the earth

spins around. Mother earth. Weighed down

by bones, I yearn for the hollow bones of a bird
so that, like a pelican, I could follow rivers to a lake forming

in the Australian desert; I could grow fat on fish flourishing there.
More likely, I will grow old here in the land of 10,000 lakes

where loons have always flourished, their tremolos
cutting the darkness.

MIRIAM WEINSTEIN

Twenty ways of looking at my life

1. I was born on an isthmus between two lakes and learned to swim like a seal.

2. Abundance swam through my childhood.

3. Growing in a world where anything was possible, my parents inspired dreams of abundance.

4. Grandparents, Great-aunties, and Uncles pinched my cheeks wistfully smiling; muttering to each other in a language I did not understand.

5. Yiddish cadences dotted the tones of the English they spoke, and laced the language I learned at home.

6. In grade school I learned not to use these words.

7. My mother's words — *Clean your plate* — were followed by a common refrain: *Think of the children starving in China.*

8. I looked at the mashed potatoes and slivers of brisket scattered along the rim of my plate. I saw Chinese children with straight caps of black hair.

9. I settled under oaks that reached towards heaven, and I dug. I dug and dug and dug in the moist black dirt. I dug through vines and roots in my pursuit — China —on the other side of the world.

10. Television news brought stark images of China and Russia into the homes of middle America.

11. Black and white TV. Black and white photographs. Black and White. Good or Bad. Freedom or Communism.

12. The Bomb. The Arms Race. The Space Race. Communism in Cuba. Adults whispering in solemn tones as I hovered, shaking, in the hallway. Russians arming the island with weapons. Weapons pointing directly at my bedroom window.

13. The movies — my window to the world — for one dollar, my friends and I spent summer days in an air-conditioned movie theatre watching the same movie playing again and again

14. Again and again. And my days spun around

15. and around. And, it's not black or white. There are many shades,

16. shades of grey. I could have been born eighteen years earlier in a ghetto in Poland, a *shtetl* in Russia, a crowded one room apartment in a nameless Romanian town. Unlikely, yes. Impossible — no.

17. I would be another clump of grey ashes swept from a Nazi incinerator. Many heroes became clumps of ashes.

18. Me. I am not a hero. I am anxious; sometimes timid and weak.

19. What, then, would be the possibility of me? Of me writing this poem.

20. Such happenstance in a the world of endless possibilities.

BRITTANY MISHRA

Flame

like a sheet of paper
once creased
these hands
never again the same

with each breath
another notch
to count down
one more day

each wrinkle
an origami
rustling
a thousand cranes
each year
a thousand more made

and in the end
all
like me
will rise into flame

WILLIAM PITT ROOT

The Day

The day the sun rises twice
our oldest dream of fire come true
  fire that burns forever
  fire no water can quench
 fire whose light welds our shadows to stones
fire whose oceanic flash turns a sky full of birds to ash

Aeons after the last of
our one-eyed prophets
has chanted
  into that permanent darkness
 there will be no archeologist to unearth
such countless minute embers as still linger among the omens

So I make this mark on silence now
knowing there will be none to speak
  none to hear
   once the clouds are rising in our eyes
 against those suns surrounding us
like the thousand thousand trees of life all clad in flame

JOHN CANADAY

David Nicodemus

Physicist, Trinity Test

Dear Mami,
            I am not the same who wrote
you yesterday. The storm has passed. The sun
beats fists against the canvas of my tent
and shakes dust in my eyes with every blow.
I saw a thing last night. I cannot say—
or having said, can't send. You won't know what
a while. But even were I there and free
to talk—I have no words. Or only words.
I don't know what I saw. Frisch said, "A red
hot elephant upended on its trunk."
The other fellows laughed.
                              My rhythm's off.
I saw our village ashed, the men's school burn
again, remembered how the gusting winds
spread pinwheel sparks. The great bass temple bell
on Mukoyama woke us. Cook helped pack
my wicker case. You wedged me in a second
sweater, hid us in the bamboo grove.
We watched while father fought the flames, filling
our honey buckets at the shallow well,
not fast enough. Smoke smudged his preacher's skin
a devil dark—his face a Hannya mask—
as though some jealousy had conjured up
the flames that swallowed almost all he loved.

131

"Heathens," he might have said, but never did.
He proffered a Trinity, but they preferred
the human godhead of a young marine
biologist. Warlike and practical
and proud, they always had too little faith
in higher powers. Even father's aide,
old Murayama-san, socked all his cash
in dentures, buying gold teeth one by one.
Old samurai, he had the kids pretend
Hirose-gawa was a castle moat
and taught us how to swim with just our feet,
imaginary swords held overhead,
his leather shako leading and, bone-dry,
its draggled plume. But father thought he knew
God's will. He spread the Word: "And he rebuked
the winds, and walked upon the waves dry-shod"—
that Christ might be a light to heal blind eyes.

I thought so, too, but planned on getting proof.
A pal and I spent all day laying cable,
sweating our sins away in blazing sun.
Come dusk, we found an empty base camp hut
and stowed our stuff before the storm began.
The roof was tight enough; the instruments
stayed mostly dry. But then brass bullied in.
We packed and grumbled till some G.I. perched
like a sacred lion on the next hut's steps
shushed us: "The General needs his shut eye." But
we couldn't help the engine being cold.
We gunned it till the crankcase glowed, then beat
a tactical retreat to watch God's will
from a hillside twenty clicks away.

　　　　　　　　Our friends
were there already, and we sat together
waiting in a deep obscurity
of darkness, like ghosts on a river's brink,
shivering on the damp earth, fearing, longing
to hear the boatman's cry.
　　　　　　　　And suddenly
there came a golden heat of sunlight down
and a purple and a royal light shining,
and I knew that God had blessed and damned us,
granting everything that we had wished.

JOHN CANADAY

David McDonald

Rancher, Alamogordo, NM

And it was quite a while, y'know, till they
begin to talk about the cattle—how
their hair was turning white on them, like frost.
The way we noticed it was if a cow
was lying on her left side, well her right
would get a brand from particles of fallout
falling there, causing a burn just like a scald,
and then the hair, instead of growing red
like on a Hereford cow, would come back white,
the way a saddle burn shows on a black horse.
And old Mack Smith, that owned the general store,
had a cat just as black as the ace of spades,
till that thing grew white spots all over it.
He sold it to some tourist, for five dollars
I think it was, as a curiosity.

JOHN CANADAY

Edith Warner

Ran a tea room for Los Alamos scientists

As season follows season, I sense a change,
though subtle, in the earth. Like the thin veil of green
that mantles the desert after rain, a change
has come upon the land. Or else, I hope, the difference is in me.
Now when I smell the Russian olive's bloom each May,
when the woods along the river fill with its rosy scent,
another odor teases my palate, faint, vague, but inescapable—
like the hint of bitterness in milk that will soon sour.
Now when I hear the wind in the salt cedar's feathery leaves,
another sound frets gently in my ear, almost inaudible,
like the whispered passing of a rattlesnake across dry sand.
And now when I see children in the pueblo spreading sheets
beneath the piñon trees to gather nuts, high on the edge of sight
a brief metallic glint catches my eye, then vanishes,
and I stop, and the veil falls, and I listen for the bee drone
fading in and out on the drifting wind. And if
I have not heard it yet, I know, I can't forget, I might.

AARON LEE

Future Tense

after the Erythraean Sibyl

No. I did not always see how things began,
and yet I could not avoid
being distressed by what I did see.
That I yet snatch a word
or phrase or two out of the fire
the way paper clutches at ink,
may prove some comfort to me at the end.

That I sometimes lose enjoyment in
my morning walk or a cocktail in the evening,
also leaves me dispossessed.
Things have not improved as long
as I can remember, and so it is unlikely
the outcome will be any good.
Don't tell me otherwise.
Though I wouldn't say there is nothing
that lifts my heart. But how it is now:
redundant children, politicians trading blows on TV,
how bad news drown us in real time—
such things insist that the end will arrive,
and none too soon.
What we have made of the past
can never be erased but each of us,
being practical, carries what we can bear of it.
Sometimes I wonder if I can step away from it all—
leave the future behind as it comes home to us
and I write it, just now, with my very own hand.

EMMET O'CUANA

Game Theory

Speaking in tongues to your neighbor
Simple lives divided by walls
Speech reduced to babble,
Pride in blindness,
Pride in deafness,
Clinging to known unknowns,
Demigods wearing shirts and ties
A mythic world mapped
From one end to the other
Reports of Pan's death are exaggerated
& Oppenheimer burns in atomic hell

PAMELA USCHUK

Genesis Revisited: The Chernobyl Buffalo

for Mary McGarvey and the buffalo

Some 150,000 square kilometers in Belarus, Russia and Ukraine are contaminated and stretch northward of the nuclear plant site as far as 500 kilometers. An area spannning around the plant considered "the exclusion zone" is essentially uninhabited.

You would see dystopia come true as your skin,
if you could walk these glowing forests growing up
through pavement in the abandoned city. Mushrooms
crack sidewalks, vines and bushes
chink condo walls while bourgeois houses sink like stumps
into a wilderness that would excite Jeffers, Thoreau or Muir
as much as frighten the ghosts of my greatgrandparents
irradiated in the path of the fallout.

Through the girdered skeleton of the nuclear plant
Is a perfect view of the rotting skyline and,
restored by once-extinct beavers,
the labyrinthine channels of the Pripyat Swamp that stopped
even Ghenghis Khan's bloody march.

Now, a few researchers roam The Exclusion Zone,
heft Geiger Counters that click like an explosion of typewriters
tapping obituaries for buffalo bones, tree limbs,
phosphorescent soil. But, what they discover is destruction
that begat Eden complete with mutant angels—
packs of gray wolves, buffalo,
moose, sturdy deer herds,
white-tailed eagles, ravens, and miraculous
reincarnated beavers—pristine and leafy beyond their scientific dreams.

Against toxic apartment walls, crumbling schools,
an echoing hospital, wolves curl
against howling winter snows. Come spring, buffalo
graze at ease between sprouting deciduous trees
that were once shopping malls.

How many decades have we feared apocalypse
born from splitting atoms to incinerate our enemies?
Who thought we could play tag with the sun and win?
Perhaps, the self-destruction we craft is
precisely what this planet needs to heal, to spawn
ozone we continue to deplete, clean up multitudes
of poisons we've shit all over our gifts.

Think of the restored without us—the smooth lope
of wolves over clean snow, buffalo
and their spiritual eyes we exterminated world-wide,
the wide leaves of rainforest trees spreading
instead of urban sprawl, generating what
we could breathe deep to live,
what we tried to kill, divine.

PAMELA USCHUK

Of Simple Intent

"The desert can be all things to man but above all it is a symbol of what
   has been most deeply denied in man's spirit...a bright mirror wherein they see the
      arid reflection of their own rejected and uncared-for selves."

Laurens van der Post

Sunset blasts the San Pedro Valley
where mountains are cryptic primordial tongues
comfortable in a desert
our thirsty words are useless to describe.
What they tell us is like a stone
of simple intent in our hands.
              In inescapable heat,
heat is the mirror that charges
each pitch of land and season.

Who would call this place barren cannot know
the endurance of Live Oak,
Manzanita,
yellow flowering Mesquite,
whole nations of wildflowers
thriving among rocks after rain.

We are house-weary
tired of the same news—
                    drive-by murders, terrorists, the
genocidal arc of Middle East wars,
soaring defense budgets for doomsday weapons
that can detonate the world from outer space.
Titan missiles glow underground
like Minotaurs to be restored
for the final sacrifice of a burning world.

We climb over heat-split stone, follow
the small scat trails of rabbits,
skirting turpentine bushes
that might hide a Gila Monster
or a rattler's lair.

By chance we find a huge Yucca tree, bathed
in the tangerine blood of last light.
Sword-haired and flat black
as a buffalo's back, it seems
to twist while its three faces muse,
unmoved by a dervish of wind.

Overshadowing us on this hill,
each of its shaggy arms ignite monsterous beauty.
Here is a Titan we can believe in, rooted
          in the ancient landscape of intuition
          that no computer can imagine.
Radiant with unprogrammable light
this is the power that names us,
compelling as desire,
shifting in its old bowl of shadow
          and prophecy, backlit
by desert's blood-copper tides,
even as warmth leaks from the world.

PAMELA USCHUK

Rafting the River of Death

for Joy

At current level, we floated on a piece of tin, some thin
metal Texaco sign given to us by gods we could't see
to keep us dry and eye to eye with the drift of the dead—

dismembered whales, dolphins, polar bears and oceanblown
birds, chopped up and overtaking us in the river
pouring from the base of Alaska. The known wilderness

was skinned of trees, plundered beyond dreams. Like
a crazed ice floe, the eye of a whale and its nebulae
of surrounding flesh whirled close enough for us to see

the vast intelligence dyed into the paralyzed lapis nexus.
At first, I was repulsed by the span of man-centered carnage,
massacre, the demise of wildlife on such a Grand Old Party scale,

but your eyes told me how sacred these parts
and beautiful. You said, *touch them. It is all
touch.* So I reached across heartbreak to stroke the eye

beyond corruption, my hand a neon wand of fear, my heart
spasmodic in its bell of loneliness. Perhaps it was then that I
could join the dead or was simply comforted by communion,

touching the whole mouth of creation breathe into each
separate cell, a being indivisible as the universe
or the knowledge of love. I knew, then, no one is immune,

no oil exec or lumber emir, secretary of war, you
or me, knew that our spiral wires are constructed from
the DNA of twinned stars and bonded like quarks

or hydrogen molecules, interdependent as electricity
and balancing everything. In that iceflash recognition
I knew why we'd chosen to ride out destruction

on such a precarious wing, why there is no safe shore
to keep us untouched witnesses,why our charge

is the constant navigation of song through dreamdeep currents

braided with islands of beauty, of terror, betrayal, passion
and fear. Call it mystery or logic. It is all
the same. Death is what we misname.

JANET CANNON

hail to the jellyfish

we've demonstrated rallied
marched sat-in protesting
from diablo canyon to seabrook

we've blocked doorways
placed our bodies across
roads held hands around
cities walked miles without
terrestrial discriminations

we've signed petitions
distributed concerned scientists'
fact sheets publicly written
letters made speeches voted
and we haven't deterred
a single kilowatt hour
of nuclear energy production

but the jellyfish—hail
the jellyfish have done it!

they've shut down florida
power and light company's
st. lucie twin nuclear
reactor—hail to the jellyfish!

they've clogged the ocean
water cooling system's filtering
screen—hail to the jellyfish!

they've succeeded peacefully
without pomp—hail to the jellyfish!
triumphant students for martin
luther king's *nonviolent resistance*
hail to the jellyfish hail!

JANET CANNON

portrait of a nuclear family

the father is home
feeding his brain tumor terminally
with sparse scalp hair he earned in
the uranium mine of a slow death aphrodisiac
he breathed working twenty years
to buy early expiration rites

the mother is crying
in the rocking chair of miscarried conceptions
with bare normalities sinewless
in her barren womb…that doesn't bloom
the desert body of motherhood
empty with the procreation of her desire

the children are buried
in simple graves they had no occasion
to see one minute of the *fait accompli*
or hear a second of pulsation
in their fetal minds mutated genes aborted
by the nectar of technological gods

their adobe house glows
even on new moon midnight
with the cologne of destruction dancing
the jig on geiger counter dial needle
stuck on maximum register the bricks
homemade from corporate profit high tailings

ALINE SOULES

Half Life

1945, Little Boy explodes over Hiroshima
Fat Man over Nagasaki

burns, radiation sickness
nursing children suck poison in mothers' milk

U.S. military confiscates Japanese film
bans John Hersey's *Hiroshima*

requires Japanese to take classes
on the value of a free press

Japan renounces the right to make war
without parliament's approval and public referendum

Americans are taught bombs spared lives
because the war ended sooner

DNA mutations, stunted growth
tumors, leukemia

Workers from pipe-fitters to physicists
build nuclear plants and stockpiles

2015, Japan votes to allow military combat
for the first time in seventy years—protests follow

world news covers remembrance ceremonies
students interview survivors, learn

fingertips of the dead caught fire
that spread through bodies

blackened skin sloughed off
like blanched tomatoes

plutonium 239 alpha rays
exploded in lungs

&&&

2011, Fukushima Dai-ichi nuclear disaster
employees try to stabilize the plant

governments weaken standards of radiation exposure
claim human contact is below harmful levels

skin contamination, endocrine damage
depression, anxiety

2015, the International Atomic Energy Agency concludes
no discernible health consequences are expected

Japanese officials tell pregnant women
not to worry about radiation levels

thyroid cancer, miscarriages, stillbirths
cancer in babies around the Pacific Rim

Japan's Labor Ministry confirms the first case of cancer
for a former Fukushima employee

McClatchy News uncovers effects of the cold war
on U. S. workers at nuclear plants

governments hide radiation records
praise workers for their sacrifice

beryllium contamination, allergic reactions
breathing problems, death

&&&

shadows still remain
from below bodies vaporized
on Sumitomo Bank steps

skeleton of Genbaku Dome
heart of Hiroshima Peace Memorial Park
pierces the sky at ground zero

MARY GILLILAND

harp of the wind

harp of the wind

heft of the fire

intelligence of the water

now   ?
nod   now

the Senses cannot detect
Radiation
unseen as the Soul

Here   is   our grief

o u r m o m e n t of grief
o r   m o'
∧   ∧
u   ment

the Emperor's ancestor
the Dragon King
beat the bones out of the Jellyfish

MARY GILLILAND

In legend

In legend
Curie's radium
often drove
the later experiments
Radioactive elements
seldom glow   The rays
are actually
tiny particles
much much finer than dust
Lose a particle, change
into a different element

Traditionally
energy
has been termed a fundamental property
of matter

Any minute now
matter is no more
than a fundamental property
of energy

Mme Curie
receives
transmits
transforms

MARY GILLILAND

Make the symbol

Make the symbol   Say it 3 times while you
strengthen hamstrings   Relax hip flexors
                              on
Beach St Rt 1 Atlantic Ave Pacific Ave
                              River Rd Falls St Riverside Dr

RN
one of the densest substances that remains a gas
                              (under normal conditions)

naturally occurring

the only gas under normal conditions that has only radioactive isotopes

                              how do I prove this
                              and to whom
                    Rn
                a noble gas
                colorless
                odorless
                tasteless

                (through the forest out to the waterline
                (over the plains toward the great divide

no passing zone caution stop

                    if I am no longer eligible
                    to buy Rx coverage
                    what do I do on

Alameda Blvd Zuni Rd Candelaria Rd
            Indian School Rd Coors Blvd Lead Ave Coal Ave

            radon daughters
            solids, not gas
         stick to dust particles
     and thus to airways of the lungs
    Won't come clean   Don't wash away
  Anybody's basement   Can have magic rocks

MAUREEN ANNE BROWNE

Hibakusha

A-bomb survivors

They had dug themselves
in like rabbits; staggered
out into ash and bone:

the doctor never tried
to save his wife
from being burned alive;

the daughter stayed
under cover rather than
go to find her mother;

the woman refused
one layer of her clothes
to a dying child who was cold.

In tents and shacks they try
to rebuild their homes.

It isn't long before
the blackened stumps are fruiting
camphor and willow buds;

street-cars clattering,
children at school again,
cafés serving sushi;

workers rebuilding
the prefectures, tangerines
in the market piled in pyramids;

the people worship in a new
cathedral, but shadows remain,
the phantom voices do not fade.

MAUREEN ANNE BROWNE

Nagasaki

A young woman
stands in the aftermath
disorientated –
everything in her world
has turned to rubble
in shades of black:

the cindered streets
are still hot;
charred bones lying
alongside melted roof tiles,
deformed sake bottles,
warped frying pans;

the stench
of incinerated flesh clings;
the only semblance
of another human being
an image, burned
into a concrete step;

she cannot cope
with something this grotesque
terrified there is nothing
to hope for left.
Her senses quicken –
in the air, Chrysanthemum.

SILAS OLA ABAYOMI

Hiroshima and Nagasaki

Seventy Years after Atomic Use.

Mushroom smoke enveloped
the cities,
within minutes of detonation,
several thousand died from
burns, radiation, and heat
Little Boy-brought upon-
Hiroshima and
Fat Man's gift to
Nagasaki people;
seventy years after,
Japanese are
still wailing.

Oh! Little Boy,
how little were you?
Hiroshima, you reduced
to ashes,
her population you cut in halve,
her buildings, structures, and
personality it stood for,
you reduced to rubbles.

Fat Man-your wide
round shape-
was your strength,
your weight, length,
height and
object in you-Plutonium-
made Nagasaki feared you.

Little Boy and Fat Man,
you left behind people-
with severe burns, radiation-
diseases, injuries, malnutrition,
ruptured eardrum, and
genetically deficient human cells.

Little Boy and Fat Man,
even in retirement and
now that you are sleeping
in death,
Hiroshima, Nagasaki, and
Japanese are still mourning.

Seven decades after,
memories of August 6th and
8th, 1945 still haunt and torment
the land of reigning emperors with
history of three thousand years of
continuous rulership.

The land of Meiji is yet
to recover from political,
social, and cultural hemorrhage
placed upon it by Little Boy and
Fat Man when you both visited.

As Japanese, remember
first atomic bomb use in
warfare and walked through
dark road to the rebuilt
cities of Hiroshima and
Nagasaki,
even as they have become
cities of "culture and prosperity"
Japanese and the humankind
want to "re-emphasize the
necessity of world peace."

With confirmed
ten-nuclear-power-
nation,
over ten thousand
nuclear warheads-
decommissioned and
partially dismantled,
which can be assembled
in a jiffy,
put humans and the earth on
pathway of extinction.

As more nations now pursue
nuclear ambition with ferocity-
will it guarantee world peace or
make the world more unsecured?
With or without mutual assured
destruction MAD doctrine-
will it guarantee world peace?

The lessons from
Hiroshima and
Nagasaki are eternal
pains and cries,
generation after generation;
more so, ethical dilemmas and
moral questions nuclear weapons will
pose from generation to generation.

SILAS OLA ABAYOMI

Nineteen Forty-Five - The Year that Changed the World

Nineteen Forty-Five
let no one forget you in a hurry,
rather may this generation
remember day-by-day,
month-by-month events
that drew tears from our
grand-parents, parents, uncles,
aunts, and their contemporaries;
let this generation weep for
the pains, sorrows, and
emotional scars nineteen forty-five
brought upon humankind.

Nineteen Forty-Five
sixth year of maelstrom,
peak of bedlam and darkness
that overshadowed light;
year of unlimited rage,
year carnage, massacre,
pogrom, and genocide
became international norms;
hysteria and frenzy adopted
as public behavior.

Nineteen Forty-Five
the year voice of reasoning and
words of wisdom were lost
on human,
civility turned barbaric,
cloud of uncertainty enveloped
world of humankind.

Nineteen Forty-Five
Allied and Axis powers engaged
in fierce battle for control,
Allied delivered world from
savagery;
Europe saved from
self-destruction,
Africa rescued from leeches,
Asia liberated from tyrants,
Australia and the Oceania
saved from predators.

Nineteen Forty-Five
first time atomic bomb
used in warfare,
which changed warfare from
"total war to belligerent";
a new warfare without soul,
mind, and human heart,
ultimate desire is to destroy and
to annihilate civilization by using
"conventional weapons,"
weapons of mass destruction.

Since 1945 floodgate of wars
had opened,
wars caused by politicians
without conscience and principles,
supported by business and
economic class that lack
morals and ethics,
sustained by religions
deficient in good works
for lack of sacrifice.

Nineteen Forty-Five
world known-psychopath-
toothbrush moustache carrier,
Adolph Hitler and Eva Braun,
his frau and one-day wife
committed suicide
ending a 12-year rocky relationship
that involved several suicide attempts.

Nineteen Forty-Five
Italian Fascist leader,
Benito Amilcare Mussolini,
with childhood reputation
for violence killed at Lake Como;
Emperor Hirohito abjured his
divinity, announced Japanese's
unconditional surrender.

Nineteen Forty-Five
Germany surrendered,
divided among Allied powers,
Yalta Agreement signed by
victors-US, UK, France and
USSR;
Soviet reached Berlin on
the last military campaign.

Nineteen Forty-Five
World War 11 ended,
German War Crimes trial
began at Nuremburg;
scores of war criminals
executed by hanging and
many sentenced to life term.

Nineteen Forty-Five
Joseph Goebbels-
worst propagandist in
history and wife committed
suicide,
after killing their six children.

Nineteen Forty Five
hostilities between Chinese
Nationalists and Chinese
Communists became open,
as new hostilities between
United States and Soviet Union
soon created cold war that
divided world into two opposing
ideologies for decades.

Nineteen Forty-Five
American war hero,
President Franklin D. Roosevelt
died,
succeeded by Harry Truman;
across Atlantic, British War
Prime Minister, Winston Churchill
lost to Clement Attlee,
without knowledge or design
Trans-Atlantic relations managed
by new actors.

French's Charles De Gaulle
became the head,
provisional government of the
French Republic,
until fourth Republic came
on board in 1946.

Nineteen Forty Five
fifty-one nations gave
life to the newly created-
world body-United Nations
replacing ineffective-
League of Nations.

Nineteen Forty-Five
historic year that shaped and
changed the world;
seventy years after
mankind is yet to recover
from lunacy Nineteen Forty-Five
follies placed upon mankind.

All traps set decades ago
have created today's
dreaded octopus that
no one can tame.
Who heals humankind?
Who saves humankind?
Who delivers humanity
from ominous dangling
catastrophe that the foundation
was laid in 1945?

If man had seen Nineteen
Forty-Five in advance with
baggage it carried,
man might have fast forwarded
or skipped the obstreperous year;
inasmuch as man has no
control over time and season,
but only over conducts and
behaviors,
Nineteen Forty-Five is a lesson,
a lesson FOR LIFE.

SARAH BROWN WEITZMAN

Hiroshima is a Name We Don't Know Yet

My mother is mixing a half-dozen muffins
this July evening. Tall in her high heels,

she creams the butter and sugar, then slowly adds
the eggs. She smells of Shalimar and vanilla

in the oven-warm kitchen. Intent, she doesn't speak
except about her own mother's cakes. I am

waiting as patiently as nine can for a heaping tablespoon
of batter for my jar-lid pan for a tiny cake of my own.

Still wearing his jacket and tie my father's reading
the newspaper. Through the glass door, we can see him

sitting in the big side-winged horsehair chair
in the bay window. We know he's waiting too

to read the war news to us as the house fills with the odor
of rising dough. Hiroshima is a name we don't know

yet. Outside the gloom sits on the porch settee
and whines like a dog to be left in.

Finally, it is time. My mother's muffins have billowed
high out of their cups, golden as the kitchen ceiling

and edged with a perfect complement of brown.
But my tiny cake, left in too long, is black, flat

and rock-hard. Oh, how I weep like a lost child
now for my childhood and that little charred cake.

SUSAN DEER CLOUD

Atoms

for Erelene

Every weekday on the far side of town
my sister eight years younger than I
wakes to her alarm's pre-dawn buzz,
barely able to move because her body
hurts in every atom and her neck,
once broken, locks up.

Every darkest hour, five days a week,
she wakes this way the same as our father
once woke, shaking off a dreamtime
sometimes tortured with nightmares,
the same as women and men all across
America wake and instantly want

to weep because they must go to work
at some shit job for little pay (everyone
knows if you complain you get fired).
Everyday my sister awakes in the bedroom
where I first saw her, newborn,
in my mother's arms, 1959

right before the 'Sixties made the scene
and we all felt hope again, believing
people really could soften life's meanness,
stop wars like "The Good War" our father
was wounded in, prevent poverty,
racism, sexism, dismantle

the nuclear bombs. I marched against
the Vietnam War and for the poetry
of good causes because I didn't want
my baby sister to ever cease smiling
the way she smiled that January evening
I bowed my face over her eyes

completely blue, irises
and even the "whites."
I wanted life to blaze
like the sky of her eyes for her,
to bring Peace and Love,
not the worries I had because

I heard my father cry out in the nights,
the bullet repeatedly entering his chest,
because I had my own nightmares
after air raid drills at school
and the Bay of Pigs when we feared
the Soviets would soon drop

the atom bomb on Manhattan,
a prime target and us only
a hundred miles away sure to die
of radiation. Every weekday
my sister groans out of bed,
limps stiffly to a cold kitchen,

brews coffee then sits outside
to watch the sun rise effortlessly,
leaving a trail of roses above
the east horizon. Yesterday
she phoned when she dragged home
from work, wept she was afraid

there'd be a nuclear holocaust after
the latest Taliban beheading and Putin
making bare-chested threats. I consoled her
until we white-haired sisters renewed
our vow to forever see roses
in a newborn sky blue on azure.

SUSAN DEER CLOUD

Hiroshima Schoolboy: Tankas in Four Parts on the Anniversary of the Bombing of Hiroshima

I.

It shone like a bird.
My best friend danced out to it.
I watched by a wall.
My friend waved at the strange wings.
He laughed as the dark egg fell.

II.

I turned blind at first.
If only I had stayed blind.
Friend shadow on stone
after the egg cracked open.
Pretty chrysanthemum cloud.

III.

In time the funerals.
We lost all words, even hell.
I became a wall.
The mothers wouldn't look at me.
Why didn't I die, their sons live?

IV.

A bright bird he was.
His raven's hair shone unruly.
He'd be a poet.
Oh, friend, nothing touches me.
Except I bow to your fire.

JOEL ALLEGRETTI

"Hiroshima!" I Cried

<u>Dramatis Personae</u>

Speaker One
Speaker Two
Speaker Three

Speaker One, Speaker Two and Speaker Three stand side by side before the audience as follows:

> Speaker One, stage right;
> Speaker Two, middle;
> Speaker Three, stage left.

Speaker One and Speaker Three wear white shirts and and white slacks. Speaker Two wears a red shirt and white slacks.

Speaker One and Speaker Three lift their heads skyward. Speaker Two's head is bowed. All three extend their arms from their sides, palms up.

The Speakers deliver their lines as if in a trance and at the same pace. The lines are in sets of 23 to represent 8/6/45, the date of the bombing of Hiroshima: 8 + 6 + 4 + 5 = 23. Speaker Two's concluding line, however, is in a set of six to represent the sixth day of August.

Speaker One:

Light heals sin. Light heals sin. Light heals sin.
Light heals sin. Light heals sin. Light heals sin.

Light heals sin. Light heals sin. Light heals sin.
Light heals sin. Light heals sin. Light heals sin.
Light heals sin. Light heals sin. Light heals sin.
Light heals sin. Light heals sin. Light heals sin.
Light heals sin. Light heals sin. Light heals sin.
Light heals sin. Light heals sin.

Speaker One intones a second complete set of "Light heals sin" during Speaker Three's recitation.

Speaker Three:

Light peels skin.
Light peels skin.
Light peels skin.
Light peels skin.
Light peels skin.
Light peels skin.
Light peels skin.
Light peels skin.
Light peels skin.
Light peels skin.
Light peels skin.
Light peels skin.
Light peels skin.
Light peels skin.
Light peels skin.
Light peels skin.
Light peels skin.
Light peels skin.
Light peels skin.
Light peels skin.
Light peels skin.
Light peels skin.

Speaker One and Speaker Three recite, respectively, a third and second set of their lines during Speaker Two's recitation.

Speaker Two:

Light steals kin. Light steals kin.

Speaker One falls silent after the third set of "Light heals sin."

Speaker Three falls silent after the second set of "Light peels skin."

The completion of both sets is to be timed to coincide with Speaker Two's 23rd "Light steals kin." Speaker Two then delivers the closing lines.

Speaker Two:

> Light steals kin.
> Light steals kin.
> Light steals kin.
> Light steals kin.
> Light steals kin.
> Light (*pause*) steals (*pause*) kin.

VISHAL AJMERA

Hour of Darkness

Hour of Darkness
world fractioned in parts; in shambles
stirred and aghast.
Struck with consternation
tagged 'nuclear depression'.
Weapon of mass destruction
humanity seeking restoration.

Impact so deadly; nuclear disgrace
only blood and burns, cries around.
Smothering humanity
in the fog of sound.
Emotions dead, extinct another race.
War conspiracy ?
or treason unjustified ?
How can 'nuclear' as strength emphasized ?

Flora and fauna; murdered to death
no traces of last earthly breath.
Unfertile land, polluted heavenly sky
nuclear erosion;
the only reason, why!
Nature's plight, never human's delight
unending gloom, nearing sight.

Nuclear- free living!
Can world ever disarm?
or; fighting battles of glory
ever lose its charm.
The momentous day never so far
wrapped in pages of history
'nuclear era' with sinful scar.

ANCA MIHAELA BRUMA

If...

If one Atom
was out of place,
I would see you...
in a different Light!...

I am trying to create a Haiku of You
but my language is riddled
with malapropism...

J.C. TODD

Imagining Peace, August 1945

No clouds mar this Sunday picnic. My father
and his brothers laze in Adirondack chairs,
loosen heavy jaws and sing through heads of beer
"I Want a Girl" and "Mairzy Doats." It's over,
the war is over. Jim and Vic already
home alive. Edmund and Freddy on their way.
No one will call Lil Mueller's boys *those Germans*
anymore. No one will fault my father for
a crooked neck that kept him from joining up.
Each night he slipped on a yellow CD arm
band to scan the Atlantic from Long Island
beaches, civilian look-out for Nazi subs.

After the A-bombs, they rejoice with icy
Rheingold and just-raked steamers whose shells tilt up
like an empire of faces raised toward
a hiss from sky, a flash that quenched astonished
cries. The men of my family tip littlenecks
down their throats, lift mugs of golden pilsner,
call and beckon, *Some pretzels, Bessie. Ellie*
bring more beer, to the women who wind among
them like a garland bearing food, my mother,
my aunts, flowery in aprons, dispersing
the largess of a just war's end. I am one
of many cousins underfoot, cranky and
curly-mopped from heat. We're picking fights. *Clam up*
or else, the first idle threat of peacetime
issued to us little ones born into war.

J.C. TODD

Reading the Dark in the Dark

Late, under covers, headlamp
a fire in the comforter's cave
shining light on silhouettes
burned into Hiroshima's wall,

a face would fly up from the book
like a bat's, human, but oh—
cheek smeary with eye-melt.
And still flies into nights,

shadowy messenger
of a dark that hides in me too
unless I keep reading it,
draw it toward light.

ELLIE DANAK

In 1986

clouds broke out in blisters,
a radio voice repeated
that children like us
and birds like stars,
were dying, after that
our sleep hardened.

MATTHEW DAVID CAMPBELL

In the Wake of Nuclear Testing
in India and Pakistan 1998

for Amy

Walking to lunch in Bangor, Maine,
I'm tripping over words,
trying to tell you about the paleo-mammalian
and reptilian brain layers under the neo-cortex.

Like a lizard you turn and stare.
I'm not getting it right now, maybe later.

Why? You tell me you're concentrating on walking.

An old man on a street bench waves us down.
You walk on as I muddle toward him.
He says, *Can you spare anything to eat?*
My eyes lazily look for you,
defeated by your fading back.
I say nothing. Walk on.

When I catch up to you I'm naked, carrying two bowling balls in one hand
and a loaf of bread in the other.

You bend down and stick my calf with sowing needles.
I tell you not to make it any worse.

You are mad now.

I order samosas, pakoras, and aloo-mutter:
tell the waiter to make it hot.
You tell me we're off cue today.
I tell you the hinges on the door are crusted with dirt.

The food is perfect, I want to tell you we are eating the silence of disaster.
There's a poem in us.
I can't find it. I order a Coke.

The waiter places the Coke next to my water.
You leave early for work.
You apologize for a *not so good lunch.*
I say *it was good. Our first communion. It was good.*

MARGARET CHULA

Inundation

The earth hums, squeaks, groans. A young boy practices his violin, notes flat and resigned. Preschoolers take out their blankets for a nap. A waitress dips her hands in soapy water. Farmers work the soil before flooding their rice fields. Two friends drink green tea and gossip. For some, these are their last moments.

Another rumble. A factory siren. A dog howls, then lurches like a drunkard on uneven ground. Asphalt cracks. Buildings sway. Dishes crash. Tractors tip. Power lines tangle and rip. Computer screens go dark. Office girls scream.

Hokusai's wave rushes towards them—swallowing boats, tiny fishermen, trucks, houses—everything, everyone. *There's got to be some way out of here.* But there is no *here* left, no uphill exit from the gullet of the wave grinding its teeth on timber and power lines. No way out.

MARGARET CHULA

restless autumn sea

restless autumn sea
remnants of Fukushima
arrive at our shores

KATH ABELA WILSON

Atomic Tanka and Haiku

scintigraphy
from the eternal fire
a nuclear spark
of insight to see
the breaks

Hiroshima Day...
a shakuhachi cracks
at every node

nuclear family
fifty years later still
his fallout

KATH ABELA WILSON

precipice

why should the statue
look at its watch now
as if it had a premonition

I'm the protector
walking in sky I hold
you away from inevitable

carry you up stairs
with no destination
never down

while the statue waits
impatiently checking
the time

cling to me
let me keep you away
from what is to be

always to be
it falls incessantly
red rain

past is caught
in a downpour
I hold it back

future
is moons falling
full to new

we won't see them
I've caught you in
this meteor shower

of now

KATH ABELA WILSON

recollection

I hold my ears
closed all the way
against the broadcast
ordinary
so that the recurring horse
can nod
into dream-gold mountains
his inquisitive snort

I hold my ears closed
hours against
officialdom
against the who and what
so masterful landscape
might speak to the horse
in dream-purple evening

as long
as my ears are closed
I can fit the horse inside my head
it neighs
and feeds on significance
feeds
on the forgotten

On Expressions and Interpretations of Manzanar
Poets on Site
2008

KATH ABELA WILSON

following the sun

following the sun
passion's fire
nuclear fusion
in the stars so many secrets . . .
the atom of our love

nuclear medicine
that small part of you
that becomes me
our bones of contention
grafted pure

nuclear testing
climbing the peak
I can see
the cold spots in your heart
I've always known

renewable energy
of the nuclear family
his fallout
clean up transform
into a whole new life

KATH ABELA WILSON

Inside the Atomic Clock

"The moon"
he said
"is beginning."

ticktock
of the atomic clock
magnetic moments draw us closer
enabling our anatomically
precise timing remotely to sense
our wave length reference cells

"Beginning moon"
we call it"
he called to me from his car.

Open-windowed he grinned
the moon shape at me
it was over his head.

excitation
in a vapor our decay time
limited by collisions

While he talked I sat on a bench
attracting moths ticktock
in the lamplight.
We turned to fireflies
"It's the first few nights,"
he said.

excited in our non-linear process
we detect
the uncertainty of environmental factors

"On these nights
the time to plant.
Fortunate nights," he said.

what magnotometer
measures (in our tiny application) what
excites us directly
ticktock
in our coupled
resonator system

I wondered, did he say plans?
"They will grow well
in the dark."

no matter, it's all the same
to the spin degree of freedom
the timing of the frequency

hyperfine at which
our total atomic moment
can oscillate

LARRY BLAZEK

Lashed to the Wheel

Give not into temptation
that which there is no desire
huddle not over iron ovens
in which there is no fire
poison not the fields
that give you food to eat
burn not the wooden bridges
that support your feet
You're at the mercy of the wheel
one step away from the stone
if you should fall upon the wheel
you're alone
Do you think credit costs nothing?
Do you live prosperously?
Do you trust the government?
Are you free?
If you think you're safe from nuclear waste
you're living in a dream
If you think you can drink petroleum
you're insane
You're at the mercy
of the wheel one step away from the stone
If you should fall upon the wheel
you're alone

M.S. LYLE

Last Days of the Machine

Sing danger
        habit of revolt
        magnified ecstasy of aggression
        splendor serpents roaring

electric earth vibrating in space
agitated revolutions   fervor orbit   axis flung across horizon
into
the
eternal
nocturnal

BENJAMIN GOLUBOFF

Curtis LeMay Interviewed c. 1983: A Remix

World communism – that's their goal and they frankly admit it. They keep telling us, and telling us, and telling us that over and over again. Mr. Khrushchev even took his shoe off and beat on the table at Geneva and told us that he would bury us. So we are at war with communism; that is their goal. We are not shooting at the present time, but we are at war nevertheless.

Frankly, the world
is on the table
at the present time.
They keep shooting
over and over again,
telling us at Geneva,
that the shoe is the goal
and that communism is beat.
Geneva would bury us:
that is their goal,
telling us frankly that the table
is off-again on-again,
telling us over and over again
that we beat the shoe.
Nevertheless, the world
and the shooting are not over.
Admit it, Mr. Khrushchev:
war is the goal.

BENJAMIN GOLUBOFF

Curtis LeMay Plans to Strike First

At a March 1954 briefing
on Strategic Air Command
plans and capabilities for war,
SAC leader General LeMay
was asked how those plans
fit with the stated policy
of the United States
that it would never
strike the first blow.

LeMay answered that he had heard
this thought expressed may times
and that it sounded fine.

But considering who started
the Revolutionary War,
the War of 1812,
the Indian Wars,
and the Spanish-American War,
"it was not in keeping
with United States history."

LeMay emphasized that he
was not advocating a preventive war.
He believed, however, that
if the United States were pushed
far enough into a corner,
it would not hesitate
to strike first. [1]

[1] From Ronald Schaffer, *Wings of Judgment: American Bombing in World War II*. New York: Oxford University Press, 1985.

LAURA SWEENEY

Lessons Learned in the RFETS Closure Project

You plan to do your fieldwork this summer. A marginal study. Not paid by Rocky Flats or DOE. Funded by an institute of science and society. You spend time in Boulder. Chat with activists, professors, the community. Read *Making a Real Killing,* and *The Ambushed Grand Jury.* Smoke and mirrors. You have the approvals, then they say NO. What's going on? What's the thrust? Who is she? Red flag – like a fire. But your writing must be done this fall. You interview electricians, engineers, managers - from the CEO to the janitor. Because when the fox watches the chickens, you're not confident that the right things are put on paper. People fall through the cracks. Lack response from the bureaucracy. What will you do with this? A masters of public administration? Presentations, publications? Yeah, that'd be great if DOE pays attention. They're reverting to open space. Hanford is next. But you need to graduate this winter.

C. WADE BENTLEY

Lightning in a Bottle

On a
planet
in the
habit-
able
zone
around
a medium-
sized
star
the
inhabit-
ants
have
built a
machine
to hurtle protons at nuclei at nearly
the speed of light hoping the collisions
will provide evidence at last of something
long prophesied, something
that will spark fervor
and rapture
and then
disappear
so quick-
ly some
will

doubt
it was
there
at all
while
others
take
the
cloth
in hot
pur-
suit.

MICHAEL MCLANE

Litany

Strontium-89. Strontium-90. Iodine-131. Cesium-137. Barium-140. Cesium-144. Plutonium-239. Americium-241. Cobalt-60. Iridium-192. Polonium-210. Uranium-235. Uranium-238.

What weight neutrality? What heft its absence? What is test? What is testament? What is proof and what is proving ground? Where and where and where is to be lie of the land? Where its nucleus? How numerous the protesters? How deep their convictions? How intangible the line they cross? How hot the holding pens? How to behave when they are freed? How many Easters before we know them by name?

MICHAEL MCLANE

Lullaby

from the ancient blessing *Lilith abi* or Lilith away. as in a means to keep a demon at bay. they say she is beautiful. they say she is harmless. say take this pendant and keep it close. sing lullaby to forget. the song is easy. the meter a metronome. the click click click click click click so rapid. as if the very soil were afraid.

MICHAEL MCLANE

Sedan Crater #1

I.

later we learn
the tumbleweeds are Russian
Thistle

the only growth
here at the bottom
of our curiosity

they spurt from the playa
in monsoon rains
and are excised

blown a thousand
miles like all things
no longer here

their name, apropos
of everything, I imagine
the names of weeds

half a world away,
the backhanded tributes.
that they should take seed

in this, of all places,
and thrive, that is belief,
is proof above all else.

when the hole was
dug, they were almost
certainly called tumbleweeds

every word chosen
as precisely as a synonym
for risk, as a fair weather day

the smallest twinge
of survivor's guilt, faint
scent like sage over sand

and the ground opens
and still they bloom
the smallest sensitive hairs

that tell the antlion
to rise, mandibles clanking
swords to plowshares

II.
In every John Wayne
film, they are the uncredited
cameo

the slow, dull metaphor
for montage, for being
passed by

an ellipsis accruing,
bookending our hero
in his righteousness

these husks, so many
scar-faced villains
circling the camp at night

and what is the West
without this desiccation
without its thorny invader.

III.
as to the sharpened
exoskeleton, a man
croons *you've got to just keep on*
pushin, keep on pushin,
push the sky away.

these words will break
you off at the root—
there is no choice but to dig
and still the sky follows.

KARL WILLIAMS

Living at the End of Time

I'm 220-54-5337-54-43-32-21-11-8-7-6-5-4-3-2-1-zero-zero-zero-zero
zero-zero . . . (1,2,3,4,5,6 . . .)-zero . . . 9
I stood up and I've been counted here at the end of time

I'm third-string second-rate two-bit but you know what
I once had the singular pleasure of the company of a good woman but
If love is a rainbow then she was colorblind
We could've worked it out but she was too busy living at the end of time
      We're living living at the end of time
      We're living living at the end of time
      I always heard her say that she needed to unwind
      Well she's gonna get her chance here at the end of time
When the clock stops ticking there'll be no pocketpicking no more
And no pocketpickers and no liquor and no liquor store
No liquor store owner no type-A blood donor and no place for Mr.
Burke to work
Cause there'll be no blood given to no one living and no more Mr. Burke

Now when the clerks stop clerking that's when it all gets murky to me
Will there be time after timecards that's what I'm waiting to see
When we're all blown to pieces aunts uncles nephews nieces and the undersigned
There'll be nothing cooking and no one looking No hands clapping and
no minds snapping
No trees to hit the ground and no one to hear the sound
And even if you could imagine the universe spinning round
If there's no one to see it that's good enough for me – it's the end of time

We're living living at the end of time
We're living living at the end of time
I ain't got no future but at least I know it's mine
Here we are at the end of time
Now some folks say they don't believe
And some folks say they can't conceive it
Some act like you can just deny it
Others say if there's a better bomb then we better buy it
Some folks say that we can win it even if we don't begin it
Well you may be afraid and try to hide it
Or you may be the one to authorize it
Or from your thoughts you may succeed to drive it
But there's one thing you can't do . . .
And that's survive it

There's breadlines in the headlines as the deadline comes in view
The finger of a glutton on the button Ain't there nothing we can do
But holler from our squalor for a dollar while they're handing out
Guggenheims
To some Mahler scholar in a collar who's living tastefully at the end of time
He's living at the end of time
He's living at the end of time
Waiting for that burst of hyperactive sunshine
We're living living at the end of time
I've always said there's something attractive about radioactive debris
You might say that einsteinium is just fine-ium with me
Let that fermium wreck my sperm-ium and curl my spine
I've reconciled realism and masochism here at the end of time

One day some misanthrope isotope gonna throw a rope on you
You'll grope for hope in your horoscope when you start to feel like a
walking barbecue
You'll try to cope use special soap maybe even call the Pope
But he'll give you the same old line

208

And when you're sliding down that slope faster than an antelope
You might write me a letter if you can still find an envelope
You might ask me if I think there's any hope
But I'd have to tell you Nope – you're living at the end of time
          You're living living at the end of time
          You're living living at the end of time
          Look at it this way: it's a permanent solution to the same old grind
          We're living living at the end of time
I might cut my toe off and pin it to my ear
I might go on a rampage steal your baby for a souvenir
Wind up in a tower with a gun adding red to a landscape that's too drab
Or I might just stay in watch the tube have myself a Tab

Down by the Gitcheegoomie she saw through me so clear
Once I was a protester now I'm an investor I fear
I hit the skid then I almost overbid when she said
Are your kids and your investments in line
I bought them all new clothes and I sent the wife a rose
But she only moved in close and the way she juxtaposed
She had me so discomposed I had to pack my nose to get me through the
end of time
          We're living living at the end of time
          We're living living at the end of time
          Somehow somewhere we must have signed on some dotted line
          Now here we are at the end of time

GRETCHEN FLETCHER

It's a Delicate Task to Sort the Garbage at a Nuclear Era Dump

found title, New York Times, October 24, 2009

Here on the Pajarite Plateau
outside Los Alamos, NM
(before that name came
to symbolize an era of secret R&D)
where rowdy boys ran the grounds
of their ranch school, the US govt.
put up in haste a lab that would produce the bomb
that changed the world. On the isolated mesa
it "seared the sky and melted the desert"
at the Trinity test site, setting off
a story that reads like a backwards version
of "The House That Jack Built":
The government put up the nuclear reactor
where scientists made the plutonium
that went into the bomb
that was put in the plane
that dropped it on Nagasaki.
Now workers in white full-body suits
excavate as carefully as archaeologists
the 6-acre dump in the desert,
unsure of what they will unearth
in the soil of this radioactive repository
in Technical Area 21, determined to make
the mesa clean enough to build homes on.

At the same time 6 otters are being released
into the ice-cold water of a river in NM
in an effort to return the mammals
to the historic range they had disappeared from.

ALAN BRITT

Lucky Ones

Orphaned by 50-caliber rounds.

Armless, legless,
torso gone missing.

50-caliber thoughts overwhelm
one's sense of decency.

Armless, legless,
torso gone missing.

50-caliber CEOs unlatch briefcases
filled with worthless stocks and bonds.

50-caliber governments
draw the line
when it comes to global embarrassment.

The 100 senators see what's coming
and dodge bullets
from small calibers
hidden beneath the stockings
of crazed soccer moms,
of Walmart cashiers,
of teachers and professors of cool clear water,
of dogs, even,
those primordial slaves of love.

So, 50-caliber planets
from which aliens sometimes descend,
keep your distance!

Do you have 50-caliber thoughts?

Or are you one of the lucky ones?

ALAN BRITT

Planet Called Earth

(Or Resisting the Oligarchy)

If Democracy was such a good experiment,
How come we're in this mess?
Ah, yes, Capitalism, that diseased strand
of DNA . . . greed, greed, greed!
        —Michelangelo Felipo Santiago

Follow the bomb; follow the bomb;
follow the money & you'll find the bomb.

Follow the bomb & you'll find the money.

Follow self-worth, follow anything,
so long as you don't follow the bomb.

Follow egret nests in leafless mangroves
off the coast of St. Croix,
straw akin to the Three Little Pigs' first shack,
which is the only bomb shelter
most of us can afford.

Follow what you see, taste & feel,
then douse it with a healthy dose
of individuality. Follow, follow,
follow until you're exhausted

from following. & after you've
commenced with mercy faith,
after you're blistered & mortgaging
house #3, plus wife who knows what,
& kids running all over the place,
step off the grimy, rain-soaked curb
naked as a proverbial jaybird
& proclaim that totally in the dark
citizens of the USA won't keep you
from clanging the bells of freedom
high above surveillance satellites
tattooing your planet called Earth.

ALAN BRITT

The Great Nation

Right now we're at terrible odds,
which does no good
(or a little).

But peacemakers preach tolerance
in all its glory.

Peacemakers are patriots too.

MICHAEL WATERSON

Mad Princes

In '69, unbeknownst to Congress
And the public, Nixon adopted a pet
Stratagem, a secret plan designed to get
Ho to the peace table by feigning madness.
The game was on. In Moscow, war was chess.
Nixon favored poker with a high stakes bet,
An unstable isotope of Russian roulette
That some might call madness mocking madness.
For three days nuclear bombers skirted
Soviet airspace waiting for instruction –
Pretext balanced on knife-edged reality –
While unaware Americans flirted,
For a ruse, with mutual assured destruction
As the antic Dane met Machiavelli.

JULES NYQUIST

Malan

(a sestina)

Chinese
desert
flower
unfolds
to blossom
Mao's A-bomb

His wish for a bomb,
a nuclear weapons test base, China's
is seven times bigger, blossoms
over the U.S. test base in the Nevada desert.
The Great Leap Forward unfolds
starving workers eat the wild flowers

Malan is named for, a desert flower
rising from the ashes of a future bomb
a new town of ten thousand people unfolds.
With help from the Soviets, China
rises her pioneer ashes out of her desert,
to assemble thousands of workers, blossoms

to resurrect Cheng Ho's Fifteenth Century, blooms
fleets of sailing treasure ships, flowers
spreading inventions of Second Century paper desert
origami birds, gunpowder bombs
once the largest navy in the world, China
rises again, magnetic stones, compass-like, unfold

to tell her future. Mao's wish unfolds,
an A-bomb test within ten years to blossom
(with three months to spare) the People's Republic of China
joins the nuclear club on October 16, 1964. A white rose flowers
in history, the giant physics experiment blows
up , forced to bloom from the Lop Nor desert.

Testing blossoms for 32 years with desert
detonations, the first one code named "596" unfolds,
is named after June 1959, the time when the bomb
given to China from the Russians and blossomed
in trade for Tibetian uranium, turned into a wilting flower
suddenly cut off by Khruschev. So China

builds her own bomb, lighter and better than the U.S. Desert
winds and Chinese fortunes willed to unfold.
At what price blooms Malan in the parched desert?

JULES NYQUIST

Party Boy

In reference to the painting by the same name by Brian O'Connor

and so you are
sitting in a corner
dunce of the party

boy spent with
fists pounding, raw
knuckles, bloodless

war drones, shadow
of your former self
dark and worn out

as ever, a game, you
didn't mean it, really
only wanted to teach

them a lesson, it was an
accident, a mistake
to bomb from a B-36

over Albuquerque,
turbulence! grab
the nearest handle

the nuclear bomb bay
release hatch
it was hard to hang on

for your life, trigger
wasn't in, thank god you
got out with only

an explosion and a warning.
Pity, was it you
drinking beer

in the Moscow Marriott
executive lounge on duty?
Your security clearance

may be revoked.
Sit in the corner
on a stool six miles

from the Grand Canyon
entrance and mine
uranium for greed.

Did you ever notice
the beauty?
The American

people want to
know why
Daddy bailed

you out again
dead weight
missing your pants

remove your gloves
and protective goggles
as you kneel

by the names
of the dead
Everlasting.

JULES NYQUIST

Roasted Pumpkin

In Hiroshima, the day of the blast
Mr. Tanimato was dismayed
to see the shelter building razed.
In the garden, Father Kleinsorge
noticed a pumpkin
roasted on the vine.

They tasted it and it was good.
They were surprised at their hunger
and ate quite a bit.
They dug up several potatoes
that were nicely baked
under the ground.

The asphalt of the streets
was still so soft and hot that
walking was uncomfortable.
They found several bags of rice
and one of the people with them
had cooking utensils.

In the park, Mr. Tanimoto
organized the lightly wounded women
of his neighborhood to cook.
This morning the city was bustling
with 245,000 people.
Now, in the afternoon,
a mere pile of residue.
Some could not keep the pumpkin
in their stomachs.
Mr. Tanimoto and Father Kleinsorge
and the women cooked enough rice
to feed nearly a hundred people.

TIFFANY ROSE NAPUTI LACSADO

Manha (Chamorro for Young Coconuts)

I lay in the sand
Looking high above me
I see two young coconuts
Who have not been touched by man

Who do not worry about their harvest
To be plucked and torn away from their mother's leaves

Who do not worry about their husks being cracked open
Or their milk being sucked dry.

They hang there
Strong
Innocent
Pure
Green as their mothers leaves.

They do not worry
That one day man will come
To crack them open
To scrape out their young meat
Just
For the pleasure of being a man.

They do not worry about their mother
The toxins being offered to her
Her roots forced to soak up the poison

They do not worry because they are
Strong
Innocent
Pure
Green as their mothers leaves

I know that the whispers of the wind
Will bring them knowledge of their inevitable fate
That the winds of war
Will transfer to them the weight of the world
That rests on the shoulders of their mother
That the echoes of the bombing
Will expose them to the radiation of their own milk.

Yet there is faith
There is hope
There is love
There is resistance
They will hang in there
Strong
Innocent
Pure
Green as their mothers leaves

MARIKO KITAKUBO

After Fukushima (a tanka sequence)

cobalt blue
was my favorite
color…
until I could see it

in atomic waste

toumeina/ao wo mottomo/ konomiitsu/
genshiro naini/miraruru madewa

when
will my later years
start?—
a mother cat has babies
at the ruined village

bannen wa/itsu kara naramu/ haison ni/
oya neko ga ko wo/unde irunari

a year later
    little by little
      he starts
        to talk about the Tsunami,

      sunset on the debris

ichinen go/potsuri potsuri to/katari somu/
        kano ootsunami/gareki no yuuhi

    how silent
      the light rain
        of radiation —

    we continue searching

        for his parents' bodies

after the storm,
    harvest moon in a puddle
late friend
  he'll be able to see this
      from a cloudless sky

onaji tsuki/karemo tenkara mirudarou/
    arashi no nochi no/mizu no omote ni

sounds
of the stream
in my homeland—

Strontium is soaking
into the placenta

furusato no/seseragi no ne wo /omoi itsu/
Strontium/*shimuru taiban*

cherry avenue
my late mother's favorite...
is there
another world?

petal drift

fukidamaru/ano atari kara/kakuriyo ka/
haha no konomishi/sakira no namiki

emptiness
of the pigeon nest—

weak rain

makes me calm

in spite of radiation

blue sky
    or mushroom clouds,

    the last view
        our future
            Saint-Exupery

song
  of early summer—

    my motherland
      will be a coffin
        of the stormy wind

hatsunatsu no/gaku sosogaruru/sokoku nari/
        yagate wa kaze no hitsugi to naramu

there were
  days when I told
my dream…

    are you there now?
        Betelgeuse

yume nado wo/katarishi hi ari/imawa mou/
    nai kamo shirenu/Betelgeuse yo

PEGGY ZABICKI

Men Jumping

Do you remember
Back when there were children
Back when the sky wasn't yellow and black with gray sunsets,

Back when you could plant seeds in the ground
And they would sprout into flowers and vegetables,

Back when you could go swimming
In the lake
And you could go outside
Without a mask

And you could look up at the blue sky
With its pink and orange sunsets
And not see birds falling
And dropping at your feet?

Do you remember?

Now I see men jumping
From old buildings
Because they can't hang on anymore.

The ones that stay, get tumors and tears
for their trouble.

Dry dirt and dead bones.
Even the golden calf is gone.

HARVEY SOSS

Mollusk Man

He may be the last of the squeaky wheels,
Demanding grease and getting bupkis.
The unoiled supermarket carriage
That he rolls out of a parking lot,
Now his by eminent domain, tips
Under the weight of his belongings.
Everything he owns or has scavenged
Is in that basket, a cardboard box
Serving as shelter perched on top.

Proud fisher of souls, with no one
To capture this Kodak moment,
He opens canned food with a sharp rock,
Unencumbered by mortgage or neighbors.
He can go anywhere the mood takes him.
If there were postapocalyptic postcards
He could be seen with his pushcart
Making his way, lumbering his pilgrim's progress
Over the devastated landscape.

HARVEY SOSS

Rumors of Invention

Talk show hosts can talk of nothing else.
Bearing word of a rumored breakthrough
To alchemize us from fossil fuel fetishists
Into cleaner, clearer version of ourselves,
Time and *Science* go flying off the shelves.

This, naturally enough, terrifies
Fierce champions of the status quo.
Side deals are made with the incurious,
Authorizing Black Friday sales, a run
On stores of enriched uranium.

When the irradiant dust settles,
When we all glow like clock faces
Winding down to an alarming time,
Headlines again crowing noisily
Of the rise in high school body counts,

Survivors among us can expect to fall
Out of lust with invention in perpetuum
And back into the old ways of disturbia,
Picking up right where we left off
Dystopian habits we had come to love.

SHELLEY MARIE MOTZ

This poem is folded

"If you fold a thousand cranes, your fondest wish will come true."—
Japanese Proverb

This poem is folded
For hands sick with radiation.
It is formed silently.

Every crease shouts:
Health. Happiness. Longevity.
Every line bitter.

This poem doubles back.
Recollects
A child flying out of the blast

Like a colt
when the bomb explodes
And black rain falls.

This poem is a raft.
It floats under Misasa Bridge.
Bears paper lanterns burning with children's pleas.

It wants to take the world to Hiroshima:
To hear 10 million paper prayers;
To lay 10 million paper cranes

At Sadako's feet.

JENNIFER BALACHANDRAN

Never Spoken Of

the decade he spent helping the US of A
make weapons-grade plutonium
how they stored the waste   which had no place
but in the rows of temporary monuments
called tank farms   how it seeped
an underground cloud blooming slowly
toward the water   the nights he lay alone in grey chambers
when his body wasn't safe to touch humankind
how he waited for the day his father would die
so he could come home to the farm of milk
he had to be strong enough for his gut to take
the blow of the blunt edge of an axe
he'd return and never speak of these things
his children would not ask
he'd return   he would not poison the milk

M. IQBAL DHADHRA

The Globe in Nuclear Claws

Oh, cruel hawk
Why de ye walk?
On a poor ant
Dancing chant
Under thy claws
Nuclearic paws
One three an 'seven
Growing 'o be eleven
Playing holocaust
Destruction vast
Heroshimic dance
Gulping world finance
The *poor ain't alive*
Until you survive
Hunger and disease
Quad increase

M. IQBAL DHADHRA

Nuclear Proliferation

Some countries have bond
To make the Earth pond
Of nuclearic water
Contaminated daughter
And keep the door ajar
To cause brutal war.

JENNIFER MET

Fallout

in the white dress which is as cool and
evil as a glass of radioactive milk…

–Lynn Emanuel from "Like God"

an image upon which people always linger but
growing up in 1950's New Mexico she says it
was commonplace to Geiger Counter your milk
to live with the dark threat of radiation poison
and she didn't give it much thought beyond that
context—I guess—how in the milk a tint of blue
is normal—until you look—and then it seems so
white that it's impossible and you imagine gray
slipping through and what you think you know—
the outside appearance—is wrong and deceiving
like how this excerpt suggests that God is in the
dress or how back in college while I studied DNA
half-lives and other things I hadn't given much
thought as to why hospitals were white but one
theory suggests that albinism is genetically linked
to sterility—and here the roots of the poet's lines—
our mother—warm and life-giving—in reality
sterile and thus not ours and of course the obvious
fear of our own diminished effect or what Freud
would call castration and when my lab partner
accompanied me back to my dorm room and we
found the microwave running—door open—the air

full of unseen waves and he stuck his hand inside
to see if it was really on and it didn't hurt but turned
his finger black for the rest of the semester and then
I never saw him again—I didn't give it much thought
but now I'm starting to worry a German nightmare—
a "doppelganger" story where your shadow separates
itself and turns against you—cancer—and I watch
others eyeing the dark clouds gathering over Sendai
full of radioactive evaporation from the flooded plant
something that you can't give much thought because
what can they do—they think—what can I do—
and can radiation be called evil when it doesn't feel—
has no malicious intent—really what could God do—
even knowing the split beginning inside the safe body
of these clouds threatening rain and starting to shadow
black—we all just watch—cool as radioactive milk

JENNIFER MET

No-Go-Zone

I am reading a book—real research
a break from the short you-tube video
eye-candy I have been calling work—

about the animals left in the no-go
zone—those radioactive kilometers
in Fukushima Daiichi's shadow

where there are dogs and horses—creatures
left behind—cattle trapped in stanchions
livestock abandoned—their owners

evacuated and the horses unable to run
from their stalls—drowned and their legs
broken—dogs dying from infection

after being cut and scraped by the wave
others starving—left tied up at home—
to stop disease the dead cattle are sprayed

with lime—stray dogs that were left to roam
lonely will now be euthanized—except for
there are guerilla rescuers entering the zone

to save them—those that can't ignore
the suffering—ignore radioactive exposure
defy legal ramifications—the book implores

and I skip the rest of the chapter—
it is too much like a commercial—one
of those long ones on late at night—a blur

of spotty and emaciated bodies stunned
barkless—trusting—all milky white eyes
bare ribs and mange—the ones

where I change the channel and try
not to go back—long enough that I'm sure
it is already over—that they have already died

JENNIFER MET

Medium

"[I] wanted to use the irony [but had] reservation about how beautiful it was."
—editor Francoise Mouly on Christoph Niemann's "Spring Doom"

when I first see Niemann's illustration I feel
the ability to show truth in beauty must be absurd
how could an artist capture anything real
in the Japanese brush style usually reserved
for depictions of nature? but the New Yorker cover
is like a dream—a moment of insight preserved—
a night's sprig of cherry blossoms antler
the page—radiating pink through the darkness—they
are not the popular Somei Yoshino flowers—
those five petal blooms we immediately relate
with Japan—but trefoils—the irony—how wild
cherries native to Japan's forests display
many petals that appear smaller and more mild
in color and concurrently with the leaves—
but how the symbol we associate with the isle
was cultivated during the Edo period—achieved
by man and not nature—how nearly everyone
forgets this—natural symbols—too—are conceived
by artists—the perfect irony! what he has done—
remembering the origin of the nuclear disaster
even as his symbol—like blossoms—becomes
real—ironic no one will remember the tsunami waters
or the radiation that created his petal's mutation

that no one will remember man's part—another's
vision—warning signs once adorning every coffee table
but already littering the gutters
like so many extra petals

Words

What if words could
feed hunger, stop the missile's
flight, guard the ancient pine
from the saw's steely bite?
What if a poem could stop
blood running,
its breath help fill
another's lungs?
If words ran down our throats
like brandy, hot trail
giving us strength and courage
not for battle, but for peace;
if angry words and bullets
could fly backward,
be reabsorbed
before they did their violence.

What if *O* and *TH*
leapt off the paper
into the pot and bubbled
into broth, rich velvet
on your tongue,
softening the echo in your belly?
What if the sticks of *N* and *T*
rose up and made splints
for broken limbs,
if I could peel *A* and *G*

off the page to make a bandage,
if *U* and *C* could form a poultice
cooling any bruise?

And why not?
Why can't good words
be a warm hand wrapping
your cold one?

Say *brother, sister*
and lay down your arms.
Say *world*
whole world
and take care of each other.
Say *same breath*
same life
and feel the wind filling
each living thing.
We only have to say the words
say them
say them now
together all of us:
world
whole world
which we love.

KARA PROVOST

Warcry

A sorcerer in the guise of rain
conjures up earthworms,
glistening.

I try to place my feet slowly
to avoid their moving bodies; still
their death is certain. Forced up
for air, their flesh dissolves in water,
leaving sidewalks strewn with corpses
once the sun returns.

Bombs rain down
in Nagasaki, Benghazi, Damascus.
Caught between deaths, the people keep
surfacing for breath.
Go back
to your black rich burrows.
Go back to the arms of the earth.

But safe lairs have turned to graves;
plagues and rains awaken
in us. The tooth of the plow devours
green heads in the fields:
we consume   ourselves.

KARA PROVOST

The Failure of Kindness

I want to live steeped in kindness.
I remember when I was a child my friend Alissa
had a little capsule filled with sweet herbs, a breath freshener.
We each took a turn sucking it, sweetness of dried flowers
filling our mouths so our breath came as a cloud of petals.
I'd like to spread kindness like that,
in each petalled breath
I take or share.

When I was young in Reagan's America
I would cry at night, thinking
about silos and bunkers filled with missiles—
evil crayons in a box,
their sharp snouts lined up, ready
at the push of a button. I wept
seeing a dead dog, bloated
on the side of a road,
anonymous in its suffering.
I'm still crying for that dog
and all its relatives—
the roadkill deer and smashed turtles,
new children born into a world still
at war, the wife with the broken lock on her door
afraid of the growl of her husband's tires in the drive,
that man with the matted hair who sits
on the college career office steps
every afternoon with his empty cup,
talking to the air.

If I could ask one question
and get its answer:
how can we live in kindness
and what do we do when kindness fails?
How can we bear the million cruelties
small and large we wreak, and what does it mean
that we bear it?
I am still crying
the same pain, still writing the same poem
and I haven't yet changed the world.

SHARON COLEMAN

Cold Angels

They begin human. They hear it
first in the ink that makes everything
small   clear   lined up
ink like strong thread
that sews up tight
a messy world.
       Cold angels begin
their ascension before knowing
it. One day in a university or
laboratory, they are chosen
a check by their name
when a colleague objects
and they won't.
They ascend in white coats
given to them when they pause
after injecting fire
into a patient's veins and before
the exact measure of dilated pupils.
Cold angels swallow only once
keep records   listen
for it more.

Listen for what keeps them
from hearing human anguish.

Cold angels ascend to laboratories
of war, study,
and pour vials
of basic elements
of creation
split and joined.

They ascend, believing
they know
what human specimens
about to be injected with radiation
or incinerated
could not possibly foresee.   They ascend
feet grounded
as a measure of more height.

They ascend
as their cheeks flush
with the cool blood
of an inside joy.

They ascend
pouring vials
of eternal peace
on humans below.

When they descend
to the destruction,
they observe but don't cure
human writhing.
They make of cities
unparalleled
natural laboratories.
They swallow twice

and either return wings
to those who, arms crossed,
won't take them
or lower their gaze
to keep records
and listen
for something more.

Cold angels write studies of prophecy
and seal their lips
seal their notebooks
open them
seal them
open them, seal.

Cold angles drink the science of death
of all nations, dilute
results in the waters
of many voices,
cross doubly from land
to land to conjure
new laboratories.

And when we write
we cannot help
but listen
for their prophecy
as it lies encrypted
between our lines of ink.

And we wonder:
what can we do
with their next message
before it's delivered?

SHARON COLEMAN

first snow after the end of the world

concrete again sand-like, buildings down in ruins, our bodies down, what still stands or slumps slowly becomes a forest of light in new darkness—a walled window, a gauze-covered saint on a cracked billboard. iron-rod skeletons, towering remains in a maze of rubble.

we hover dizzy, hold out hands to our ghostly likeness, fingertips skim fingertips skim our eyeless love—as our bodies lie in frozen beds of white. ficus trees grow from a jagged glass frame into light. below, a shadow burnt into stucco of an angel incinerated mid-flight.

walk through a city opened at its seams, gathering a crust of white. walk through words no longer breathed—they've slid down a collapsed balcony to the street's seared tongue. trace false steps we couldn't erase before taking them. trace false moves before cold covers more.

DAVID ANDRE DAVISON

Nuclear Impact

A dream not fulfilled, a life not complete,
The reality of hopelessness, the emptiness of defeat.
How did this happen, what could motivate the hate?
Civilization was destroyed, peace offers came too late.

A misunderstanding at a press conference, an insult perceived,
Yet, it was only a reporter's question, the motive not believed.
The dictator felt his honor sink, he was embarrassed on stage,
His people saw him as he was, full of hate and rage.

He lashed out at the reporter, and killed him where he stood,
People tried to help, they did the best they could.
Our president grabbed the dictator, but got a knife in the chest,
The dictator escaped, our countries patience to test.

Our troops on alert, guns and missiles at the ready,
The dictator did the same, his mind was not steady.
Who fired the first shot, nobody knows for sure,
What happened next, was nothing more than a blur.

Bombers took to the sky, missiles fired at our towns,
Was it by accident, or a premediated attack to bring us down?
The explosion was strong, sending a mushroom cloud to the sky,
The dictator had used a nuke, but no one understood why.

Our military responded, launching missiles through the night,
But by daybreak, the nuclear clouds hid the light.
A few people escaped, by hiding in a cave,
Some survived the attack, but the crops they couldn't save.

Many died of radiation, their skin melted away,
The scream of infants, in their mother's dead arms lay.
Finally, life was wiped out, not a single living soul remained,
All that was left, was a planet that radiation stained.

The lesson for us, is really quite clear,
Words we speak, might invoke prejudice and fear.
They say that words can't hurt you, but this isn't true,
Even a single utterance can bring destruction, to me and you.

The world must destroy their nuclear arsenals, the power to kill,
Or someone might elect a leader, who seeks a psychotic thrill.
A nightmare scenario, a horror movie come to life,
Who realizes the evil, the termination of child, husband, and wife?

PHOEBE REEVES

Continuously Dancing

To live till you die
is to live long enough.
                    –Lao Tzu, trans. Le Guin

My heart, I lie—the waves control
the sea. The river wears down the bedrock
like a donkey's harness rubbing away the skin.

Under the bomb's thick casing, its metallic
heart waits to trade electrons in a generous
expansion, flash burns continuously dancing.

In the bang zone, windows wait to shatter and
buildings to dance like potential daffodils
in a spring thunderstorm. In the space between

a concrete wall and a dandelion, I hide from
the Ten Thousand Things. Traffic lights are
continuously dancing their three note waltz.

Cabs with shot brakes halt and go in screechy
counterpoint. When the bomb is released
by a lever or a button, pulled or pushed by a human

hand attached to a human being, given
an order over shortwave in code written by aging
Navajos with no one left to talk to, paid

by bureaucrats whose starched collars
press the loose fat of their throats uncomfortably
all day long, all the clouds in the sky bend

their faces to the ground. The bomb has a million
hands on it when it drops and below a mother
is making breakfast for her daughter, who is

tying and untying the red ribbon on her braid
and asking questions ceaselessly: Mother,
why is the sky blue? Mother, where does the cat

go in the afternoon? Mother, when will I be tall?
Mother, how many stars in the sky? And where
do they go when the sun comes up? Mother, before

I was born, I was sleeping inside you?
Was I crying? Could I speak? How did I fit there?
Her questions float like cherry blossoms

across the courtyard and her mother, half
listening, smiles and kisses her hair,
the top of her head.
                          I would rather not keep going.

In the worst of my dreams, this child keeps
asking her questions as her hair bursts
into flame and the skin, the muscle, the fat

each peel away, away from the epicenter
until only her charcoal shadow on the kitchen
wall is left to ask where her voice went,

and the cat will never come home and the mother
will never eat breakfast and all the hands on the bomb
are left wriggling uncertainly in a trail down the sky

like lost stars, continuously dancing. My heart,
I lied—I must remember her, this imaginary child,
dancing with her arms held over her head, red

ribbon hanging down, singing a child's song
in a high clear voice—her voice is the only
flame that can illuminate this night.

PHOEBE REEVES

Trinity

Los Alamos: July 16, 1945

Men wait in the trenches, cover their eyes
or their testicles, and calculate wagers
based on blast force, TNT equivalence, the heat

they feel on their faces from ten miles away.
This moment redefines the nuclear
family, doesn't it? Father God,

Mary the Mother, Infant Jesus—or is it
Father Man, Mother Plutonium, Infant
Destruction? The air does not ignite,

only the desert and our minds, as we burn
to see the holy family in our reflection on
the Trinitite's greeny glass crater.

Oppenheimer struts and tilts his hat.
Passing the whiskey, Bainbridge guesses,
"Now we are all sons of bitches."

PHOEBE REEVES

Helen of Bikini

"At first Reard had tried to persuade his usual models to take part in his poolside show. They all refused...but he soon found a suitable model in Micheline Bernardini, a strip-dancer at the Casino de Paris."
The Bikini: A Cultural History, Patrick Alac

Helen. It's an apt name for this bomb.
Helen of Troy bore the burden of war
and witnessed men like these tear
their lives apart for her, or at least, that's
how they told the story in retrospect. Anything
can be blamed on a woman's face, plausibly,
and the other men, those whose houses burned
and whose children were sold as slaves
in the victory rout, shrug their shoulders and understand
how Agamemnon could burn a city for a woman.

But this Helen does her own burning, erupting
thick necked out of the Pacific, with upturned
boats on her throat for ornament.
She is what they fear, and what they manufacture
to hide their fear.

How natural, then, for a French fashonista to pin
his future on her new surname, her new
fallen city, Bikini, and pin that tiny name
on his tiny idea—an exposed ass, triangles
outlining nipples, and the fabric, inevitably,
not floral, but newspaper headlines
in a parodic pastiche over Micheline's thin pelvis.

Micheline, Helen, any woman is now of Bikini,
altering ourselves from the inside out for invisible
forces and headlines that
cover us like a wave
coming back into shore after the blast
and displacement.

Things look different from Bikini. We can't
stop ourselves from digging through the hot
sand of what we're told is paradise, looking
for something we know lies beneath.

FAY AOYAGI

Three Haiku/Senryu

Hiroshima Day—
I lean into the heat
of the stone wall

***

Hiroshima Day
multi-color threads
on the weaving machine

***

hand-cuffed lobsters
in the water tank
A-bomb Anniversary

MIRIAM BIRD GREENBERG

We Knew Nothing Then

We knew
nothing
but that we must
do as told, that no harm
would come to us. We knew

we were working
towards peace, and we moved
everyone off the atoll. Thatch
houses, outriggers, everything
that was left behind

was burnt.
Then, for 23 days we did nothing
but swam, ate ice cream, slept
in the sun waiting for a tug on our fishing poles
cast overboard in the luminous

water. We were making
history without our knowing.
Why, then, did God give us power
of doubt? The sea turned mist,
our left ships blackened in the blast. The ocean

was a landscape painted
with minor fires. Why

did belief cleave
  to us so strongly? The Geiger counters'
constant irregular ticking

as we passed before them
    was like the tallying of fates
        of each of us,
            every object
one by one.

MIRIAM BIRD GREENBERG

After All This

The mountainsides
are empty, the crags
uninhabited.
                    Ash pits
have melted to dirt
beneath the fallen leaves. There are no shots.
No firelight
but yours. No train whistles
                    anymore,
or mail routes, no
riverboats or gasoline for chainsaws
or the dirt bikes
that had hummed across the valley.
No pack mules stepping carefully
sideways over the rusted chassis
of dirt bikes. No bullets,
no hunters, no fish
                    flashing
in the river. There is no one to track you
to your shelter, to steal your dog,
if you had one,
                    for food. No one
to learn your name and say it after moon
rise. The communiqués
of the mountainside are spoor and paw-
print; they pattern the ground
                    just beyond
firefall. Without fear, the act of flight,
what would you have?

MIRIAM BIRD GREENBERG

Utopia

The utopia we'd imagined—
of cottonwood water-tracing

and oak-grove windbreaks
(bounded by wrecked strip malls
edged with barbed wire, helicoptered
all night by tobacco-chewing
militiamen)—
                showed its false front

like dirt-yellowed teeth.
                Million-
watt moons swooped low-slung
over our hideaways, spotlighting
runaways and the bedrolls

abandoned by vagrants
in the overgrowth, jungles
we'd hobo'ed and the dim hooch
where I sleep when the tide

goes out of my life
for a while. Our broken-up fire
pits were littered with bones

of small game like, when, as kids
on ponies,
                    we chased thicket-
bound coyotes and rabbits
with our badly-bred foxhounds
baying (longhaired where ticks
made their nests
                    in neck-wrinkles
and paling belly-skin), field dressed
critters with a jack knife
to spit-roast on the creekbank.

                    The quarry
where lately I gather mushrooms
earlobed along shallow shaded pools
is a cliffside. Amid a honky fantasy
of Indian afterlife I check my snares

on obscured outcroppings
where cacti tufts keep others (trap-
setters, poachers, snake-
oil salespeople with beaded
hair and souring hopes, half-
imaginary

                    but some part true),
away from my catch. I count
constellations in my eyrie

some nights as helicopters loop
down into the blast-emptied pits
beneath me, unseeing the eye-
lights of others' in their own perches,
tear-edged, worrying their hem-
fray.

What promised
land would these creeks and ravines
harvested for gravestone, for keystones
and curbstones, ever be?

By now the kudzu-claimed cemeteries'
granite was long-scavenged
for shanty-stoops or sunken
back into faraway earth, swallowed

by the soil like a lure-weight.
                    Subterranean
names carved on the stone
sought (like lures) the bodies that bore them:

ghosts rise, moss-fringed
and plain-faced, from the dirt—

decaying suburbia
fills the emptied underground
they've left—they pace, eagle-eyed
for half-smoked cigarettes, hunting

the fallen-in avenues
of a city they've been gone
too long to have ever,
in their first lives,
come to know.

ABIGAIL CARL-KLASSEN

Shock and Awe

03.20.03   01:23:20

[+   ]

                              03.20.03   01:23:25

                              [+]

        03.20.03   01:23:27

            [+   ]

            03.20.03   01:23:30

                [+]

            03.20.03   01:23:31
            03.20.03   01:23:32
            03.20.03   01:23:33
            03.20.03   01:23:34
            03.20.03   01:23:35
            03.20.03   01:23:36

ABIGAIL CARL-KLASSEN

After the Universe Breaks

Every shopping cart, every bag of aluminum cans and every
pack of cigarettes ever sold is coming down on your head.

Every hair net, every mop bucket, every mess, every cleaner
and every tray of dirty dishes is coming down on your head.

every steel toed boot, every no-slip shoe, every box cutter and every
piece of anything ever assembled is coming down on your head.

Every syringe, every 40, every condom and every piece
of plastic in that empty lot is coming down on your head.

Every brick from every building that you ever built
and then abandoned is coming down on your head.

All the piss and all the shit from every single open
sewer on the planet is coming down on your head.

Every bomb every bullet every toxic chemical ever
sprayed every tear gas canister that says made

in the USA. Anything that I can see. I will grab
with both hands. Everything in my reach and everything

out of my reach. Everything that you dumped
and then blamed on us is coming down on your head.

ABIGAIL CARL-KLASSEN

Emma Goldman Falls in Love (with Tolstoy) at the End of the World

If there won't be dancing at the revolution I'm not coming—E.G.
Such chances arise, and they alter and direct a man's whole life—L.T. "After the Dance"

Yes, he is a pacifist, but does he believe
       in dancing? I don't know
                   if I could love a man
                        opposed to both war and dancing.
Would I choose a man, like my other
       men with their hands on the trigger,
                   bracing themselves for the end of the line
                   dance, over this man
with empty hands with open
       hands? Not a word
                 to say about dancing, except that once
                   while drunk, he watched a soldier
beat a man to death. With nothing
       but his hands. And he still remembers
                 how the flies circled the body. The mass
                 of blood, after the dance.

RICHARD JARRETTE

Beso's Dust

The wind touches
Beso's coat.

Earth is a donkey
rigged to carry everything
until everything dies.

Then it will carry dust,
Beso's dust,
whirling in the wind

if there is wind

RICHARD JARRETTE

The Sea Duck

How many killed for cotton, oil, terrible ideas?
My feelings shoot out but only so far.
Some days I sense the worms of the earth
at their work and I see leaves trembling,
feeling no greater than one worm, one leaf.
The sea duck reads the passage of the Trident Submarine
with its feet and makes a little quack at the stars,
bobbing above cold trenches and creatures
flashing in the sonorous deeps.

RICHARD JARRETTE

To a Sacred Statue

With no one to bow,
kiss your feet, or pray to you,
what would you mean?

We'll take the birds with us
and you'll be as we once were
to your stone eyes.

Perhaps you'll join us
in the dust devils some day,
if there is day.

ELIZABETH HOOVER

Attempt

after Imogen Cunningham

She studied the art of the tea ceremony
in Nagasaki before the war
and said that, although technically perfect,
she lacked something—

the translator struggled for a bit
then settled on *sad sentience,*
but it was more—the beauty
of imperfection, the absence

of desire, a hint of perishablity.
Something I search for
here on Geary Street all dusted up
in midmorning light shattering

glorious in the broken windows
of an abandoned shop.
When I first started taking pictures I was terrified
of missing things, struggled to capture

the haze that collects over a morning
making love, tried to keep
the thumbprint shadow under the nub
of his collarbone. Now I consider the light

its shifting syntax, the way the glass adds
a playful grammar, before I swing
my camera off my shoulder. He is just
a ghost I draw through dripping fingers,

flashes of white on the negative
bring choked love-calls to my throat.
If I get the angle right,
this photo will have three layers of glass

and my reflection nested in architectural lines:
machinery of my hands, ruin of my face.
The quality the woman spoke of is elusive,
and must contain that which is dying

and that which is exuberantly alive.
She said she never achieved it.
She stopped practicing
after the bomb killed her family.

As I watched the film she brought
I wondered, what could I give her
for her story for her sorrow.
Why use a machine to make a bomb

into a brilliant moon that resolves
silently in majestic clouds?
All around me perfect shadows
balanced compositions go unphotographed.

I stand in this back alley
finding not perfection
not tranquility surrounding emptiness,
but the memory of his face

turning from the dark hallway
into the bedroom where a window
illuminates his cheekbone
darkens his eyes.

The light twists into an improbable arc
slicing the frame—I let it pass.

ELIZABETH HOOVER

Letter to Albert Einstein

The girl holds her mother's neck
as she runs to the Urakami River.

In the city the skin of her people
softens the footfalls of soldiers.

Some stand completely still
without faces to cry on.

She watches the strange flight
of a crow—one wing burning.

She doesn't know photos of her city
became flash burns on your palms.

She doesn't know about the opening of atoms
or the way intention vanished at the test site

but she knows they can only watch
as her skin darkens to purple

and her mother's paper cranes
drop on fields of black snow.

MARTHA SILANO

Rondeau for the People of Nogents-Sur-Seine, France

We could not say missile, *even among ourselves. We called it our dear one.*
To give it a name gave it power; we called it anything other. Once
there had been hay and castles—sugar beets, wheat, white asparagus;
a strange crop rose from the fields of black dirt, crop of concrete towers.
Some of the people, as always, said no, tried to keep the brilliance

from their town, the noble intentions of science. What of reverence
for the healthy cell? The wrens and robins keep singing, children balance
on a bridge above the Seine, jumping toward the steam of twin reactors.
We called it our dear one,

played down the part about the devil's pact, the lack of conscience,
our daily complicity, the drive each day to the plant, distance
the whine of evacuation sirens, docimeter's clicks, Strontium-laced
milk, inedible *chevre*. We do not speak of them, invisible spinsters
butt-naked on the bank. No gaping. No alarm. What a sentence.
We called it our dear one.

MARTHA SILANO

Damage Status

My polonium, your magnetism. My governess, my garret; your Rue Cuvier, your aromatic woods. Me: the stilled flickering stars; you: feverish heat; us: opposite of stilted, a French-windowed Fontainebleau, tourmaline and topaz, main-squeezing quartz, or let's math it: tight quarters equal high-frequency vibrations. We vowed in lovely blue with bicycles, with heather and gorse, returned to the lab, to X, and the loves kept coming—the unborn/unknown balancing the known. My constant current, your unchangeable. My pitchblende, my nameless, our 1/10-gram proof; your tumults, our intermingled script. What gleaming! What fission! What detonation (your/my prize). Anemia, hysteria, sexual decline: the things we Curies would cure! Marriages that strain breath, burn skin, glow with flowering failure. Chain reaction of aches.

MARTHA SILANO

Early Sunday Morning Glosa

Pity the planet, all joy gone
From this sweet volcanic cone;
peace to our children when they fall
in small war on the heels of small war.

Once home to 120,000 people, the Zone
of Alienation contains nearly 200 ghost towns.
On last count, 197 returnees were living
among barn swallows with eleven deformities—
swollen breasts, mottled plumage, mouths
that will not close—calling card of Strontium.
In the town of Pripyat, thirty high-rises
hold televisions and toilet seats too hot
to turn on, too hot to sit on;
pity the planet, all joy gone.

Be careful where you step, be wary
of the Safe Living Concept, selective
resettlements, revised delineations.
Reconsider that guided tour to sunny
Chernobyl; Plutonium's half-life's
24,400 years. Place a headstone
on eco-tourism, on Belarus's farmland,
wildflowers more toxic than you know.
The steam that wafted over entombed
this sweet volcanic cone.

Some say it's our limbic system's
craving for hormones released
during brave and violent acts.
Some tell their people what's
making them sick is worry, stress.
But the birds with bent tails
don't know they're living
in a contaminated zone. Pity
the ones who suffer most: the small.
Peace to our children when they fall.

So many numbers, such dreary math—
easier to think of something else,
not the yearly thirty tons of spent
fuel rods with no safe place to go,
not the weasels with multiple heads.
Our grief stacks up like bricks, scores
of mold-ridden temples. Don't pray
to a saint, don't expect a burbling spring
to fix your damaged genes. No savior for
small wars on the heels of small wars.

KATHLEEN HELLEN

Trees with No Branches/ Flowers with No Names

—for Nobuo Miyake, Takeharu Terao
and the Hibakusha

One::
A yellow finger like a bone rose out of smoke and pointed
to the sun the clocks stopped the world went white
a thousand winds rushed in

Two::
Glass that didn't shatter melted bodies burned to mattered
sticks floating bloated buildings shrugged
collapsing in the radiant waves

Three::
Something in his eye besides his eye turned in
he called for his wife the tattooed pattern
dangling blackened husks the sleeve of skin

Four::
Flowers grew to excess keloid cherry
blossoms falling out of iris
with a head bigger than a human's barren stem on top

Five::
Maggots hatched in wounds that wouldn't heal
the woman indistinguishable from man
as it was in the beginning, in the end

KATHLEEN HELLEN

Pictures in Bufano's Garden

for Saito Masakazu

The survivor shows the pictures he has drawn
in colored marker and
the student translates into English.
A halting word-for-word to explain
the barracks that were hit— and himself
left for dead in the trenches of a crematorium.

Pictures that a child might draw:
Stick men in explosion, a young man's face,
red with burns and ruined, the glass and wood embedded.
Another face to show the ones who did not make it:
Four eyes, two noses, two mouths.

Pictures tell what he remembers:
Wind and blood, a moment hotter than the sun—
what he remembers but he cannot say
in English to the small group gathered
in Bufano's sculpted garden.

With tripod and a timer now
he takes another picture,
another moment he has translated to image:
The students' faces— eyes, noses, mouths.
Another picture for himself, with himself in it.

KATHLEEN HELLEN

Bonsai

The space is open silence. The tray—
        a flat clay stunned
This dwarf implies: disaster
A wind
                that flings to shore Hokusai's tsunami
                    that sends defeat
           that strips to leave the least

bare branch that bears the keloid of the cut
The ancient roots reduced

                trained to contain
the great design
        diminished in the mutual arising
Shears, benders, cutters

How to make us small? How to graft the new to what is sacrifice?
The changing of the clothes. The hard prune
            These small trees mimic
survive
dis-
    figured

FERN G. Z. CARR

Chernobyl Undone

Pripyat, Ukraine – a ghost town
inhabited by the elderly,
content to compromise
their remaining years
for the sake of the familiar;
a rogue nuclear reactor
entombed in steel and concrete,
denial;
inordinate incidences of
childhood thyroid cancers,
babies born with no eyes or limbs,
Geiger counters spitting out
roentgen readings
thirty billion times normal,
cleanup crews transformed
into sacrificial lambs,
rescue teams bombarded
by gamma radiation
a hundred times more powerful
than the Hiroshima bomb,
the world's worst nuclear disaster –
incineration,
no containment facility,
a nuclear reactor's roof
explodes with unprecedented fury,
Alert! Alert! Core meltdown of
Chernobyl Reactor Number Four!

incompetence,
disregard for safety,
experimentation,
1:23 a.m., April 26, 1986,
the early hours of the morning,
workers' families sleep
in the neighbouring town of Pripyat –
they enjoy a quiet night,
a peaceful night.

FERN G. Z. CARR

In the Beginning

Silence, then from the void, cosmic chaos –
atoms belch across a universe
pulsating with Mephistophelean
fury of infinite proportion,
colliding in a drama of fire and brimstone,
coalescing into a primaeval plasma soup
from which the embryonic stuff of life
creeps onto cooling shores
instinctively replicating,
evolving into erudite, sophisticated
beings learned in technology,
brashly overconfident and dangerous,
desecrating and vilifying the sacrosanct,
flinging matter into infinity and
strewing stars into oblivion.

FERN G. Z. CARR

Fukushima

pink cherry blossom
petals drifting to the ground –
radiation sickness

DONALD ILLICH

"Don't Pass Go"

When I was nine I didn't go outside.
I played behind my house's back window,
opposite a coffee table where I built
castles out of blocks, knocked them down,
re-assembled them in new shapes,
sharper towers, broken drawbridges,
moats where crocs ate everything in sight.

I monitored the placid backyard,
a field collecting wagons and soccer balls,
green and flat during summer months,
covered with snow and pinecones in winter.
The seasons would fill with gold light
if bombs fell on the Air Force base,
melting grass off the mowed lawn,
freezing the slush in black fallout.

The ALERT sign at the base's barber shop
would glow its red letters, pilots jumping
from their chairs to lunge into cockpits.
Each B-52 carried nuclear weapons
destined for Soviet targets on huge maps
they didn't remember to include people in.
I'd see them soar overhead, shaking
the furniture, stopping the clock's hands.

290

Then my parents would bring out board games
for us to quietly enjoy in their bedroom,
not arguing with each other like before.
Once during a car trip to church they said
if missiles flew Griffis would be hit first:
no lingering around the earth, poisoned
by radioactivity. We'd burn to ash
in the time it took to watch a sitcom.
Instead, I'd move a tiny car across
railroads, while mom picked up a card
telling her to: head to jail, don't pass go,
give your son a hug, tell him goodbye.

DONALD ILLICH

Griffis Air Force Base, 1982

Houses are broken up like the jets and skies.
We are familiar with symbols, bars, stripes,

oak leaf clusters, eagles. When stars decide,
we will all disappear. Bombers will lift off

to snow nukes on the other side, who we don't
know, who never harmed us except this once,

flinging missiles, fingers of death that want
to press on our necks. What they don't know

is we're afraid to lose our pulses, like they are.
That we've seen movies of mushroom clouds

where the enemy dissolves, bakes in the sun.
Our houses are the perfect spots for the end.

Blue and pink, streets named after weapons.
Systems that demand we become shadows

on the walls, looking forever into the distance.
But not tonight. We can have ice cream, soda.

The flakes outside don't melt, nothing burns.
We open the green freezers, touch thick ice.

DONALD ILLICH

Plane Overheard at Griffis Air Force Base

Beyond a wire fence a pond floods the grass,
soaking the field with life, frogs, and shells,
on the edge of a dairy farm, a barn's dark
red seen through the mist in the distance.

A few miles away bombers start an exercise,
jetting down the runway then rumbling
with thunder over the captain's car, his son
following the storm's passage through his window.

The plane's shape cuts black death over the sky,
beneath it the farm rushes deeply into life.

COLIN DARDIS

Let the Polite Clapping Begin

When the trumpets sound
and seven billion feet feel
the earth moving under them,
there will be polite clapping.

When the ground slithers and tussles,
trying to shake off the iron stakes
and concrete clothing we have robed it with,
millions will watch the violent undressing
via their TV and computer screens,
even though it is their feet
the earth rumbles under,
and they will never think to look down
and witness the vibrations for themselves.

The destruction of cities
will be taken for entertainment,
bookmakers running the bets
on which continent will go first,
mouths will coo at Armageddon
as the ultimate firework display is seen
from every front porch;
warmongers glad over not having to deplete
their stockpiles of nuclear warheads
to help create such a spectacle.

The lands will be festooned
with the pointillism of mobile phones
capturing the event for a posterity
that never comes.

Let the meek inherit the earth;
perhaps it is the foolish and the ignorant
who are lucky not to realise
the arrival of their own deaths.

COLIN DARDIS

Schism

I open my mouth and the rain gets in,
words washed of all color before vibrations reach any ear or disturb the molecular
  composition of any of God's construction.
Teeth feel the acid; raise my head to allow sunshine's tongue
  to come clear out all this tongue-pollution, throat as cooling tower
  smog-station, and my heart the nuclear generator.
I'm gargling on my own waste, trying to dump me at the bottom of a foreign sea
  where no telephone wires can reach and the postal service holds no code
  for; where no sun crowbars the corals.

With the sun, I am indomitable to any anchor or albatross, refusing to
  sink, one-man
armada cannonballing against all invaders; my song reverberating through
shoals of seaweed, outlasting any siren.
Gone is the alienation of the dark ages, vanquished to obliteration;
I am open to the world: my heart, my mind, my mouth opens and the rain gets it,
  vaporizing in the heat of my verse.
The sky opens and God's crazed star of wonder will never blind me again.
I know of shade. I know of great shelter.
I know the weather systems and the mystery of how they move around the
earth, their
misery looking for bare heads to copulate with.
No weight of great rainfall is any match against the force of my stature.
I will not bow to the deluge. I will not buckle to the bucketing thunder.

I am showering in the great cadence of the days, singing happy tunes; and however wrinkled my skin may get, my spirit will remain fresh.

The rocks under the waterfall do not hurt me.

Watch me swim, buoyant and free, lifted by the sunlight.

Praise be the sunlight!

Long live the sunlight!

COLIN DARDIS

and the statisticians
keep on counting

580 billion wasps in Britain
and the honey bees are going extinct:
something is going wrong.
7 billion souls on earth
with so much genius taken out when young;
so many dismantled hearts
without any reconstruction;
countless unspoken words trapped in silence
contrasted with a melody of cries from the afflicted;
hungry plates offered in supplication
given piles of junk food astounding in their emptiness;
unrecognized gifts of bedroom heroes
amongst stinking throngs of celebrity dross;
something is going wrong,
the horror of beauty lost
against recorded blood-letting.

JOSEPH HESS

Gargantuan

The A-bomb dropped, and the sun
burned not in anger.

Teller shook Oppenheimer's hand
before testifying.

The poets learn from the blinding
darkness of caves

while outside, the sun
burns not in anger. The churches

promise the earth to the meek
but none are so a blue face is born

to a peeing in baby pools
graduating to a slow dissipation

in a father's eyes, and the red sun
burns not in anger

as forever a child remembers
a yellow dress

spit from the mouth of a giant
Japanese, radioactive monster

he saw on a Saturday
matinee he always watched alone.

JOSEPH HESS

Life on Mars

Mars has old grooves.
They're always *new*, here,

on earth, like Jenny driving
her lover around this

town. God gave me one
gland for sex and war,

and I've re-crossed all their
intersections. When earth

becomes like Mars, I'll
internalize the dry, creviced

lake beds like thoughts
of ex-lovers that awaken us

gasping with sudden apnea—
the roads not taken, the roads

gone, finally leaving us
the dried grooves in a terrible

new desert heat.

JOSEPH HESS

Black Eyes (The Last Courtesan)

The beast grew stronger

living in a high rise above

the desperate, hot city

the starving

called her black eyes

the last courtesan

the fleshy goddess

of the last capitalist

a storm cloud crackled

she could not remember

into the past

a time before

like a trail of smoke

pleasing the owner

rising in the night

he paced the high rise

stories remain

looking down on the starving

beneath the tower

and mumbled about a God

among the milk crates

one day his body guard

descending from gladiators

while his head was bowed

imagining another time

smashed his head in with a gun

before the becoming

        she pleased the new owner of

her black eyes wandering to

        the windows on the starving

people below

        and the high rise air

suffocated her so.

NINA LEWIS

Half Life

In the early hours
as humans curled in sleep,
Reactor 4 explodes.

Fire burns for seven days
spews radioactive particles
overseas, wide span of terror.

Liquidators came,
exposed to terrifying levels.
Two years to clear-up
working in blocks of 90 seconds.

Time now stands still
reactor building suppressed
by concrete tomb,
sarcophagus and ghost.

In the exclusion zone
older residents move back in
close to family graves
carrying memories
of a time before.

NINA LEWIS

Shadows Burnt into Stone

The cycle of death turns
without end,
infinite horror.
Heat strangles buildings,
kills the shielded.
Materials combust.

Fire consumes oxygen
rising heat,
lethal hurricanes
perpetuate the fire storm.

Survivors hold short
time-lines. Indirect death.
Suffer the marks,
fatal burns, blindness
unseen internal damage.

The best they can hope
is to wish pain away.

Caught in the open air,
heat flash vaporizes
human tissue,
the only remains of people,
shadows burnt into stone.

NINA LEWIS

Becquerel Town

Pripyat. Model town,
purpose built for the workers.
Abandoned.
Fifty thousand gone.

Overtaken by wild nature.
Birch trees grow inside decaying
apartment blocks.
Wild boars roam streets at night.

Graffiti artists replace the lost,
paint silhouettes of ghost population.

Disaster creates the Dead Zone,
a fairground, due to open five days
later. Never used.

Dominating the horizon
the immutable power station
absolute ruler of this empty town.

AMY BRUNVAND

Let the Cows of Hope Live!

After all the people were evacuated
From the nuclear exclusion zone
At Fukushima
Hungry cattle roamed
Through soggy ghost-town streets.

Cows born to be killed for beef
Became accident debris
Tainted life
No longer useful for food
They were to be butchered and buried.

A farmer, dodging police roadblocks,
Caught the cows by their ears
Gave them names,
Fed them yellow rice stalks,
Led them to contaminated pastures.

Human sustenance is one thing,
He said, it's another matter
Killing cows
Merely to bury our shame
At what we have done to the world.

So even though this honest man
Apologized to the authorities
For his trespass
He refused to promise
That he would never do it again.

AMY BRUNVAND

Downwind

Nevada Test Site, 1988

I hardly remember the faces
Of the women in tie-dyed skirts
Who went singing as I drove
In my sky-blue VW bus
Through the star spangled night
Across a blank Nevada desert

Don't worry 'bout a thing
'Cause every little thing's
Gonna be alright

I only remember that we woke
In a city of tents, ate oatmeal
With brown sugar and raisins
Under the banner of Food not Bombs,
Paced the silent bends of a stone labyrinth
Into the center and out again,
Pressed our painted hands to butcher paper,
Hung on a barbed wire fence
Fluttering with ribbons, ribbons, ribbons,

I only remember how tenderly
I held the wire down
So metal thorns wouldn't tear their clothes
As they stepped gingerly across.

I only remember long brown hair
Blowing in the wind
As they walked away
Towards the radioactive dust.

AMY BRUNVAND

Fallout Shelter

Where did all those signs go?
The black and yellow ones
You used to see on telephone poles,
Post offices and schools,

A Sierpinski sieve
That promised to protect us
Under the infinitely expansive
Wings of the Butterfly of Peace.

Somewhere in America
Are there still basement closets
Stacked with uneaten biscuits,
Carbohydrate supplements,

Bulgur wafers, water barrels,
The necessary Geiger counters
So that we would recognize
When it's safe to return to the surface?

Where are the tiger swallowtails
I used to capture in my net
And pin to cardboard sheets
Until their wings crumbled to dust?

I wish I had known to be gentler.
Their wings were the color of summer
Their wings were the color of war
Averted, the color of shelter.

TOM TRACEY

Nightwalk

Daisy chains and atom bombs,
Spanish steps and blue lagoons:
Everything I've ever seen
Has come to mind in empty rooms
With a view to finding you.

Swans and signets still pursue
The quiet wake of the canal.
Now I wonder how to woo
The hard-to-get of the banal.

TOM TRACEY

Infinite Jest

After the n winds have tossed us off
this nuclear paradise,
what'll we do in the muggy summer
with no kisses from each other
or a huggy mother?

We'll be on warm bench-wood
smoking up/out the finite rays,
catchin' our final cancer tan
before the next world's universe
big-bangs
again.

MADHUMITHA MURALI

Do we need it?...A thought.

Blast!! Screeching!!
Fires, flames rising
Bloody flesh erupting
Like a Volcano
Of the failed nuclear explosion
Miles far away
Became barren
That a sprout could not take birth
The fission reaction
That broke the calm lands
That completely cut off the lands
For sprouting life for generations
Think beyond
Preventing mishap
Do we need it?...A thought.

CECELE ALLEN KRAUS

Wild Asparagus

Pure cool Columbia River waters, few
inhabitants—perfect for making a bomb.

We played in the wild asparagus fields until
the government uprooted them for housing.

Wanapum river people and the white farmers
of Hanford, White Bluffs, and Richland

were driven off for nuclear reactors. Now I drive
out to the bomb-site, dun-colored and still.

Here, my father, raised in Alabama pines, patrolled
the desert in a jeep right up to Rattlesnake Hills

with a gun and spotlight, looking for spies, awed
by desert skies. As a child I saw posters

around town with a woman, finger to lips,
saying, *Shhh-hh. Don't spread rumors.*

CECELE ALLEN KRAUS

Hanford Works

In a long crinkled black and white photograph
Daddy poses with one-hundred tuxedoed men.
A grin offsets his body honed lean in cotton fields.
Somewhere on the Illinois Central between Birmingham
and Chicago or on the North Coast Limited to Pasco
he became a stranger in a strange land,
and in the shadow of Hanford's towers,
policed atomic energy workers made mad
by loneliness and beer—welders, carpenters,
construction crewmen—poor men from Oklahoma
and Missouri with skills useful for bomb building.

In the bar he'd open a hose to stun drunks off to bed.
Quartet harmonies quieted him until Mother and I
reached the Pasco station. When classical music called
he joined a chorus touring the Northwest. By then
he'd settled in Richland, a town pasted and thrown
on a desert landscape right along where the Snake
and Columbia rivers meet. We three came together
in a thin-walled prefab with no basement
or attic.

CECELE ALLEN KRAUS

Vacation Rental by Owner—#407

With a click I travel the four tiny rooms
of a cottage just like the one my family rented.
Willard Street. Richland, Washington.

Company town for workers at the atomic
bomb plant. Furnished in colors of tumble-
weeds and the Hanford nuclear reactors

just a few miles away. Gingham filters
the sun. A widened doorway—living room
to kitchen—suggests a spaciousness

I know does not exist. Irrigation yields
a small yard. The owner writes: *Backyard
is a work* in *progress—a little weedy.*

I think of plutonium choking body
cells, clogging blood flow to the brain,
and wonder: can I pick up a key,

open the door, find Mother singing,
the four o'clocks blooming? Claim shelter?
When I was a child, the government

told us to cower in case of a bomb:
*place a table in a corner—
crawl under.*

ANNETTE C. BOEHM

The Homemaker's Rain Dance

Go right now, layer the house with books.
Sixteen inches for ample shielding.
Accidents are happening
everywhere to everyone;
it's a wonderful time to be alive.

Fallout: a light dust. Wipe it off.
Scrub and peel inanimate objects.
They will be perfectly safe to eat.
They are too small to hurt you.

Locate salve, powdered milk,
a hammer. Get on the floor.
The State Orchestra's Conelrad rendition
will continue
for an hour or so.

ANNETTE C. BOEHM

This outdated future —

Tuck it back into the particular spaces.
Where you found it. Let's pretend it
never happened, and I never learned to count —

One's a deviation, an unexpected rain.
Twos: anomalies, two yolks in one egg.
Threes, incidents, are no reason to duck.
Fours have consequences: one of us has to die.
Five's accident is the talk of the town.
Sixes reach past Metropolis.
Sevens eat Belarus and Japan.

ANNETTE C. BOEHM

Greater Noctule

Tonight my body is shedding me,
or the opposite is true:
I'm loosening my hair, my skin,
my bones thin as a bat's.

I meant to say
my heart is a geiger counter.
Drumbeats contract into ticks;

where is your echo, your radium face?
Where are you, songbird,
my sweet passerine?

LUCILLE LANG DAY

The Product is Safe

The manufacturer's representatives say
a child could throw it against
a wall, or drop it off the roof,
and it wouldn't break.
In fact, it's guaranteed
to be found smooth and shiny
in the wreckage of a plane.

But used as directed
it will vaporize cities.
Whole populations will disappear.
The sky will turn orange.
Even watching from a distance
will melt your eyes
and turn your skin to ash.

Then the sky will turn black
and all the flowers
will return to the earth,
their petals falling in darkness
amid the troubled breathing
of the last warm-bodied creatures
to crouch in the snow.

LUCILLE LANG DAY

Where the Radiation Goes

When an earthquake cracks
a reactor, iodine molecules
ascend. Tumbling in hot wind,
they drift to a grassy slope
where mottled cows graze.
Soon children will drink milk
that scintillates like a galaxy.

A woman opens an umbrella,
but broccoli, lettuce, mustard
and spinach are suddenly
bathed in strontium rain.
There's nowhere to go except
earth, sky, and sea—algae,
fish, clouds, birds, trees.

Radiation from a test in China
ends up in Utah and Colorado.
Fifteen years after Chernobyl,
the isotopes were still found
in stalks and delicate gills
of wild mushrooms gathered
by picnickers in France.

LUCILLE LANG DAY

Fear of Science

I have no fear of Dolly, whose genes came
from the nucleus of a starved mammary cell,
or of tomatoes sprayed with gamma rays
to kill maggots, worms and *Salmonella*,
or of mice whose mutant myosin disrupts
the alignment of muscle fibers in the heart.

Nor do I fear the frog and carrot, cloned
from mature cells long ago, or the outdoors
where cosmic rays bombard my DNA
and radon gas emerges from the earth,
or people with hypertrophic cardiomyopathy,
whose heart cells are in disarray.

Should I fear grana stacks, where chlorophyll
molecules capture light in an oak leaf,
or the sunbeam itself—dancing photons
arriving after a long journey through space,
or the beat of my own heart, squeezing
blood one way through its four chambers?

I don't even fear the way neutrons
from a uranium nucleus cause fission
of a second nucleus, changing mass
to energy, making a chain reaction possible,
and certainly not the electrical signals
traveling like thoughts through silicon chips.

What I fear is the imperfection
of the human brain, quick to anger,
oblivious to the needs of frogs and carrots,
mice, oaks, sheep, confused by too much
or too little dopamine, unable to remember
clearly the color of manroot, the cry of geese.

YUAN CHANGMING

[fissuring]

Between two high notes
The song gives a crack
Long enough
To allow me to enter
Like a fish jumping back
Into the night water

Both the fish and I leave no
Trace behind us, and the world
Remains undisturbed as we swim
Deeper and deeper in blue silence

Upon my return, I find the music
Still going on, while the fish has
Disappeared into the unknown

YUAN CHANGMING

[pomegranate]

As long as you have ample blood
Filling in your cells, your heart
Will never fade
Within your fine structure

A rosy inner being:
Each sarcotesta is inflated
With juicy passion

YUAN CHANGMING

[25th letter]

yum yum yummy, you have
become so addicted
to this juicy alphabet
you can readily get high
high within your hairless skin
as yellowish as the bank
of the Huanghe River
less sleek than a china crane
but more fragrant than a young yucca
while its pronunciation can lead you
to the very truth you are pursuing, its shape
can grow from an unknown sprout
into a huge Yggdrasil, where your soul
can perch on an evergreen twig, cawing glaringly
towards the autumn setting sun

YUAN CHANGMING

[word idioms]

No belief without a lie
No business without sin
No character without an act
No coffee without a fee
No courage without rage
No culture without a cult
No entrance without a trance
No epicenter without an epic
No Europe without a rope
No freedom without a reed
No friendship without an end
No fundamentalism without mental fun
No heritage without a tag
No glove without love
No ghost without a host
No groom without a room
No infancy without fancy
No life without if
No malady without a lady
No manifestation without man
No mason without a son
No millionaire without a lion
No nirvana without a van
No passage without a sage
No pharmacy without harm
No plant without a plan
No prevention without an event

No product without a duct
No recovery without something over
No restaurant without rest or rant
No sight without a sigh
No slaughter without laughter
No splurge without urge
No spring without a ring
No substance without a stance
No think without ink
No truth without a rut

YUAN CHANGMING

[you have a dream]

You will be sad to depart from us tomorrow
At an antlike moment in the smallest space
Where you will become used to singing aloud
With a throat wider than your belly, the song

Of a frog with only one tone and one pitch
A song about your dream flowing with leeches
In a ricefield. Yes, you will have a loud dream!
You will dream of humans who will no longer

Try to catch you, skin you off, barbecue you
Or eat you alive as they do with their own
Species; you will dream of jumping
As high as summer stars, and as rapid

As winter winds. You will dream of
Equality, equilibrium and equanimity
Yes, thank his Song, thank God Almighty
From human catch you will be free at last!

YUAN CHANGMING

[birds of disparate feathers: a confucian call for commonwealth]

Come, come, you peng
From the Zhuangzian northern darkness
You swan from the Horacean meadows
You pheasant from under Li Bo's cold moon
You oriole from Dufu's green willow
You dove from the Dantean inferno
You phoenix from Shakespeare's urn
You swallow from the Goethe oak or
The Nerudan dense blue air, you cuckoo
From the Wordsworthian vale, you albatross
From the Coleridgean fog, you nightingale
From the Keatsian plum tree, you skylark
Form the Shalleyean heaven, you owl
From under the Baudelairen overhanging years
You unnamed creature from the Pushkinian alien lands
You raven from near Poe's chamber door
You parrot from the Tagorean topmost twig
And you crows from among my cawing words

Come, all of you, more than 100 kinds of
Birds from every time spot or spot moment

Come, with your light but strong skeletons
Come, with your hard but toothless beaks
Come, with your colored feathers, and flap your wings
Against Su dongpo's painting brush strokes

Come, all you free spirits of nature
Let's join one another and flock together
High, higher up towards mabakoola

PETER MARCUS

The Comforts of Amber

Smoked fish hang from wooden racks along the shoreline road
to Lake Issy-Kul.
           Bodies split. Gills partly open. Trout
perch and pike oily to the touch.

                For sale at the higher elevations
glass jars of apricot jam and wild honey in golden variations.

Women wrapped in floral head scarves, wave
their fleshy hands
          beseeching passing cars to pull over.

What was and what will be, matters less.

        Three months from now our bodies heavier, encumbered.
Skin turned the color of jarred paste

               as we drive through mountain snow,
past frozen lakes, wind gusting its Soviet-era radiation.

              August sunlight ladling the day.

Melon rinds and tiny, intact skeletons nonchalantly tossed

from opened windows

on the summer road to Bishkek.

Only fish-smoke lingering pungent on fingertips

as if in advance we had touched

our own pyres.

PETER MARCUS

Basho and Togoe After the Little Boy

Flocks of white geese, flocks of white cranes—
…before….after….One lurid cloud
roiling aflame. No time to surrender.

On a distant mountain, in his simple cabin,
an unknown monk sweeps
cold cinders from the furnace of history,

sweeps from his mind's-eye
the countless eyes aghast,
blinded by an unknowable light.

For those whose flesh did not peel
instantaneously away, *Togoe wrote "Give Back
the Human."* But how to give to those

whose flesh was smelted,
enduring thermal burns, leukemia,
melanomas, ulcerated skin, convulsions.

The world remains explosive:
Kalashnikovs', grenades, car bombs, landmines, drones,
flung rocks, hurled stones.

Few rowboats anchored among the moonlit lotus blossoms.
Few friends adrift, sharing wine and verse.
No black-crowned heron's love song for the dark.

In a world of one color the sound of wind.

PETER MARCUS

When the Light in Dreams is Identical to the Light in Death

I'd just returned from a bus tour of the mass graves at Baba Yur
with an hour stop at the Chernobyl Museum with its photographs
of a radiated humanity. Thyroid cancers, gross deformities, rashes,
workers in protective suits raking, shoveling and tossing out debris
as if performing mundane yard work. On the road to Pripyiat, we
passed deserted farms and in town center amidst derelict apartments,
the driver spotted a wild boar foraging beneath a rusted Ferris wheel.
Neither images of genocide nor toxic-leakage disquieted me more
than Tommy's disembodied voice. His body shelved in a Bangkok
morgue, kept cold for an upcoming autopsy to rule out overdose
and foul play. While I lounged in a three star hotel in Kiev with beets,
bilinis, herring and crème' fresh on the breakfast buffet. That night
I slept with the Archangel Gabriel hovering above the rows of empty
contamination suits till wakened by an almost inaudible voice saying,
I'm alone now. Outside my hotel window I count seven construction
cranes and the golden domes of two Orthodox churches. Tom never
said goodbye and neither did I. Poor connection? Lost signal? Does it
always end like this? Or had Tom, by sleight of language, reversed the
pronouns to make certain that I knew, I didn't want to be alone either,
which is precisely what I was: a tourist within easy reach of lingering
radiation and anonymous piles of Jewish bones, following the hush
of his words. Watching the summer dawn through a fifth floor picture
window, scanning the hilly, tiered horizon. All these unfinished
buildings pocked and skeletal like honeycombs abandoned long ago.

YUN WANG

Dreamscape

Mad men were counting down
to detonate the planet.
Dreams directed us to
Tunnel Number Two beneath the sea.

On the other side: a land of white
lotus.
We learned to live without eating.

We conversed in poetry.

The explosion carried our oxygen
iron, magnesium
into opaque
intergalactic clouds.

We grew translucent wings.

YUN WANG

Futurescape

Thunder of applause
followed by rain on the desert.
A single yellow flower
opens from a cactus palm.

A child sleeps.
Oars navigate an opal sea.

The Sun will die in five billion years.
Ten million spaceships will depart
from its white dwarf corpse.

A kiss sparks
beneath a canopy of cherry blossoms.
Electricity of one thousand faces
carved in breathing stone
rushes from Notre Dame.

Protons will decay.
The Universe will dissipate
back into a sea
of space-time foam.

Child, you are the guide
in my journey. I climb on
the boat of your laughter.

RODNEY TORRESON

October '62

Under the yard light
Kruskchev lowers the flaps
of his schapska
and beats his chest.

Kennedy swears behind the barn.

Where car lights follow
the gravel's curve,
I see the flexing shadows
of fences.

Mother says I may never wake.

I think the circles
my life makes
are accidents:
glass marks on the dresser.

Bombs chirp on the lawn.
Catthe stretch
their necks toward the sky
and try to say moon.

JASON BRAUN

Ode to The End

In *The Gita*, God made his visit, bent a boy's ear
with argument for war, and fears were redefined, threats outlined.
This script primed itself in testament, tethered to fire's ascent
sublime from the hand holding flint and fission.
Einstein laments we must surpass where the Germans went,
so diligent their descent, lining up, down in uranium mines.
In 1939, Einstein signed and sent the letter to the president.
All past winters compressed into a momentary event,
its torments falls on them all: the sirens, the death rattles,
the weight of water dents the sunken battleships.
Einstein called the peacetime doves to dine, converted them serpentine
quick as Saul's became Paul as his horse bucked and kicked.
Paul rose to squint, repent, and take sacrament
after three days spent blind, limp, sunstroked, seizure-gripped.

When the first crop of his test bombs dropped,
Oppenhimer beamed proud, then distressed as earth rocked:
I am become death, the destroyer of worlds.
Scientist stole the whole fire and the olden cipher from god's workshop,
our theft grew to the church choir lungs' blessed breath,
then sprung the organ's bellows' bass cleft.
The pews on the left sat rapt, the right's feet stomped and hands clapped.
Dissidents shouted and fixed a protest to represent:
one world or none, one world or none.
Dresden and Tokyo burn in firebombs so quick,
so quaint, soon that mechanized doom topped.

Loading the bomb on the rack, they name their toy Little Boy.
They slapped him softly, strapped him in hopes
like swaddling clothes of their chosen one.
He learned to burn x-marked maps with joy and the hunger of a sun.
His tongue of flames cast shadows that flicker past
and thrash skin, organs, and bones from a runner's back.
The flack incinerates all but where his silhouette hung
quick then dead, his head rung by tick-tock of an atom smashing.
But today sitting on rocky stream not far from Nagasaki—
there's a bridge that zigs and zags to lose ones ghosts'.

DARYLL MICHAEL WILLIAMS

On mother's lap

Cold and tightly wound
    Deserted onto a pile of remains,
    The child sits the colour of dead leaves
        Or scrap of bone
        Head only a burden

Heavy lids and heaving breath
    Hold a spine that is
    Bending like a plastic bottle
        Spilling tap water
        That has dried long before

Smelling of a gutter spillway
    The child needs to rest his head
    On mother's lap
        Or any lap
        That can spare the time

Flaking and dry
    Much like the land
    Now risen to his neck
        Where he fidgets
        From the flies

Burnt patch
      Reminiscent of a chapping lip splits
      Right at his belly
         Right at his navel
         Right at his hunger

Plunging down onto the corpse and
      Tugging at twisted varicose and torn tendon,
      The vulture finds the colloquialism
         Organ beneath the rib
         Life beneath the death

DARYLL MICHAEL WILLIAMS

the dead tree gives no shelter

Rising upon the wasteland

"what branches grow
Out of this stony
rubbish?"

questioning,
lithification and
potential that only
whispers now
wind-whipped dust
around the inhospitable
arval

ERIN ROSE COFFIN

Outage

"Radiation is [..] naturally present in our environment, as it has been since
before the birth of this planet. The sun and stars send a constant stream of
cosmic radiation to Earth, much like a steady drizzle of rain."
– From The Nuclear Regulatory Commission's *Frequently Asked Questions*

Three times a year, we take one
of our two nuclear power stations
offline to complete routine maintenance.
We work sixty-hour weeks, work

through velvet nights, work while our wives
and husbands find new ways to sleep
alone. I see Karen – her static-shocked silver
hair, her fur-lined slippers – only in the mornings,

after a long drive home that feels like science
fiction. The brightening world turns upside down,
bleeds silent purple. We live our days in tandem,
particles colliding in drowsy attempts to compound.

She is forever concerned, warns *exposure*, frets
isotopes and iodine pills. I tell her that it's nothing,
that it's in everything all around us. I tell her
about the steady drizzle. Now, she glares skyward,

wary of storm clouds rolling, distrusts constellations.
Once a year, we get to bring our family to the plant,
give them a tour. I point to the colossal turbines,
shout over the sound of steam unimaginable.

See? I fling my arms wide open. *There is no reason
to be afraid.* The reactor roars and her atoms rupture.

GUS ANDREWS

Shadows

Shadows burnt into the ground
Tell a story with no sound.
A story that will outlive man,
and damage dealt by his hand.

Burnt and barren forever more,
After have stopped the pangs of war.
The water won't drink nor damned dirt grow,
And the starving youth, all will know.

A scar upon the face of Earth,
Of scorched rubble, mangled dirt,
And shadows burnt into the ground,
Tell a story, with no sound.

NATE MAXSON

Preemptive Strike

A crack appears in the machinery
Quiet unlit wound
A break in the façade
Disproving infallibility once and for all
Like a curtain opening on the magician early
And yet
It is there
Spread open over gears and wires like something coming out of the sky
A crack appeared in the machinery, a bluebird began to sing
And then stopped
Like electricity
Even devotion has its limits

NATE MAXSON

Rocket Science

We used to send monkeys
Ahead of human test subjects
Brief astronauts to test the water, blow on the soup before swallowing
Into the substance: an evolving arrow with sudden green buds/ atremble
Not from the sky, no
But through it, a sub-audible whistling not for our ears
Animals across the horizon, down below it's summer with no preparation
The shattering of windows (canaries of the sound barrier) precedes the
actual impact
Has that ever struck you as odd?
An object falls from the sky, as it was meant to be
As if it thought it was the first to escape
Downright comforting though
Compared to what happens when it vanishes before detonation leaving
only shattered glass
Nobody knows
Where they go, these iron causalities
And (just between you and me)
Most civilians don't know the difference
They may as well be ghosts
To be safe, clean and cost-effective
Nowdays it's rockets and children first
Headfirst into the future
Because firing one backwards takes a lot more effort and we just don't have
those kinds of resources these days
Still, there's that mosquito-pitched air raid siren that hums: someone has/
someone has

So for the sake of stability we memorize   in catalogues the bodies of
Orpheus and Lot's wives (only one of whom had a name)
And we need the ripe human machine, always moving ahead
Plucked gently from the rodeo, never looking behind
Where every clown is a winner
Slow talkers need not apply
Someone has/ someone has, not I said the pilot
It is assumed that the origin point is the Trinity Site
But what if the trajectory goes back farther?
Patient zero frequently renamed, reassigned
Patients One (maiden name zero) and beyond are fuel for rumors and
nutrient-rich, black garden soil
Anything will grow
Between wished-upon falling satellites
Anything at all (even wooden horses)
Just be sure to buckle up/ the indicator light has come on meaning there is
no more smoking allowed in the restrooms
Because time is fickle, a fickle liquid
And these are shallow days
Public swimming pools too crowded to swim
Antiseptic/ half naked
In a nearby highrise apartment: Eurydice plays cards with Medusa not
looking up from her hand but unsure if she should be afraid/ if an ending
is predetermined, may as well make it strip poker
Someone has dared/ loose a rocket into the substance: fire is always a
breached birth
There's a science to landing on your feet but that is not our science, against
the limit of sound and light you can live in a year longer than it actually
exists but be prepared for that familiar whistling: incoming
Look at them/ looking up/ at us looking down: closer/ someone has dared
In the beginning we would send dogs

NATE MAXSON

Rendezvous/ The Fire

Meet me tonight at the event horizon,
The part of town where most of the houses are barricaded with shopping
carts and tricycles
Against what?
It's only me out here, only us
So what scientific curiosity are they so afraid of?
Ella,
Meet me tonight
And we can discuss the rumor that one of us got a lobotomy to look younger
or guarantee reelection

I never denied that all those Bruce Springsteen songs I used to listen to
went straight to my head

And yet, tracing white line headwound scars (almost disappeared)
One has to eventually confront who these circus tricks are for
What audience,
And what constituency…
Ah but that's all in the future
Still liquid

Not here,
You lie in bed, wounded by something more ordinary than I have the
stomach for
Time (rather trite, I know)
And that moment I went spinning across the road during a short respite
from traffic

You'll get your dancing shoes back, I promise
I know my guarantees are naive
I used to think the night of the living dead was on its way
But it was just the Leidenfrost effect
A song stuck in my head
It's a fancy word for when water droplets hit a surface so hot they evaporate endlessly
Until the heat eventually dissipates

Now about that lobotomy:
Meet me tonight at the edge of the future
Where I vaporize back and forth forever, the same way when I'm under your breath
Past the combustion-engine sound of our subtle escape
It can all be explained (though sometimes I sure hope it won't be)

But look:
Sometimes the rings of Saturn touch Brooklyn like a stereotype
Something distant shimmering in the west
Leidenfrost Effect
(I love it when you talk to me in German)
It's a heatwave before heat
How curious
Like thunder, a timelapse
The effect/ the signal/ the sudden/ the equation/ you're half vanished now: the fire

CAROL BARRETT

Baby Teeth

after Kathleen Flenniken's *Plume*

Imagine them all laid out on silver trays,
each tiny cusp sent swift as an arrow

from Cupid, rows and rows of successive
generations, originating near Hanford

on the Columbia, moving along the wind's
impartial trajectory, farms laden

with Idaho potatoes, Montana river valleys
where trout still arch, flick rainbows in the sun.

Recall that insignia infant on every box
of Gerber Baby Cereal, the blue shadowed

lock of hair. Maybe you hadn't heard
about the rebate Gerber promised

for baby teeth, mailed in, perfect pearls
innocent as little bronzed shoes.

Hooded figures calculate how many
radioactive isotopes are showing up

over what range of motion, what increments
of time, and silence. In this plutonium

town, tumbleweed blows in bundles,
children dress their dolls for tea parties,

run toy trucks over the dusty backyard
grass under filmy light from the place

their fathers inhale behind locked doors,
decades, if they last, samples of morning

urine in milk bottles set out for collection
on front porches. Downwind in Longview

my father estimates the thickness of lead
for the basement fallout shelter where

mother has stacked rows of canned
peaches, gallon jugs of water, sleeping bags

in case the Russians drop their bomb.
But the fallout has already come,

and teeth be told, it's American.

MARK LABBE

Trinity Test

The ground
came to life.

It writhed and shivered
and heaved and bucked
and maybe it screamed
but who can be sure.

It twisted into clouds,
spiraled into smoke,
and gasped until
it became an inferno.

Still, they nodded
and smiled
and winked
at the thing that was
better off dead.

RICHARD VARGAS

Godzilla

he was a big schlep
half dinosaur/half rubberized foam
but they needed to give
the real monster we had
unleashed on them a form
easy to understand,
powers that made sense
(the way his radiation-
glow-green-breath leveled
the city as his roar sounded
like one of those horns
God's chosen people would
blow to knock down the
walls of their enemies)

of course we bastardized
the original, softened
the images of the burnt
and vaporized
instead gave ourselves
Raymond Burr smudged
with dirt and a bandage
around his head while
he played the poster boy pipe
smoking american observer
a presbyterian Hugh Hefner
surrounded by foreign

hysteria and chaos
but never forget
we made Godzilla
gave him the power
to destroy and resurrect
so when he comes for us
appears off the shores of
San Diego or New York
returning like our prodigal son
expecting to be welcomed
with open arms
we will have no one
to blame but ourselves
and justice will be served

FATIMA AFSHAN

The Rain of Fire

Ashes filled the void in the melted skulls.
To make a child sleep, an elegy a mother lulls.
Acid rain is no more charming for a jaunt.
Gloomily the humans cum skeletons haunt.
Mines of talent rest beneath the ground.
With dust and stones the remains can be found.
Frightened are the hearts that remained alive.
With crippled bodies it is hard to survive.
Dreams mingled with dust, and hopes with ashes.
Recalling the eerie crash every heart smashes.
How they were deafened and blinded in a blink!
Their parents and children blazed in a wink.
Armageddon saw they before it actually came,
making the generations disappointed and lame.
The nuclear attack devoured the flourished lands
Leaving broken atoms in their burning hands

FATIMA AFSHAN

Heaps of Broken Skulls

When embers began to rain down,
the craniums of the living beings
changed into tiny fragments
of flesh and blood,
only because of some selfish motives
of political minds.
Piles of rotting hands and decaying legs
found here and there,
Heaps of skulls lay bare in the sun,
some toys and cradles melted into dust
extinguishing the sweet memories
of someone's chuckles.
the houses that were built with bricks of love
and cement of dreams for the tiny tots
Turned into rubble and ashes
black as the night.
Careers ruined,
lovers separated, children orphaned,
old parents lost their hopes.
Poisoned living creatures spitted blood,
generations were gifted with disabilities,
contaminated air to breathe,
filthy water to drink
and polluted soil to crop upon
making them emaciated for ages
and the nuclear power hailed....

LAURA MADELINE WISEMAN

After the Bombing

I didn't invent the neighborhood trolls. I didn't make them my bumps
in the night. As a girl, my mom said, *Your troll friends are only using you.*
She said, *Talking shit about me, huh?* She said, *I wouldn't marry a troll. Not
again.* I used to think all the people were bad and were trying to catch me
at my badness. I used to live without a gasmask on, without an air purifier,
a water purifier, a grocery that promises purified food. Each day, I try for
politeness, to not interrupt or stare. I say only kind words. When I must
walk outside, I chant mantras. I didn't start the stories about trolls, didn't
start the films, never even knew about the books. For years, it was only
trolls in Hogwarts, trolls in Disney, troll muppets who crossed the desert
to die. Now there are trolls in the neighborhood in collars and chains.
They bellow at the neighbors. Their clubs smash the windows of cars. I am
the type of woman who thinks I should run out in my pajamas, the ends
flapping around my shins, and wrap my arms and legs around them, hold
on tight to calm whatever it is that quakes inside. I did once and one bit
me. The scar is keloid.

LAURA MADELINE WISEMAN

Digger Troll

I went with him into the hole. I was trying to be with him, the way anyone might follow a lover, the one we hope would touch us in darkness. I wasn't seeking words, or a game I could letter out like scrabble, building language from what I had. He never spoke. We scrambled down ramps made by machines, ankle turning earth, soft where wind collects. He carried a shovel, a pair of gloves, a rag to wipe what might be found. He shuffled. His hunch was the kind that marred old men, the homeless, those demented by drink. He moved earth to see what might be hidden inside. Dogs followed us, but the streets were empty, the sky. Not a radio burbled. When he handed me the shovel, I had to dig. He corrected my hands. He showed me where to strike with the blade. I tried not to look him in the eye. They were rebuilding this part of the city, opening what had been impossible to reach. He kept his hands on his knees as I sweated. Finally, he took the shovel from me. When he found what he was looking for, he threw it at me—some piece of glass, some evidence of what had made him, what was done before this.

LAURA MADELINE WISEMAN

Troll Ashes

When we arrived again at the carvings, you scattered half the ashes. The other half you wanted to save for our yard. I said words before the seal and you said words, the bone bits white against the brown of fall. I asked you if the trolls had a way of haunting, of coming back, if this one might come again at night. You shook your head and took me home. You held my hand, took it really. I didn't say no. Still, it's strange to sleep. To find a bed and stay without roaming, without listening for what shakes, bodies hitting walls, things exploding above. Sometimes the troll that lives under our neighbor's porch calls to me. His voice is the voice of cities bombed to destroy what's underneath. He wants me to look so I look towards nothing. Our yard shivers half-dead. No one tends the stones, collects the dropped limbs, stops the cash crop going rogue. I look towards nothing and see— porch of glass window, porch of junk to be dragged across concrete, porch of blacked tools—then I go inside. Because you thought it best, we frosted every window and moved my bed across the house to the spare, where I sleep now, really sleeping.

THOMAS GORDON REYNOLDS

Prospects

when I am alone and,
the bitter summer night,
hangs about my nostrils
like a drunkard's breath,
courting veins
like the pull of the moon,
massive and far,
a weight on my too human soul
like a miller's stone
to which my horse is chained,
we alone, standing where others once stood,
with the light of your heaven's small eyes
prickling my back like cat's claws, kneading,
or the place roses were, thorns,
decorated with blood.
The thought of love, you, life, time, fate,
red like a raised welt
on my heart or wrist,
or the gnawing of wolves
having brought down something big.
The place where we felt hope,
like a dead man's house
torn down after his passing,
and I see history
has stalled with it
is fast-cut with the bomb-flash negative,
the grass heat-brown,

the creek sky-starved,
the stones kicked over,
the wind across the dreadful heart
scraping the earth's insides
and mine,
featureless with grief
like a Los Alamos sun rise,
like an ancient sea,
like the washing of a wall
or like the dead desert dreamt us
and now it wakes,
and we and you and I and us and all of it
two thousand years
of beauty, war, and love,
art, death, kings, building, ships, and lives,
and my true love
are swept away by matter's empty hand,
let break,
blown far,
and even the earth forgets
where love grew,
and even love forgets
who we once were,
and in our bitterness and brilliance
we nod
at Time's great philosophic insult:
that now we know the truth,
and that knowing the truth
does not help.

MARK HUDSON

Radioactive Water

The Japanese nuclear plant,
had a radioactive leak.
They'd stop it, but they can't,
radiation is making them weak.
A tsunami and earthquake,
created March madness this year.
How much more can humans take?
is it God who we really should fear?
The ocean is a radioactive lake,
for the Japanese I shed a tear.
It brings us all heartache,
is Jesus ever going to appear?
Why would he punish Japan?
Could it just be a coincidence?
Would we be glad if it happened in Iran?
Will there be more incidents?
This is worse than Chernobyl
worse than the disaster in the Ukraine.
The Japanese people are so noble
why must they have such pain?
In America, we don't suffer,
we complain about our life of ease.
We all need to get much tougher
because radiation is in the seas!

MARK HUDSON

Three Mile Island

Three Mile Island was an old event,
no one remembers the accident.
It won't take long,
before it won't belong,
in the memory of the innocent.

CHERYL STILES

Recalling Oppenheimer

A cloud
this particular cloud
clouds over the wing of a plane
a puzzle of snow
and snow drifts below
It's March
and I'm flying over Washington DC
toward Baltimore

We knew the world would not be the same.

Clear
clear air
over the wing of another plane
a puzzle below
fields of salt and sand
I'm flying
on my way
from Germany to Singapore
flying over the Iraqi plain

We knew the world would not be the same.
Some people laughed, some people cried.
Most people were silent.

In childhood I watched on television
the footage from Nam

rice fields and clouds of napalm
M16s firing
troops on the ground
the ominous click click
of helicopter blades
sulfurous orange-red clouds
long lines of body bags
lowered from transport planes
young widows
clutching their perfectly folded
American flags

We knew the world would not be the same.....
I remember the line from the Hindu scripture,
the Bhagavad-Gita. Vishnu is trying
to persuade the Prince that he should do his duty
and to impress him
takes on his multi-armed form and says,
"Now I am become Death,
the destroyer of worlds."

Now the broadcasts
are of sandstorms
unmanned drones
buildings in a forest of flames
snipers on rooftops
missiles
fired from vessels
explosives
wired to vehicles

More clouds
shard
shrapnel
shroud
More troops
on the ground
A thin line of green
still comes
from the north
from the south

> *I suppose we all felt like that,*
> *one way or the other.*

Amber waves of grain
jungles
rice paddies
these sandy plains
From paradise a storm
a storm is always blowing in

From paradise a storm
> *I suppose we all felt like that*
A storm is always blowing in
> *one way or the other*

Notes

Italicized lines are from Robert Oppenheimer's comments on the detonation
of the first atomic bomb, code named "Trinity." From Richard Rhodes' *The
Making of the Atomic Bomb* (1986) and Len Giovannitti and Fred Freed's
The Decision to Drop the Bomb (1965).

"From paradise a storm is always blowing in"
after Walter Benjamin's *Theses on the Philosophy of History*.
A Klee painting named "Angelus Novus" shows an angel looking as though he is about to move away from something he is fixedly contemplating. His eyes are staring, his mouth is open, his wings are spread. This is how one pictures the angel of history. His face is turned toward the past. Where we perceive a chain of events, he sees one single catastrophe which keeps piling wreckage upon wreckage and hurls it in front of his feet. The angel would like to stay, awaken the dead, and make whole what has been smashed. But a storm is blowing from Paradise; it has got caught in his wings with such violence that the angel can no longer close them. The storm irresistibly propels him into the future to which his back is turned, while the pile of debris before him grows skyward. This storm is what we call progress.

PAUL BROOKE

Red Forest Twisted
Insects Toxic Wolves

From the meltdown, a plume rose one thousand meters high,
Blood-red, dangerously beautiful, fuming uranium and graphite.

Even before the burial of the Red Forest, people were evacuated.
Whole cities. Schools without students. Churches without God.

Clouds of radioactive dust flamed across Europe, like Rorschach
Tests, ebbing, morphing in connivance with hot winds, and packed

In its wake, mutations arose: unalike antennae, bizarre wing folds,
Illogical symmetry, even spiders mis-spun their orbs, webs odd

And mis-stitched. Mortality heightened. Now, the marrow
Of wolf bones, the limbs of acacias, the organs of swallows

Carry toxic concentrations. Unnatural selection, an impure
Experiment blighting the land. Natural selection, a set of workers,

Plodding, dependable, methodical, unwavering. Time. Generations.
Massive numbers of generations. Beyond all human comprehension.

On April 26, 1986, the Chernobyl Nuclear Power Station exploded causing
tens of thousands of acres around the reactor and its organisms to be exposed
to hazardous amounts of radioactivity. Some claim it will take a million
years for the area to recover.

"In 1990, she [Hesse-Honegger], the illustrator of the insect to the right] traveled to Chernobyl itself, collecting insects from within the exclusion area around the sarcophagus of the nuclear reactor. Out of the 55 true bugs she collected, 12 were malformed" (Thompson in 26 April 2014 *Smithsonian*).

"Mutation is random; natural selection is the very opposite of random" (Dawkins 41).

KELLY CHERRY

Eniewetok, 1952

Elugelab, an island off the atoll
of Eniewetok, disappeared forever
when scientists set off a hydrogen bomb.
A fireball like a gigantic fear-blanched face
stretched its mouth and swallowed the horizon.
It changed the sea to red, incarnadine
as well-water turned to wine in Canaan,
but the sea was not effluence of pressed grapes
nor a miracle performed by Jesus Christ.
The island itself blushed red; burned for six hours.
Elugelab was gone. When Teller heard
the test was a success, he telegraphed
Los Alamos: "It's a boy." (Original
his mind might be but he clung to societal convention.)
Upshot? We'd lost our opportunity
to coax the Soviets to the table, where
both sides would forswear hydrogen bombs.
The H-bomb—flagrant harbinger of Doomsday.

KELLY CHERRY

August 6, 1945

The boy perched on the steps.
The day was fine,
a day made for perching on steps.

After the bomb, the boy is gone—
not fishing, not to school, not
called by family or playmate,

just gone, his shadow burnt
into those stone steps,
himself mere air.

At the same moment,
language comes to an end.

We cannot speak, our voices crack
and break, our tongues stumble
through the ruins of the tower of Babel.

KELLY CHERRY

Pikadon *"Flash bomb"*

The blast boiled flesh from bone,
ground bone to grit, flake, and shard.

What more is there to say?

White light in silence,
the moment suspended—
a woman changed to air—

What more is there to say?

Like a dog with a bone
winds shook the city.

What more is there to say?

A man carried his eyes in his cupped hands,
palms open, as though his hands might see
what he could not.

The still living
envied the dead.

What more is there to say?

Black rain fell.
What more?

The sickness began.

GONZALINHO DA COSTA

After Basho

Chalk white moon, a disc of pooling light.
Round old pond, stillness unruffled,
Bird tucked inward. Behind
Embankment of clouds, a frog leaps—
Touchdown in water!

Black sky bursts, broken,
Beatific placid mirror shattered
By splash of a big blast,
Droplets, tremulous,
Subatomic particles scattering,
Tsunami unleashing gamma waves, X-rays,
70,000 instantly dead...

Genbaku Dome, UNESCO World Heritage Site.

JOHN SOKOL

Prisoners of War, 1956

my brother
with armies of plastic men
planes armed
with Tinker Toy bombs
and me Godzilla
crushing his tanks
his Lincoln Log forts
when out of his throat
an air raid fills the house
and alerts my father
who bounds the steps
and smacks me to bed
where boredom
rolls me over onto my side
to roam the labyrinth of grain
on the closet door
as time ticks away
to the sounds of my father
in his basement shop
building I figure
a cage for me
warnings of wood
and hammered spikes
that scare me enough
to hide in the closet
where I open a box
he stores in the cubby

behind some clutter
I find some pictures
I've never seen
dead soldiers
rotting in mud
missing arms
missing legs
faces gone
empty ruins
mountainous piles
of empty shoes
barbed wire
mass graves
overflowing
rows of matchstick bodies
naked on frozen ground
human cords of wood
burn my eyes
I can't move
so crushed
by weight of bodies
among which I am one
shaken and hammered
bombs exploding
metal to metal
blade of dozer
picking me up
and the corpse beside me
breathing my name
my brother
shaking my arm
shouting
get up get up
Dad says
it's time for dinner.

JOHN SOKOL

A Thousand Years from Nowhere

The dinosaurs, too, must have thought "this is all about us"
as they watched the sun come up on each millennium.
At least vanity wasn't their downfall. For a thousand years
before their demise, a tar pit was no place for reflection.
They had a better excuse for their flawed instincts:
their brains were the size of walnuts.

But what of the hairy mastodon, stopped cold in his tracks
by an ice age that left him stiff with humility, and without
an inkling of how that pristine buttercup we found
on his tongue left a lump in our throats?

Perhaps the Sumerians held an essay contest, commemorating
the year 2,000 B.C., and maybe a boy from Babylon wowed
the judges by slipping a world of wonder and wisdom
onto one clay tablet, while a hundred war-horse scribes
chipped away at those same old pictographs about themselves.

And speaking of wonder boys: Alexander the Great
(323 years before the year 1) was already gazing longingly
into the mirror of the future. By the time he was 29,
he had razed Thebes to the ground, crossed the Hellespont
to crush the Persians, destroyed Tyre, and reduced
Persepolis (a wonder of the world) to a heap of ashes.
He, too, must have thought the next millennium would be
all about him. He named thirty conquered cities after himself.

And in 51 B.C., Caesar had a lot of Gaul. Then, along came
Jesus, and everybody stopped counting backwards.
But there was an endearing quality to those people
who counted the years backwards. We have a sense
that they knew their place in history; that the future – to them –
wasn't so all-important. Or, as they may have said, in Latin:
"Conquer if you must, but be happy!"

And, Hitler, too – that quintessential, type-A "forward
counter" – thought the next millennium would be all about
him, so he jumped the gun – by 60 or 70 years – and started
counting: Jew after Jew after Jew after Jew . . . and, today –
in Bosnia and Kosovo, in the Sudan, and Rwanda
(or, just spin the globe and point) – we see what Hitler hoped:
that history is an opportunity drawn in blood.

So who will blame me, for driving home tonight, through
these blessed woods, and breathing in all the sweet humility
that hangs in these trees. Who will blame me for listening
to Dwight Yoakum, on the radio, singing "A Thousand Miles
From Nowhere," while I sing along, and try not to think
about all this millennial madness; all the dread and loathing;
paranoia, xenophobia, and rage? And who will blame me
for thanking the stars that I love that moon
that shines through that hole in all this darkness?

JOHN SOKOL

Thoughts Near the Close
of Millennium

In this expanding universe, everything is leaving everything,
        yet there is no center
from which any of this leave-taking leaves; the middle
        of every departure
is everywhere. Microcosmically viewed, it all looks a lot like
        the pores of Dizzy Gillespie's cheeks
when he blew his horn. We're spinning away from the sun
        and the stars
while Ceres moves away from Jupiter and Neptune moves
        away from Mars.
Everything is leaving its immediate neighborhood, gathering
        more and more distance
for itself, like the furthest quasar, that — 18 billion years ago —
        said goodbye to Proxima Centauri.
Even Nancy down the street is leaving Charlie and the kids.
        Like everything else,
we're forever blown away by that first Big Bang. We're stuck
        in the atmospheric saddle
of a slow-motion explosion, like that one at the end
        of Antonioni's *Zabriskie Point,*
where that floating olive might be the earth, and if we slow down
        the slow-motion (slow it,
geometrically, down), we can witness that olive decomposing
        and watch entropy eat it up
while we consider that all those little anatomizing volcanoes
        and olive-quakes of it

might be comparable to the shifting and colliding of continents
     which have slow-danced
to the music of the spheres for billions of summer nights,
     crashing their own weddings
and feasting off each others' tectonic plates until the next big
     bash: all of which is just the drop-of-an-olive
in a martini glass compared to what it would take to understand
     what I'm talking about
is the energy that is the black hole of me that sucked this martini
     so dry that no light exists,
and now the pimento of that olive is the pit of my stomach
     which seems to have multiplied
in density a thousand-fold, like a pellet of buckshot become
     shot-put,
or maybe, like — at the core of a white dwarf — that teaspoon
     of matter that weighs five tons.
So maybe all this wonder and worry — and all this speculation —
     is futile, because, here it is,
New Year's Eve again and I don't think I need to overstate my
     point.

ANTONY OWEN

Sketching of an Atomic Horse

In pastures of blank white pages
someone captured a nag through graphite
rubbing it's lead mane in the dropped stars' corona.

Pencil on page is a cruel stable:
a nag lapping troughs of her wounds,
the hurled tongue black from ghosts of grass.

There is no shame in falling twice -
a palomino rain stampedes the thoroughbred;
art reels the drowned foal from eyes.

ANTONY OWEN

Letter from the Sun to Man

Dear Human, I am dying slowly yet you murdered my sibling wind.
You took her last breath on August sixth and ninth, your sun blew it back so fast
it made my children vapour and shadow. Some of them made rivers in the
sky, estuaries of red mixing with black rain - like cardinal cloaks spilling
rosary beads, yet this was not the blood of God, this was yours.

Dear Human, I am dying slowly, like that girl and that boy, and that boy
and that girl, and to save ten thousand pages - for there are no trees left
- let me say there is nothing here but death. Look at my daughter moon,
her face looks sicker - she has seen a doll made of flesh, kokeshi white and
limbless like moon. *Oh what have you done dear human?*

Dear human, this new flag of Japan shows my face - I am limbless of rays
like my daughter moon. Our empires are islands of hibakusha conquered
in their wars of altered blood. My orphan nephews shall be peaceful now,
please listen to the silence of Nagasaki streets and the noise of Nagasaki
streets will disturb you like typhoons of Hiroshima butterflies.

Dear human I am dying slowly,
yet I shall outlive you with your Mother
Earth.

Notes: hibakusha = atomic bomb survivor

ANTONY OWEN

The Fisher's Daughter

Some things drag us back sad and heavy
like gipsy wagons concealing a cargo
of painted - over myths that peel us back to grain.
Some things wake us in our temporary deaths -
the bracken of my chin my wife gets lost in
kissing closed eyes, her pencil-case prince.
Some things break open like Hiroshima clouds -
daffodil bulbs glowing out from trespassed darkness;
this is me, my love, head bowing to so much death.
Some things translate us from the font of human bone
carried by a fisher – his daughter's dress with a ghost
of her handprint flashed against the flora.
Some things never change like those who dare not look,
who make their nuclear families in brittle little hamlets,
and teach their children never to play with matches.

HEATH BROUGHER

Chade in Mina

You will eat your dinner of imitation crab meat
and generic sushi from the truck-stop; this roundtable
of concoctions and mixtures of toxic things mutate,
transform and transmogrify;
Manmade pollutants disturb the world,
rub nature the wrong way—

these defiled bones and guts and toxic toys
and food swing way off hinge and into the bizarre,
mutation after mutation—

"Momma my three legs, Dada my tenth neck,
Nana my vomiting up of overly tampered-with chemicals"

the extant Manmade dent in the Earth
has soaked deeply into the soil and sky;
mutated children or just plain dead babies everywhere;
this is the dying down; these are
the toxicology reports run amok
with unsafe chemicals—   so where do we go from here?
just survive; try to live through
the enormity of it all—   these poisons so deeply ingrained
in land, in air; a colossal intertwined coalescence of Manmade toxins;

there will be no easy fix,
no sudden magnanimous cure
to what we've wrought and taken
into our bodies and the Earth entire.

the toll of a mangled Earth rings loudly;

Sickness
rises.

HEATH BROUGHER

Nuclear Baby

My mother breathed contaminated air
while I was floating in the amniotic swimming pool of her belly.

My mother was pregnant with me during the Three Mile Island crisis.
She living only a forty minute drive from the power plant,

nuclear air swept into her lungs and spread to my tiny alien body.
Her umbilical cord, a soft hypodermic needle injecting radiated air,

atomic nutrients, straight into my buttonless belly.
I was born into a world of nuclear waste. Nuclear skies

and clouds pouring acid rain. Nuclear particles whisking along the
toxic breeze.
I came nascent and pink into this world gasping for my first breath

among the atomic poison that blew cold and mutagenic
along the air-paths of my hometown.

MARK J. TULLY

shade

pamphlets
of
empire
blotted
in
final
refute

MARK J. TULLY

white sands

legacies slain seeding besickened
bitter haze heroes betrayed

KHADIJA ANDERSON

Ossuary

If it weren't for the bones
We could have flown without a plane
Used our long hair as wings

Glittering blonde in the lightning
We could have flown without a plane
If it weren't for the bones

Glittering blonde
We could have rested on the wind
If it weren't for the bones

We could have rested on the wind
Let 600 mph gusts take us
Into the sudden black rain

Gusts would take us
Into a spectacular cloud
A shimmering pearl ossuary

KHADIJA ANDERSON

Shelter

Here is your shelter decay
You who made me lawless & hoarse

Left out to be disappeared
Shifting in the new dark sun

Hoarding water around you
Boots cindered and clean

Ready to disguise yourself
In earthquake or storm

Heat and debris
glitter with trinitite

Wires hum in the crazed wind
Door locks gratuitous

Wind ravaged prayer flags
Stinging near the place

You always claimed sacred

KHADIJA ANDERSON

We live on an island

It's romantic to live by the water
while drowning

Families have lived here for generations
houses full of things

It's a place of isolation
like the underworld

There were 30 suicides of young people
in the past year

You know what they say
war has been declared

DAVID ANTHONY SAM

Cloud Chamber

The spin of the atom is imprecise
but knowable.

Its parts we create in accelerators
can be seen in a cloud chamber

only as white streaks.
And these white streaks

can be known only by a camera,
quick eyed, digitized, permanent

in image, not transient
like the fleeting illusions of eye.

How do we know anything is really there?
The infinitesimal

is all space and nothing.
How can you see through

all the apparent solidity
to the precise spin within?

Numbers are like eyes,
but careful, certain.

Equations balance the world
in a careful scale,

weighing energy with thickness
and the motion of the light.

Equations have the power
to liberate the eye.

And photographs can capture
the eye's transience

and contain it in patterns
of ghost streaks.

Precision of spin.
Careful quantity of result.

Specific power to each sphere.
Waiting the liberation of the eye

in waves of light so perfect
that the eye is blinded.

As if, unbidden,
it had sought to view Diana

at her bath, or dared
to watch, uncovered,

the hindquarters of God
as he strode through the mountains

seeking his final freedom.

DAVID ANTHONY SAM

Alamogordo - July 16, 1945

The sun rose twice today.
Why call it Trinity?
At Alamogordo, the first sun
boils in a brown cloud.
The Destroyer of Worlds.
The second sun seems rather smaller.
We watch the cloud of the first
dissipate—who understood?
We understand the process,
sort of; but some feared the chain
would never cease until
it had consumed the world.
Perhaps it won't. Shiva.
Shattering himself into a thousand
shapes and forms to wait
behind the illusion of the second
sun, until the rising of the third,
the Terrible One of many names.

DAVID ANTHONY SAM

Nuclear Winter

Time for a new season,
a weather made of skin
and muscled with human motion,
but still rhythmed to moon phases
and the rise and dip of sun.

You can't make that season;
but if you can, find it
in the way you breathe January
cold and send back clouds
out your nostrils and lips.

And you can find it in
the throb your blood does,
and the angle of the eye
to shadows and horizons,
and the touch of hand

to powdered snow whirled in wind.
Time for a new season;
but too much of the old
hangs in the drop of flat clouds
and the drop of your face

as the tissue releases with age.
Another planet would have
another season. But will this one?
You must know if there is time,
for we have cut the clock

to inches, and laid our lives
out hostage to deep burrows
where missiles lurk,
ready to cold the world
in winter smoke forever.

BEKAH STEIMEL

Maybe the stars have mythical names

for our streetlights
making wishes on bulbs that flicker and fade out
our point of view is the worst seat in the house
our point of view keeps us lonely and smug
ask the dinosaurs about arrogance and watch them blush
we are just ants stepping on ant hills
our guns, our wars, our nuclear weapons
our pollution, our capitalism, our endless shoulder shrugs
let's hope the stars are making wishes for our survival

Tonight I believe

there are no self-made sinners
it's the denial of love
that strangles a conscience
goodness can be murdered
just as evil can be nurtured
and groomed
we are all victims
and every victim
was once a perpetrator
and every perpetrator
was once a child
there are no clean hands
in this world
we should all be pointing
dirty fingers
toward one another

BEKAH STEIMEL

I've never written

weapons grade poetry
potent enough
to infect the masses
I simply bury small explosives
and wait for you
to stumble upon them
and get blown away

ELIZABETH DEBUNCE

Lullaby in Six Parts .

1.
Midnight whistles as we pass through the cities.

The scattered tracks lay burnt behind us,
and I watch the exhausted coal-shovelers
fold the soft black steel like bed-sheets
and stack them in the rear of the locomotive.
To be used for later.

A muted sun drips crimson across the peaks of the mountains.
Residue of gunpowder thickens the walls. The dust of Bangladesh
clouds from our white hair. Human remains.

2.
On the train,
my father threads his wounds with a piece of barbed wire,
sterilized with lighter-fluid.
Burn victims floss their teeth in the reflection of the windows.
The scabbed lips, melted limbs, avulsed eye sockets bruised or bruising green.
Mothers finger-comb their daughter's matted hair
so they will not have to be shaved to look like boys.

3.
Having read the obituary section of the newspaper
for a family history lesson.

Black vomit.

Moments of silence. Moments of chanting.
Moments of prayer. Moments of emptiness,
every face staring into the black landscape
behind the glass. Vacancies at the dinner table.
Moments of weeping, followed by a moment of dark laughter
that peters off into a red scream.
A kaleidoscope of healing.

4.
The nail-beds of our neighbors are still black
from clawing through rubble and ashes
to rescue their whimpering dogs.
The waiter lays out silverware
that glistens like my grandmother's bones.

None of us can stomach meat, still.

5.
Midnight.
Night fall. Falling night. Night. Night.
The whispers of parents shushing children.
Warble of the train.
I dream of the sound of mothers weeping.

Midnight,
I dream you fill the rivers of Bangladesh with black ribbons.
Filaments of your mourning fabric
draped over our house windows, strewn across the sky, slathered in our insides.
Your whistle is a siren
as we pass Gazipur, through Tongi,
finally Dhaka. Calling for the alive
as well as the dead.

Midnight siren.
On the horizon,
a body appears over the crest of a hill.
An elderly man,
limping under the weight of
his wife's lifeless body.

6.
We cross the border. The last of the war is left behind.
My father puts his hands over his ears and howls.
Howls.
Midnight.
Howls long into the night. Despite comfort. Despite threat. Until he has
to be gagged.
So we can pretend to sleep.

ELIZABETH DEBUNCE

How to Make a Monument

They are deconstructing Enola Gay today.
February, the month of love
and death poems. Virginia
fills its fields with red flowers
and aircraft carriers.
The first cheer goes up
as the name is revealed,
a second as the hammer hits the steel.
there is a point at which it is indistinguishable
if the screws go in or come out.

The thing my mother never taught me
about loving.
I have been reared on
portions of lost loved ones:
my mother's married name,
my grandmother's hands,
how my father never cried.
How, years after my grandfather's brain rotted away,
my grandmother stood in their bathroom,
scrubbing his dentures clean
until her fingernails covered them in blood.

Someone recites a poem from *Enola Gay*
over the loud-speaker.
Passing to the south side, the scars
of red paint are still visible
along the flank and nose
from the 2003 protest.

In Virginia,
the third cheer is softer, as the first panel
folds to the earth.
Crowds stare as the great hunks of metal
come screeching down.
Someone reads the lists of the dead over
the loud-speaker.
There is a point at which it is hard
to hear the screams over the screaming
of nails.

The pilots leave the pieces where they fall,
like severed wrists, thighs,
the cheeks and eyes of children.

On the anniversary,
my grandmother holds his teeth
until they come apart in her hands,
names each one after a great-grandchild.
She does this instead of prying each of her own
free, one by one, and hiding them in pillowcases.

The field fills with scraps of metal.
The deconstruction has stopped.
No one moves except the children.
They run amongst the ripped and torn pieces,
having found a museum.

The thing my mother never taught me
about loving:
the vitality in destruction;
how you name a bomber
after your own loved one.

ELIZABETH DEBUNCE

After, Japan.

In Kokura, I imagine they hold festivals
to the god Wind;
in Hiroshima, festivals
where they gorge the air with the ashes
of their loved ones.

Mid-August, the cities swell with cloud and smoke,
and Kokura sends up 140,000 red lanterns
and Nagasaki catches each one.

JEN KARETNICK

Sonnets for Code Red

I: 1975

Our teachers taught us to curl into ourselves
like turtles, shielded in the basements
where no windows could burst into fragments
so fine you couldn't see them glisten on shelves
of cheekbone and shin. Of course, we suspected
even then that flesh could never protect flesh.
When the alarm blared like a cymbal clash
over and over, the shells on our heads
—made only of unmodified forearms,
bones lined up to bones so young they still bent
like twigs rather than broke—could have been paint
on pavement, clouds in the wind. Oh, the harm
they meant to prevent, even as they showed
us what mushroomed in class, and how cold glowed.

II. 2015

I teach my students to remain silent,
in radar stealth—doors locked, lights off,
huddled, breath held like the bolt of a safe
in the hope that, from a childhood spent
disregarded, one of our own has not gone
nuclear. When the alarm blares, a spoiled
child lost in an indulgent household,

they remove from their pockets their cell phones
to ask each other if this is a drill
over text and Snapchat set to vibrate,
pop hidden Xanax, hyperventilate
over who might have been trapped in the hall.
We don't practice safety in case of threat.
We bandage the throat after it's been cut.

HEATHER BOURBEAU

Souvenir

Trembling, he remembered, the moment the photo was taken, in the orchard with his parents and brothers. He was four, climbing on Arihiro's broad shoulders, avoiding the tickles of Kenji, his middle brother, and giggling as cherry blossoms fell all around like feathery rain. His parents had spent a small fortune on a photographer to capture this moment, to send to aunts and uncles who had emigrated long before he was born. He had only a few moments to say goodbye to his home, to this photo that tempted him to take a souvenir of a time before the radiation.

HEATHER BOURBEAU

The Homeless Hires of Fukushima

We were nothing. Not forgotten, as much as ignored. We slept in alleyways, begged quietly, sought dignity in the corners of the city. They approached us, one-by-one, and offered us real work, but not for real pay. Who were we to choose? We were grateful to be acknowledged, given a chance. We didn't know, didn't think they would purposefully leave us unprotected. We thought we were offered a new life, not the shortening of the one we had. Had we understood fully our clean up in Fukushima, we might have asked for more, for something, or chosen to remain nothing.

HEATHER BOURBEAU

Fukushima I-VII

Fukushima I

I watch the ants crawl
emerge like tiny crocus
birds pierce the silence
half a world away, it's spring
here cherry blossoms float slow

Fukushima II

I have no patience
for the 30 years prescribed
to decommission

Fukushima III

my shiromuku
nearby, lay your motsuki
our wedding eclipsed
(your aunt gone, my father lost)
yet one thousand aftershocks
fortified our foundation

Fukushima IV

in sun, warmed, I sit
what then is more exquisite:
to survive the pain
of the last moments' waters
or to know life's small pleasures?

Fukushima V

What does the world say
when earth, water, fire hit at once?
What does the world do
when men here begin to weep?
It cries in consort,
but in a generation,
our need will be strength, not tears.

Fukushima VI

For my grandchildren,
should they survive what we've seen
and the harbor wave stole,
I wish steady earth,
calm seas that feed and foresight
so their children may be whole.

Fukushima VII

Once the world shifted
collective cries, then forgot
rubble shock, leaks found
last year's crisis, last year's news
fickle fears hinder healing

TRISH HOPKINSON

The Next State

"To remember Hiroshima is to abhor nuclear war. To remember Hiroshima is to commit oneself to peace." –Pope John Paul II on his visit to Hiroshima, Feb. 25, 1981

Every moment becomes
the past in an instant.
Our hands ache with despair,

the inability for reparation.
The unimaginable loss of thousands
imprinted into a copper etching.

The wax melted onto the surface
of subsistence. Curls of copper
burr into engraved cities

and the crosshatching of civilizations.
The ink of history seethes
into grooves, awaiting impression.

This is the first state.

Every moment becomes
the past in an instant.
One divergent force, an impression

so high-pressure, the plate
can no longer produce
a distinct replica—

the hollows disfigured, the edges
distressed. It takes years of work
to repeat the process, to resurface.

This is the second state.

We are stationed here in copper,
in dark ruts and muddy ink.
We are the products pressed

onto paper, products of all
that came before us, products
of passion and of pain,

products of art and wisdom
and learning and of the other,
the not-knowing,

and the witnessing of all
this through individual experience.
The impression is lasting.

This is the next state.

TRISH HOPKINSON

Denial

The surface of silent sorrow
where eyelids fold, half-rimmed
and wrapped sober over

Hiroshima and Dresden.
Colored by denial and closely
guarded, loss has haunted us.

Three generations unforgivable
and past knowing. An ancient
self-portrait from a different dimension

fell from the lemon tree in nameless grief.
The firestorm of emasculation heated
the force of life, horrifying, enormous,

flat, and arranged. The unmanned walls
of flame, unblinking in death-dealing—
a stalemate in exhaustion reflects

the inferno truth. The extraneous layer
more alive than not. Its body tenses, blurred
in abandon, grasping the essential,

and transforming space. It whispers
of progeny—a sea of corpses,
a field of bodies. In transgression,

the atmosphere speaks
her name again
and again.

TRISH HOPKINSON

What

after Sharon Olds poem "When"

This is what is going to happen—
the lone woman will stop the
rattle, the death breath from the chimney hearth,
when she opens the damper, then turns the urn's mouth out
with her wrists, cascading the grayed decay,
from there, the ashes flurry up and out, into the
orange remnants of autumn skyline,
she will watch from the window, as they dissipate
against the end of day, the seeping dark,
the moon's edge, sharp as dying,
its frowning tip tilted toward Saturn.
She will dust the hearth with feathers,
turn away from the sad moon, its slivered glow
and the dust that was once her lover—
she will love no longer.

DON KINGFISHER CAMPBELL

Surrender

It was on the Fourth, when my brothers were celebrating the Revolution, that I saw the end. From the sidewalk, our families on lawn chairs in a row watched fountains and flowers explode in the night. Little Shaun held a sparkler for the first time. My son, Jonathan, hands over his ears, just gaped. And I, sitting back, toes in the dirt, my love's arms around my waist, thought I glimpsed the red glow begin. I closed my eyes and imagined never opening them again.

J.R. SOLONCHE

The Anti-Tyger

Physicists at CERN, the Swiss particle physics laboratory,
have created anti-atoms made of matter's opposite, anti-matter.

Anti-tyger Anti-tyger, burning bright,
In the anti-forests of the anti-night;
What immortal anti-hand or anti-eye
Could frame thy fearful anti-symmetry?

In what distant anti-deeps or anti-skies,
Burnt the anti-fire of thine anti-eyes?
On what anti-wings dare anti-he aspire?
What the anti-hand, dare seize the anti-fire?

And what anti-shoulder, & what anti-art,
Could twist the anti-sinews of thy anti-heart?
And when thy anti-heart began to beat,
What dread anti-hand? & what dread anti-feet?

What the anti-hammer? what the anti-chain,
In what anti-furnace was thy anti-brain?
What the anti-anvil? What dread anti-grasp,
Dare its deadly anti-terrors clasp?

When the anti-stars threw down their anti-spears
And water'd anti-heaven with their anti-tears:
Did anti-he smile his anti-work to see?
Did anti-he who made the anti-Lamb make anti-thee?

Anti-tyger Anti-tyger burning bright,
In the anti-forests of the anti-night:
What immortal anti-hand or anti-eye,
Dare frame thy fearful anti-symmetry?

NORBERT GORA

The Atomic Phoenix

Hot and even hotter,
clouds of burning death
open the apocalyptic wings.

Fiery phoenix woven from
the atoms, a nuclear Satan,
turned out the light of dreams
of thousand of faces.

One flick of the wings
of doom and disappeared
the row of bird trills
that poured the joy
into the souls
contaminated with anxiety.

Hierarchy of desires,
words and thoughts
full of love have been burnt,
the flaming tongue of radioactivity
touched them, saliva dissolved everything.

Charred bodies fell
on the black soil,
one nuclear explosion,
so many lost lives.

NORBERT GORA

Do You Remember?

Do you remember
the blazing claws
of the devil of Nagasaki?

Their embrace
devoured innocent people,
their hopes on this devilish hand
melted away like a snow.

Bodies as black as the glow of murkiness
and roads pierced by the ashes
from which they arose,
in which they turned.

Breath of the atomic demon
hung in the air, high,
on a par with clouds
victimized by radioactivity.

Do you remember
the murderous grip of Hiroshima?

It was so strong that strangled
freedom, joy and purity
flowing in humans
as blood in veins,
as lengthy stream.

The grip that squeezed
the life out of people,
every emotion as drops of tears.

On the soulless bodies
there were not even a trace.

In the memory of many
remained those two hellish faces,
huge like mushrooms,
soaked in the atomic evil.

In prayers, between words,
there are hidden requests,
fervent supplications –
never again.

JARED HAREL

The Bright Side of Nuclear Winter

At last, God sighed,
and strolled Earth

delighted by emptiness,
the pleasure of being

and being alone.
He even began to whistle

those miserable hymns:
To God be the glory,

great things He hath done...
But over time,

the ground stirred.
The stench of petroleum

and charred plastic
cleared from the atmosphere.

Before long, God saw
signs of *not* death,

and sensing what followed,
vanished again.

DON NARKEVIC

The Committee for the Restoration
and Display of the Enola Gay

Only the front 56 feet
of the B-29 Bomber
will be exhibited.
Some might find the end
unsuitable for viewing
by children
juxtaposed against life-
sized photos of the burnt
offerings, flash frozen
wall clocks, watches, all
stopped, staring back
at the gawks,
faces, flawed and distorted,
reflections altering fact
to suit a victor-
ious walk through a museum,
and in the murky mirror
of an aluminum hull
the shadow image
of a child
counting rivets,
disbelieving the tour guide
as to how many
it took.

DON NARKEVIC

Fall 1962

it
is
fall
again
leaves fall
like children
falling in line
to the nearest fallout
shelter their school desks
as Kruschev and Kennedy
hammer out their falling out
shaking the tree of civilization
like some monkey contemplating
the Fall of Man as each politician
wishes on a falling star looking
to find the perfect fall guy or
something to fallback on
without falling over
themselves or
w/o falling
to pieces
it
is
fall
again

DON NARKEVIC

Epitaphs

Paul Tibbets (1915 – 2007)

My job, in brief, was to wage atomic war.

With his crew he poses, defiant
before the reflective aluminum
womb, his mother's namesake
bearing Little Boy, delivering
the Adam bomb, dehumanizing
humanity on the Eve
of unconditional brutality.

We had feelings, but we had to put them in the background.

Dear Father and Mother,

I am honored, a pilot chosen
for the Army Special Attack Corps.
In flight I am part of the machine,
but in my heart I am Hiroshima,
our hometown. I will fall
to my grave in the sea but
in the spring, as the petals
of the weeping cherry tree
in our garden, I will return.
Isamu.

We knew it was going to kill people right and left.

Early for work, Akiko squats
on the steps of the Sumitomo Bank,
watching pigeons take flight,
then the flash, bright
as a white chrysanthemum,
transforming all into shadow,
the fossil record of souls.

The city was hidden by that awful cloud . . .
m u s h r o o m i n g.

Within days Mother's burns
turn the color of worms.
I feed her body
to a bloated pyre.
Weeks later, like garden weeds,
my fists fill with my toddler's hair.
He, too, withers.
When my time comes,
my baby, a pressed flower,
Tsutsuji, my pink azalea,
arrives stillborn.
Restless in bed, I mourn.
My husband refuses
to touch me.

I never lost a night's sleep over it.

CARL WADE THOMPSON

The Curse

It came with promise,
an era's milestone,
innocence lost in a blink.
The white sands witness,
Fire—God's flame makes glass.
Scientists smile, marvel.
We have wrought this;
we are gods.
Fat Man, Little Boy,
nick names, kids' names, harmless,
mass murder on wholesale.
Science says this is good,
Necessary—for all mankind.
Hiroshima, Nagasaki,
they understand.
Of course, nips don't count.
Let them char for science,
shadows burned in sidewalks.
So much time has passed;
no one's responsible.
No one's ever responsible.
Let us bask in the glory,
the atomic age comes,
until dust, and time,
come for us all.

LAUREN BAGWELL

The End

Mother Nature gave me up for adoption
                    she was young
                                        i was
destructive.

GWENDOLYN HART

The Needle Jumps to Red

We assemble in the auditorium with the blood-red
curtain and the blue-backed chairs rubbed silver
from use, music stands still arranged in semi-circles
from last night's band concert. The superintendent faces
us, adjusts the microphone, speaks static,
adjusts the microphone again, and gives us the run-down:

In the event of a catastrophic explosion and shut down
at the nuclear plant, we will evacuate according to the Code Red
plan. The high school students will be bused to (more static)
and the junior high students will be bused to the Silver
Hills Mall. All I can think about are mannequins; their faces
blurred, mutated into blank, white circles

like pale flowers or empty dinner plates. There are circular
voids in the porcelain sinks where the water goes down
the drain in the girls' lavatory. I resurface
there after deciding that I will find a hundred
places to hide, just not the mall. I run my hands under the silver
faucet, then try to tame the flyaway static

of my stand-on-end hair. At home, things remain static,
unchanged. I pretend to eat pork chops, then, while circling
the table, picking up the plates and silver-
ware, I mention Code Red to my father, who sets down
the butter. He is an engineer at the plant. He puts the bread
away. He is calm. He wants me to understand, to face

reality. He unfolds a map, smooths out the surface
on the kitchen table, the stiff paper crinkling with static
from his sleeve. He uses a compass and a colored
pencil to draw a "contamination zone." Inside this circle,
everything would be seriously affected by a meltdown:
the schools, the mall, the baseball fields. I picture a thin sliver

of moon rising, spreading its metallic silver
light over the rusted-out buses, the windowless, open-faced
buildings. Years later, talking with my Belarus student, it dawns
on me that her mother is a Priapyet survivor. The elastic
moment snaps shut around us; we are ensnared, encircled,
by an old, cold war. Hearing about her family, her cancer, feels sacred.

I want to put my palm to her face, enclose her in the circle
of my arms, feel us cinched together by history's quicksilver thread,
pins-and-needles bouncing through me like a Geiger counter's static.

BEATRIZ FERNANDEZ

The Point of No Return

It came upon us all, not when Caesar forded the Rubicon
with his invading armies, intent on victory at all costs,
nor when Travis's battle sword traced a line under the sun
at the Alamo, certain death promised to all who crossed—
nor when Earhart, flying on fumes, radioed without relent
as her engine coughed its last over the Pacific Ocean—
nor even when Einstein signed a letter to warn a president.

No, not then. But late one night after dinner, when an eager man
headed back to Los Alamos to finish an experiment,
quite unplanned. The clever hand that had played the violin
let slip a brick too close to a cradled sphere—that moment,
when all breath left the body of young Harry Daghlian,
when his hand bathed blue in the glow of the demon's poison
core, then fell slack to his side—it was then, it was then.

Harry K. Daghlian, Jr., 1921-1945,
"The first American casualty of the Atomic Age."
(from his memorial.)

SUSAN ROSE APRIL

this happened

during my occupational duties
in Nagasaki Japan
at the edge of our camp
where survivors would come
for comic book hand outs
and sticks of gum

we'd just dropped the bomb—
everything was as flat as a pancake
and pulverized into shards
so hard to describe
what it is nothing looks like
the kids maybe

eight nine ten years old
hard to tell their age or sex
all hair fallen out
all wearing loose hospital gowns
and their skin coated in
crusts of noxema

Christmas Eve 1945
a friend of mine
walks up to these kids
we're done handing out comics
and for tonight candy canes
friend has a funny look on his face

I light a cigarette
what's he up to here?
I see him reach into the sack
and take out a couple of
screw-top tins—
joke cans you understand—

one was saltwater taffy
one was salted mixed nuts
only they were
none of these things
cans that spring out cloth-
covered snakes   *surprise!*

and everybody laughs
but these were not snakes
and it was too late
one child was disemboweled
one lost an eye
one took their unopened can

and ran

SCOTT T. STARBUCK

Napali

said she worries

about this new generation

living seven stories up

in high rise apartments

and what will become of them

cut off as they are

from Earth and sky.

They may forget

there is a pull of things

unseen by some

who balance numbers

and how, if conditions are right,

a well-placed feather

can bring down

a nuclear power plant.

SCOTT T. STARBUCK

At the Nevada Nuclear Test Site

grandmothers
are arrested,
imprisoned
      to make way
      for the blast.
A sheriff explains
      the old women
      are dangerous.

SCOTT T. STARBUCK

Plutonium Fish

Once, high above the polluted river,
sky helped water return
to its natural state.
If left alone long enough
it would come alive again
with purple-sided trout,
a green and yellow choir of frogs,
human families touching
with hands, arms, and words.
Winter didn't have to wait
half a million years for spring.

STEPHEN MEAD

After Chernobyl

Growing skin on a slab
beside a cup of herbal tea, pair
of sun glasses, book of graphite...
In her pocketbook there's a few test
tubes busy with cells from some mouse's saliva.
Through the lab sunlight bakes bricks,
sets nacreous brilliance on tables.
Later it will be even more yellow.
She makes science comfortable, homey,
talks to the surgeon, the biochemist.
About tissue cultures, she places violets.
Other lives are depending on such, heaving
with spasms, breaking off limbs.
Their bodies can't help it.
To think all this was caused by an accident,
that a halo of wands took its useful infrared energy
and became something else. To think a controlled
substance with its initial explosive potential
really happened to do that:
burst like wildfire, radiant heat melting down,
searing the nearby.
Meanwhile, about the research room
light continues to elucidate.
Lasers graft follicles, their sharp beams
a seamstress stitching. Here flesh is a fabric
being put to a test. Will it hold?

Sleuths who drink tea, conduct another
experiment, tap for healing like water
to find, if not a cure, than a means
to live on.

STEPHEN MEAD

Detonations

Whale at a submarine—
Dear deep mariner, what do you hear?
Is it people milling about, snoring bunkmates or
busy machinery, the beeping meter's pop?
If you can, to that porthole, put an eye, look around.
Are you interested? Does it make sense?
How I wish I could read your thoughts, become some medium
in order to understand all this complexity going on.
These beings aren't puppets, are they?
And their consoles have a purpose—
Exploration, correct?
So what's shooting forth?
Whoosh, such a fathomable
propellant, such a beautiful
bombshell whizzing through foam, schools of fish, strips
of plankton to hit some, some—
                What
                   is it
           just child's play
        with the weight of earth
                         oceanic
          suddenly on backs?
                            How
          to stomach, digest, breathe
              belly upward?
Meanwhile, in some desert, for research, another device
goes off.

STEPHEN MEAD

Nuclear Diary

Thanks to Andre Carothers

I light a cigarette,
little tobacco tube,
strange squared-off phallus.
Smoke stacks too, only without
smoke, in the distance, rise.
The flats leading to them
should all be mahogany.
Flats—
here a wheat field, there
an oat, the tall stalks
which might gleam,
the streams, the soil
alive with a silent
tick tick tick.
Most citizens left sense it.
How could they not?
The houses of photographs,
fabrics, flesh
busy with signals, the amok
transparent termites
waving cell-like from eyes,
from milk into bottles,
bottles to mouths...
White sound & bravery badges,
banner smiles & too aware faces

with rarely enough money
to get away, convince
a government chlorine burns
more than it cleans.
How angry, how fed up
can patient waiting turn?
How despairing, how atomic
when living in levels
science, coerced, swears
are not harmful, not as much
as thought?
Not as harmful say,
as a bullet that's left
the gun.
One's wound just overreacts.
One's blood should just
stop bleeding.
One's children
should get down from towers,
find beds hidden away,
let tongues, diseased,
quiet on waves.
Sea pleats, field sheets,
nature's grand green,
the design of peace
finds a ship, finds
a rig & a plant-
1,2,3: test
4,5,6: dump
7,8,9: bury.
I put out my cig, & finger
the sweet pistil of a lily
in the passing window of this train.

RICHARD O'CONNELL

Trinity

I saw a small boy on a back lot in New York,
crouched, burning flies alive in a sealed jar
with a magnifying glass he held up high,
focusing the fire of our companion star.

Dispassionate, like mischievous boys ourselves,
out in the desert, quarantined, sealed off
from humanity, as if we bore the plague,
like lepers to the locals, treated rough.

Prometheus pilfered fire from the gods
hid in a fennel stalk to help mankind;
which proves the gods at times can be outfoxed
or even conveniently be stricken blind.

The dawn of a new age or the death of one
-Can blinded prophet or Cassandra tell?
as here we toss this sop to Cerberus,
his three heads barking at the gates of Hell.

LIND GRANT-OYEYE

What would we do when the clock strikes twelve?

Would we dance like that little chimney sweeper
With a lone glass slipper and charred dreams
borrowed from that last fairy god-mother;
that fairy who died while base jumping off the big Ben in London?
That fairy god-mother who knows twelve O'clock means midnight,
but cannot tell if it is time before tomorrow
or time after yesterday.

Would we dance to the drum beats of big Ben,
Sway like we were in a charmed ball room
Or would we shake to the steps of Zombies
in an apocalypse ?

When Big Ben strikes twelve,
perhaps we would be busy writing eulogies and epitaphs
to rain, sunshine, clouds and winds and
color the skies with graffiti written in black.

ROGER APLON

Fifties Blues

Revisited – New Year's Day 2004

Walking down Carrer de Pelayo dodging baby carriages, Simon, the
destitute pet collector & his seven dogs & an occasional free floating balloon,
it is, after all, soon-to-be spring & I stop to sample a wurst at Des Alpes &
overhear the news: Roy 'King Of The *lonesome* Cowboys' Rogers has departed
for greener grazing absent wife Dale, his faithful-horse Trigger & us. Ellen
had her RR lunchbox, lariat & badge & her first ride, a Trigger look-alike
at the San Diego Fair & I'm sure mom had me slapping leather
back home in Chi like the real Roy with matched six
shooters, chaps & Stetson just as the fifties were
all set-up to give us the world or what
was left to resurrect after some
son-of-a-pioneer proved you
don't need much of the
old west or new
to test a man's
humanity
& Good King Roy
beat the drum
herding us
smiling
down
those happy
trails
into that
starry night
unmindful of a few
split atoms &
his good
God
gone amuck.

ROGER APLON

Desert Landscape: Roots
Clouds & Water

"It works . . .It's Beautiful"
J. Robert Oppenheimer
Alamagordo, New Mexico
7/16/1945

1
At First
There are just
His tumescent roots
Flat
      Grey
            Enamel

Working up & out
even as we talk
the muck
clay makes
of inland lakes.

Their soaring turns
this quaint
provincial scene
cacophonous:

                    an alarm
          racing
bank
          to
                    bank,
concentric whorls of water

its entire
                    mile wide
                              breath
no feeding fish could make.
**

To our left
all black & blue-lined,
his suspicious columns:
A way out?
Maps to something buried in flight? An undulating
Distraction? Wait!
Someone is already ascending.

One tentative hand,
a foot
          another
                    hand . . . So,
He's left a cleft,
Chink in the rock, a ladder? . . . Rooms?

2
Ten of us, at least,
are already lost.
More & more choose the lake.
Sprinting
they crash together,

driven to grip
their own exceptional

burgeoning
Root
**

His landscape has begun to glow:
a yellow juice
oozes over the banks.

The tendrils still
muscle up
slowed only slightly
under their new weight of bone.

They twist sluggishly
then gain height – soon
are lost to grey.
No one has thought to let go.
**

Skin & root
a faint memory now
married with lake
with clouds
With tower
slim slip of sky
these faceless acres of sand.

After a watercolor by Rick DeMont

EMILY WALLING

The Painting Fish

A fish with razor
thin fins slices through the stream,
stroking the eco—
leaving a bright paint trail
as it encourages flow.

EMILY WALLING

Nothing

is nothing but redundant.

JULIE THI UNDERHILL

The time we broke from time

In reference to my troubled rest
all night I lay awake
and hear the sap
creep through the trees
near roads I should not take

In the sky birds fly the other way
in a murmuring the sudden shape
of a fingerprint

as heat bends
a roar gathering loose
the flotsam of earth

I remember how
we looked up
before a thousand slivered blades
entered us

Without language or sound
we collapsed
as fire opened its dark center
unfolded across our shoulders
then crumpled us to dust

before that cold silence
when night found me alone

Of those who remain
who else counts eternity
from the time
we broke from time?

On anniversaries
journalists find us
extract our stories
then ask
How long until the war's end sets you free?

They stop writing
when I reply
that grief is holy
like something held close in fever

it rouses the white smoke
from our bones
extending
down to the sensitive roots
of trees

so when I take again
these worn routes
with breath held back
I live and die

CLAUDE CLAYTON SMITH

Until

Until the day that all the stars collapse
upon themselves in clouds of light and dust
(or raise their fissile mushroom heads, perhaps),
as quantum physics proves what physics must—

Until on Earth the oceans split and flood
the poles as if old Moses bade them to,
and cities lies awash in salty blood—
I'll bide my time and concentrate on you.

Apocalyptic visions slip and slouch
through history to leave us in their wake,
but not a damnéd one, in truth, can vouch
for Truth. Imagination fails. Forsake

the future, then, for *this*—the day we share
with atoms that bombard the very air!

SALLY ZAKARIYA

Victory Garden

On the 70th anniversary of the bombing
of Hiroshima and Nagasaki

Daddy worked all day in town, then
took up hoe and spade to plant
a harvest worth of groceries
in our victory garden

I didn't know what victory meant
why the window shades were black
why we didn't have enough gas
to take a ride in the old Plymouth

or why Mother called it black market
when Mr. Orndorf drove in from the farm
bringing butter, eggs, and milk
in his battered pickup truck

We kids played Bombs Over Japan,
dropped rocks in the sand box, laughed
as grains exploded outwards, tiny
sprays of destruction

We didn't know what devastation
would be sown, what toxic terror
the world would reap
from our victory

LEANNE DUNIC

Waves

Seismic. Oceanic. Sonic.

Mountains steam
wounded and wounding.
Radioactive mist
   a   nuclear   exhalation.

The Fukushima 50 –
stabilizers of nuclear reactors
prepared for death.
Embraced *bushido*:
sacrifice, loyalty, honor –
the warrior's way.

Likened to the wandering samurai
The 47 Ronin.

   Ronin – *wave man.*

NILESH MONDAL

World Shall Rejoice

"Sleep no more!
Macbeth does murder sleep, – the innocent sleep;
Sleep that knits up the ravell'd sleave of care,
The death of each day's life, sore labour's bath,
Balm of hurt minds, great nature's second course, Chief nourisher in life's
feast."
⊠ *William Shakespeare, Macbeth*

The world will rejoice in death today
Midnight gongs like broken bliss
Minions of heavens, in Hellish foreplay.

No spring shall come, no sunny May
Acid rains like scalding piss
The world will rejoice in death today.

Smokes from pyres, paint the world grey.
Corpses melt into intimate kiss
Minions of heavens,in hellish foreplay.

Escapists are extorted, a price to pay.
Anarchist ambition leads to this
The world will rejoice in death today.

Fat boys shimmer through Christmas sleigh.
Cities of dead meat steam and hiss
Minions of heavens, in hellish foreplay.

Statues of stony dictators crumbling lay
No countries left to rule or miss
The world will rejoice in death today

In churches, ghosts, hallelujah say
Prayers of salvation, tickles lips
The world will rejoice in death today
Minions of heavens, in hellish foreplay.

TRINA GAYNON

Through the Cyclotron

Our monks gown themselves
in lab coats and meditate
on subatomic particle movement
in an effort to split the world open.
Their machine pulses with a power
beyond that of any heart,
capable of darkening the city below
until provided with its own plant.

The clerestory windows
of this steel basilica, under a dome
larger than a small moon of Jupiter,
let in morning sunlight.
Beneath that dome, an orange crane
clicks and clangs, both clock and bell,
to move concrete blocks of shielding
that hold in the radiation.

A wheel chair rolls along barren halls
past painted yellow and black triangles.
At the base of her brain, its passenger
bears a tumor to the altar within a cave.
In the treatment trailer (a waiting room
dressed in plastic chairs and wild flower
posters, the hum of equipment muted)
she glances through *Time*.

When the technician wheels her
into the treatment room,
he puts plaster armor on her chest.
A fiberglass mask encases her face.
Strapped into a metal treatment chair
and warned not to move, she smells
only alcohol, not incense or candle wax.
She hears only her own breath.

Moving behind a shield, the technician
signals the control room. There they
release the beam, which can split apart
atoms, to destroy cancer cells.
Operators prefer to tune the beam
like a musical instrument rather than
an assault weapon against disease.
(So many of the patients are children.)

When this beam travels, alarms begin.
The technician moves slowly this time,
sips a cup of coffee before pushing
the button that silences the claxon.
It sounds repeatedly and the patient
begins to scream. No technician,
no operator will ever tell
how the screams came to a stop.

TRINA GAYNON

Modern Alchemy: Fall 1980

Take a cyclotron

in it bombard

a bismuth target of foil

of the bismuth nucleus

knock four protons out

with carbon beams

whipped

on a circular track

to a frenzy

dissolve foil in acid

And
Behold
Gold

Midas miracle

at more than a quadrillion dollars an ounce

like Rumpelstiltskin
a few billion atoms
angels dancing on the head of a pin

NELS HANSON

Odd Westerly

Can you feel it, a fiery breeze
invading bare branches, sense
sad and invited pain on wings

from vast ages and half second
ago, missteps we took mature
now in size and strength, frail

egg less than a single fennel
seed but the shell elastic and
swelling instantly until oval

curve casts shadow large as
a Jupiter and air dry kindling
catches from the brittle sheath

webbed and cracking in quick
spreading veins, deep unstable
faults like stirring lids for eyes

to see at last a fledgling hatch,
one blazing phoenix not rising
from ashes but toward them?

NELS HANSON

Time

Kind Noble Ghosts, I won't
cry "Wake!" You know time,
history we don't understand

but feel you watching always
from where you are to where
we are. I just ask if now it's

time to step from shadow and
speak. It's getting late and we
can't save ourselves, the air

and waters, innocent beasts,
flowers, grass, this planet all
new days we destroy again as

we destroy each other. I hear
you always whispering but if
you could talk loud as thunder

now or a hurricane, in scarlet
contrails with your fingertip
write you're still there and

won't turn away or leave in
final despair but lead us to
that place you kept pointing

toward as like ours your time
ran out and at last in a green
world we meet face to face.

NELS HANSON

Collector

I've collected many famous hats and much
well-known headgear and for my visitors'
protection keep them safely under strong
lock in tempered-steel cabinets examined
through hardened Plexiglas. Ask me why

the special precautions? Theft? Insurance
policy stipulations? Have you suffered a
very high fever or taken some dangerous
drug, swallowed unlabeled poison, fallen
sudden victim of a breakdown, mentally

collapsed? We don't want the ambulance.
Cleopatra's tiara there with raised golden
cobra about to strike will make you love
and murder incessantly until just in time
your loyal lady-in-waiting comes running

with deadly asp. Wear George Armstrong
Custer's slanted Stetson on display you'll
writhe on my carpeted floor, porcupine of
arrows as you drown in oceans of staining
Indian blood, scarlet Sioux and Cheyenne.

To the right for those less hardy souls why
not J.P. Morgan's tall black topper? Clamp
ears to starving widows' and their orphans'
screams to read once more Charles Dickens'
handwritten "A Christmas Carol" the bank

delivers each Noel Eve. Jackie Robinson's
sweat-stained Brooklyn Dodgers blue cap
freezes your veins the way white catcalled
hate echoes 60 years down the policeman's
pistol barrel. A hurricane of numbers will

suffocate your brain, every falling swirling
leaf etched with H-Bomb's secret equations
if you put on Teller's tasseled mortarboard
from Berkeley grad ceremony. Napoleon's
sideways sable half-moon crest I acquired

last year at hefty price would spark Europe
to final fire. Beside it Hitler's brown-billed
general's diadem killed former owners and
their neighborhoods: No creature breathes
but his Shepherd "Blondie". Young Martin

Luther King's straw fedora banded in azure
clanks with slave chains breaking from here
to Zambia before Ray's rifle wounds a heart
beyond repair. You've heard a silver rumor
one reclusive collector hides in a lead-lined

safe on chain deep down a mine a crown of
thorns? Yes, life's stressful and demanding,
even scary, sometimes hard. But here, don't
be afraid – Soft as flannel pajamas' touch is
this grey-felt cowboy I allow special guests

to don, one our president preferred relaxing
at his "Rancho Cielo" while Contra bullets
felled Sandinistas, Americans died of AIDS,
Russia expecting incoming rockets. A brief
moment know a heaven of pure vacant sky.

SHARON KENNEDY-NOLLE

Under Fissile Cover, Oak Ridge

The Secret City still hums in cemesto,
a prefab life lived in forties' chrome finish.
From 60,000 acres of rich farmland,
rose up the flattop houses, the complex appliance of isotope.
Y-12, K-25, S-50, X-10 –
letters and numbers multiply in dead earnest.

Feel the museum's motto, "where history comes alive,"
in the crackle talk of Geiger;
Pass displays of hard hats and X-rays, and brickbats.
All funded by the Energy industry, who cheerfully say:
"Radiation's here, there, and everywhere to stay."

In the gift shop,
Ed Westcott's war-time photos
make light of Secret City life:
Santa frisked by security at Elza Gate;
A boy sells five-cent comics at his homemade stand
to a tanned girl, idly leafing the pages
while Girl Scouts parade under the ever-energized fields
separating 235 from 238.

More enriched than uranium admits,
the secret sells well.

And what of that other city,
scorched rubble of fused roots and bones.
There's one photo,
a woman and child,
bandage bound, kimono- singed, throats swathed,
staring at the camera.
She holds the child's hand in humble why.
How long did they last?

Not to suffer the silence
a radio drones Roosevelt's Four Freedoms,
and the sacrifice asked of us all.

An Oak Ridge whippoorwill carries on the wind.

At five, the scientists pass through the gates
out to suburban ranches.

Somebody flips a switch

and in the blue hills of Oak Ridge,
a distant gloom blooms.
"A gaseous diffusion process," they say,

while the East Fork Poplar Creek,
laced with mercury everlasting,
still somehow moves
past the All-Clear.

TERESA MEI CHUC

Chernobyl Necklace

The scar is a pink horizon, sunset at the ocean. Each tree still standing in the Red Forest carries the story in its rings. Blind birds sing, calling to their mates. Broken glass, a plastic doll: the inanimate survive. How many more Aprils will that day be remembered? On my body grow mushrooms that could kill. Out of my heart runs a six-legged deer.

TERESA MEI CHUC

Love After Fukushima

I want the
courage of
the elderly who
volunteered
in the clean-up
at the
Daiichi plant

To be filled
with a desire
to live
and know that death
is a reality of
isotopes rearranging
in the body

Five years later
cesium-137
cesium-134
are still leaking
into the Pacific

Bluefin tuna
a neon green

I think I am
growing two
hearts
They beat one
after the other
in a constant
drumming with
no silence in
between.

DREW DILLHUNT

Plastic #7 [Teflon]

I put a hex on myself
just before I enriched our kitchen
with space-age polymers.

I was investigating freezers
when one hundred pounds of TFE gas
spontaneously polymerized.

I was four of a mind,
trapped and frozen, shoulder to shoulder
inside steel cylinders.

I rested on a bed of dry ice
braced myself for the rupture
of impending disaster.

/•/

I was disappointing and waxy—
a white solid soon to be revealed
as the world's slipperiest material.

I didn't worry
until I was told I would have to give up
my metal spatula for wooden and plastic.

At that moment, I began
to obsessively watch the soft surface
of cross-hatched frying pans
for any indication
of flaking residue.

/•/

It's the Cold War
I shield my eyes with frying pans
I solve my problems with separation

and correct the market slump
by counting down from 2% to skim.

I shoot television spots
as the president; I
[presciently] sport a milk mustache
to mollify our worry
over the indictment
of milk fat as an agent
of heart disease,
Soviet tests over the Pacific

and accumulations
of strontium-90
in our children's milk supply.

/•/

Nuclear physicists at Oak Ridge
struggling with the corrosive properties
of enriched uranium hexafluoride gas
were the first handymen
to plumb their pipes with Teflon.

Little Boy and Fatman made non-stick pans.
Two hundred and fifty thousand
lost in a pair of bright white flashes
meant to make sure
we wouldn't have to scrub so hard.

I tell myself:
duplicity doesn't always imply complicity.

/•/

AIMEE NOEL

Baking Uranium

Grandma's cookie jar never saw a treat
made by her own hand. She baked bricks,
instead, at Bethlehem Steel, replacing
the broken blocks of an earthen furnace.

She baked bricks with her own hands
and kept the slag-fire burning
the broken blocks in an earthen furnace.
It took $2.35 an hour and sixteen-hour days

to keep the slag-fires burning,
rolling uranium into billet bars.
It took sixteen hours a day to cut
poison into an ethereal dust.

Uranium to billet bars
to her rattling cough twenty years later.
A poisonous dust, so ethereal, yet
a weighty loss of raw material, found

in her rattling cough twenty years later.
Missing mass clung to crib sheets:
the weighty loss of raw material
hung out to dry in the mill town.

AIMEE NOEL

A Death Faster than Math

Steel men are dying, see,
faster than widows can figure
the equations. A colon closed
down + a rectum sewn shut,

equals

they carry their life's waste
outside of their bodies
in clear plastic bags for all
to see, not making it to meetings
- tallying enough numbers

equals

an absence of legs to move them
there. But the miracle of math
will weigh each limb's worth:
heavy metal + heated
elements + Cold War

equals

if their breathing can be sub-
contracted a few more years
until their pension kicks in; Dying
at graphing calculator rates, men
spike thirty years after the last (alleged)
uranium billet + rolled onto the train
- (conductor now dead)

equals

lungs to hold six more pounds
before the dosage will be enough
to honor their lives. Calculations
taken from soil, not people and
the polyps are processing +
processing + processing

equals

they'd like to provide you with
more information but those papers
were ≥ burnt paper flakes filtered
through hairs of the janitor's broom.
He'd push the files back but

equals

he's too dead for that.

AIMEE NOEL

Calculating Exposure

for steelworkers Joe Ed Lawrence and Ted Priester

In those days we took a test
for a better mill job an' the reason
that was so hard–
they had things like algebra
that you take for granted now.

Set parameters using the dose coefficients for inhalation:
einh(50) for 1 μm AMAD [Sv/Bq]

It was a mechanical test, could you read a rule,
an' then they would have the numbers
like 5/16, 7/16, 3/8 on there,
they have them mixed up.

For ingestion: eing(50)[Sv/Bq]

They say put them in order,
which is the lowest up
to the highest, quarter inch, an eighth,
an' you did that.

For external exposure: [Sv/h per Bq/cm³]

Then they asked you about if the gear is turning
to the right clockwise an' this shaft
is turning to the left or which way –
if it turned counterclockwise,
which way would the shaft turn,
an' you had to answer it,
you had to figure it out whichever way.

The solubility class can be selected
according to the chemical form of the uranium:
F: UF_6, UO_2F_2, $UO_2(NO_3)_2$ (f_1 = 0.02)
M: UO_3, UF_4, UCl_4 (f_1 = 0.02)
S: UO_2, U_3O_8 (f_1 = 0.002)

They asked you about bearings an' about seals,
what kind of – they have different kinds
of seals, leather seals, maybe plastic –
I don't know about the plastic at the time,
but anyway, a lot of mechanical questions
an' then math.

Occupational Annual Limits on Intake (ALI's) for Inhalation
Unatural (soluble): 1 µCi (= 37000 Bq, equiv. to 1.5 g)
Unatural (insoluble): 0.05 µCi (= 1850 Bq, equiv. to 74 mg)

You had to do math, add an' subtract,
multiply an' divide an' fractions an'
changing fractions to decimal, decimal
to fractions. You had to do that also.
So it was a pretty tough test.

JULIAN DE WETTE

The Right to Bear Arms

So the darkness shall be light,
and the stillness the dancing. T.S. Eliot

I like hunting, shooting at things,
at birds and bats, whatever wings
its way through here. It might be huge,
an elephant – majestic tusker, who's to care
when I bag a seal or polar bear?
Whatever breathes is now at risk
(big bore Marlin, Remington,
pump action shotgun, AK47 too)
will come unstuck like useless glue.
Squirrels limp to get away
and raccoons bolt across my path.

Swallows plunge for a quick snack,
they'll all be gone when I hit back
and stalk the happy hour, punch drunk
sated with power, muscular and bold.
I stalk all things crepuscular, young and old.
And as I've said, cats and kittens,
watch dogs, lapdogs, ducks – I'll blast the lot,
pigs rolling in the muck.

And when there is no birdsong left,
no owl nesting in the cleft – I'll load my guns
and come for you. There's nothing like
a meaty stew, all thick with gravy,
marrow bones to revel in that glorious day
when not a soul is left to pray
and bid God help me stop
as children fade away, the Piper and his guns
set off a flare to lead them on
till all that's left is barren rock and stone.

The sea no longer weeps when bones
are washed up on the shore.
The cormorant caught in mid-dive,
the fish spared for later incineration.
But here I am, the last alive and swear
that when it's dark I'll take my gun,
reflect on all the wars I've won.
Nothing, no one else will shout,
watch me do a final rout.

Except, perhaps, the last hyrax
lazing on a seaside lawn, a springbok
and a nuzzling fawn. All fine targets
in long grass, a lone zebra gored
at Sabie Pass. India's mouse deer
skulks into sight, slaughter is my sole delight –
meerkats, mink, the coast is clear
except for spattered brains and deer.

No need to plough, no mouths to feed
no more corruption, futile greed.
Makes little sense to work the land
everything poisoned, lifeless sand.

No movement on beloved's bed, no art
a smothering in which love plays no part.
There is no need for doctrine,
reality is upon us now.
We look too deeply for the faults
when these were futile all along.

A songbird had no duty, but to sing
and procreate – spread its song abroad,
then pollinate, not be cut off at the gate.
But now the lark has lost its tongue
could it be considered late?
The clockwork sparrows have had their say,
no more mating or rough play.

The final thunderings of war
imposed stark silence, nothing more.
Gunners in the cockpit flying high
have done their jobs, are last to fry.
They knew their planes would rise
then self-destruct, Armageddon's workhorses
reaping a vast crop.

Mission accomplished, smart bombs deployed.
With push button ease, the earth is destroyed.
No trees, or Eden, we've razed every spire.
We've turned back the clock, the whole earth is on fire.
The sun's been darkened, the moon's taken flight,
the stars in the sky no longer give light.
The night is still, no crickets shrill,
no voice breaks through the damp, dark chill.

JENNIFER CLARK

Ceaseless is the Work of Saint and Scientists in Russia's Los Alamos

Before he became a saint, he was Prokhor Moshnin (1754-1833), a boy born inflexibly toward God. As a monk living in Sarov, he is given the name Seraphim, derived from the Hebrew word, Seraph, meaning: to burn. And he does. Even as a hermit, Seraphim blazes for God. "Acquire a peaceful spirit," his tongue flames, "and thousands around you will be saved."

In the monastery and on the path to his hut in the forest, he stockpiles prayers of peace, bakes bread, and grows beets in his garden. Prone to being blinded by bright rays of light, the monk amasses wonders: He kindles friendships with fox and lynx. Even Misha the bear brings him gifts of leaves stuck to the hexagonal wombs of honeycombs. Seraphim feeds his wild friends from the bare, bright stars of his hands, hands he uses to claw his way up a flank of rock. There, he raises his arms, shoots off fiery rockets of praise for one thousand nights and days, eating little. He rarely winks out, but when he does, he uses a stone for pillow.

*

A hundred years later, Sarov flickers, then disappears off the map. Barbed wire winds its way around a Bethlehem that has lost its star. Shrouded in a thick cloak of fir and pine, Arzamas-16, code name for Sarov, fuses faith with human design. As scientists shepherd plutonium, the town gives birth to the Soviet's first atomic bomb. Many follow.

In 1995, Sarov slinks back onto the map, though it remains closed off. Retaining ponds pellet the landscape. Swimming is not advised. As Sarov struggles, herds of uranium wander away. On the darkest days, townsfolk and guards see an old man in a white cassock. He strikes the ground with a staff, offering a blessing perhaps, or trying to remind them what they have forgotten, that one day, while chopping wood, thieves snuck up and used Seraphim's own axe against him. Bloodied and battered, he lived, his back bent, on fire, the rest of his days.

AMY UYEMATSU

Peace Haiku

on the 70th anniversary of the bombing of Hiroshima, 2015

"A city of peace" -
Hiroshima's name before
      that deadly August

~ ~ ~

Bombs do not have hearts -
but who answers for the men
      who won't stop hating?

~ ~ ~

Who do you believe -
generals and presidents
      or silenced victims?

~ ~ ~

Cities and churches
bleeding from bullets and bombs -
      no country is safe

~ ~ ~

Love thy enemy
or these wars will never end -
     all free or no one

~ ~ ~

America's shame -
don't forget Hiroshima,
     Nagasaki too

~ ~ ~

Embrace your children -
remember your enemy
     wants only the same

~ ~ ~

Clear the sky of bombs
to fill it with songs of peace -
     our true legacy

AMY UYEMATSU

Three Synonyms for Weapons of Mass Destruction

Greed
Ideology
Indifference

AMY UYEMATSU

from Basic Vocabulary

mouth

how many bullets does it take
to fill the open mouth

how many bombs
to feed it

eye

not even a mother can know
the eye of her young son
hunting for the enemy

sun

who could imagine a light
more blinding than the sun
or that hot black rain
from an August
sky torn inside out

who could imagine we'd be
more than willing
to repeat it

VIVIAN FAITH PRESCOTT

What's in a Name?

"What's in a name? That which we call a rose by any other name would smell as sweet—,"
says Juliet from Romeo and Juliet by William Shakespeare.

After the horrors of Fatman and Little Boy,
someone decided
to give those mushroom clouds a name
like we name hurricanes.
Let's personalize them,
name them after neighbors, friends, lovers,
and even mothers.
Call them
      Charlie
          George
              Mike
                    Annie
                        Nancy
                            Harry
                                Pricilla

And someone thought it amusing
to give nuclear bombs Indian names:
      Seminole and Totem
          Apache and Mohawk
              Blackfoot and Dakota
                  Buffalo and Bighorn.

Funny,
now my own country
makes conventions
reducing nuclear arms,
prohibiting their construction—no more testing.
But who's to say that someday, a name
      like Gandi,
            Dalai Lama,
                  or Nobel
will mushroom up in irony, fire, and smoke—
trailing over all our histories,
these broken promises
      like treaties imploding
      on themselves.

VIVIAN FAITH PRESCOTT

Project Chariot

... in this enlightened age, the great powers of the earth, both of the East and of the West, are interested in human aspirations first, rather than in building up the armaments of war.—Dwight D. Eisenhower "Atoms for Peace" speech, Dec. 8, 1953 before the general assembly of the United Nations on peaceful uses of atomic energy.

Father Teller
he sits in his Chariot
holding his arms outstretched
across Ogotoruk Valley— Port Thompson
proclaiming:

> **I am the visionary**
> **I will reshape the earth to your pleasure**

this tussock of heath vegetation, this nothingness
       sedge—lichen—moss
I will unearth riches untold
       economic, politics
a deepwater harbor—can you envision it

       six thermonuclear bombs
       160 Hiroshimas
a credit to our geographic engineering
blasting America into a new age
       with a flash of white light

as hot as the temperature inside the stars

over one million degrees Fahrenheit
                    2.4 megatons, radioactive
            earth dust floating across the tundra
                the Chuckchi Sea, the villages.

You children, hear me
I will create a neo-Genesis
I will thresh them down into plowshares
and make atoms for peace.

      I am the visionary
I will reshape the earth to your pleasure.

VIVIAN FAITH PRESCOTT

Recipe for Disaster at Ogotoruk Valley

Take 6 mCi (millicuries) of Cesium 137
     5 mCi of Iodine 131
     5 mCi of Strontium 185

Mix Thoroughly

Be sure isotopes and mixed fusion products
are mixed thoroughly with sand.
Add sufficient amounts of water—preferably rainfall.

Dig Hole

Next: Bury the mix in tundra

WAIT

Pour sample water into glass.

Here, would you like a glass of water?

MICHAEL SHORB

Chernobyl Spring

in gray and yellow woods
just beyond reach
of the sealed-off cement
and metal behemoth
left behind

the eager allure of birdsong
catches at your heart,
tugs the dazzled legs of your trousers,
"come on" the plea
reaches your genes in a breath,
balances hope on the note
forward, the implied normalcy
of tenderness, the feathers extended

allow me to join my lament,
weaving into it the gradual,
sickening realization
that 99% of these birds are male,
that nature's feminine's
been strip-mined, driven into ditches

left with a hole in her wing
and no fair chance to sail,
she hesitates, hearing your
love songs and liking them well enough,
but return to those woods
in these scant times?

Walk past the way things were cheated,
when a net broke
and something shadowed
the other voice of rain.

Bios

Silas Ola Abayomi is a poet and historian. She uses poetry to create social change because of its value and power of influence.

Fatima Afshan is a teacher residing in Lucknow, India. She has also worked as an English Editor for Global Classroom Pvt Ltd. for some time where four of her poems were included in the textbooks meant for primary grades. She writes poetry in English, Hindi and Urdu languages. Her poems and stories have found a place in more than thirty national and international anthologies and magazines of great repute. She has recently won the 'Sanmati Young Talent Literary Award 2016' by Aagaman Group and 'Sahitya Gaurav -2016' by Yuva Utkarsh Sahitya Manch. She has co-edited a recent story book named 'Meri Kahani' by Lab Academia.

Vishal Ajmera is an Indian resident and Business Strategy consultant by profession. Over the years, Vishal has developed a penchant for poetry and has established himself as a successful poet cum lyrics writer; composing poetry across several genres and encapsulating various aspects of life from psychology, nature to imagery. With contributions in several international anthologies and magazine publications, his journey in the 'poetic world' continues unabated. Apart from poems, Vishal is an ardent music lover and plays guitar.

Joel Allegretti is the author of six collections of poetry, most recently *Platypus* (NYQ Books, 2017), and a novella, *Our Dolphin* (Thrice Publishing, 2016). He is the editor of *Rabbit Ears: TV Poems* (NYQ Books, 2015), the first anthology of poetry about the mass medium. Allegretti's poems have appeared in *Barrow Street, The New York Quarterly, PANK, Smartish Pace*, and many other national journals, as well as in journals published in Canada, the United Kingdom, Belgium, and India.

Khadija Anderson returned in 2008 to her native Los Angeles after 18 years exile in Seattle. Khadija's poetry has been published extensively online and in print and her poem *Islam for Americans* was nominated for a 2009 Pushcart Prize. Khadija holds an MFA in Creative Writing and her first book of poetry *History of Butoh* is available through Writ Large Press. She runs a monthly social justice themed reading series, Poets & Allies for Resistance, in Pasadena, CA.

Gus Andrews was born in Birmingham, Alabama and lived his youth in Cullman, Alabama. After high school he enlisted as an infantryman in the Army National Guard. Upon completing his training at Fort Benning, Georgia he enrolled at Spring Hill College in Mobile, Alabama where he plays rugby and pursues a bachelor's degree of Political Science and Law.

Fay Aoyagi is a bilingual haiku poet living in San Francisco.

Roger Aplon has had eleven books published: Ten of poetry (most recently *It's Only TV*) & one of prose: *Intimacies*. He's been awarded prizes & honors including an arts fellowship from the Helene Wurlitzer Foundation in Taos, New Mexico. After eight years in Barcelona, Spain, he now lives in Beacon, New York where he publishes the poetry magazine "Waymark" & is assembling *Mustering What's Left - New & Selected Poems* as well as a new collection: *Poetic Improvisations* after musical 'experiments' by composers such as John Adams, Elliot Carter, Miles Davis & John Zorn to name a few. Read and hear examples of his work at: www.rogeraplon.com

Susan Rose April lives in Maryland. She holds an MFA from Vermont College and degrees from the University of Chicago and the University of Massachusetts at Lowell. Her poetry has appeared in several journals and a collection has been published by Loom Press (French Class, 1999). Her poem, "this happened," really happened, as told to her by her father, a WWII Marine who was with the first U.S. detachments that landed at Nagasaki after the bomb.

Lauren Bagwell graduated with a Bachelor of Science in Secondary Education from Baylor University, where she now pursues her masters in Curriculum and Instruction. A spoken word artist, Lauren has competed in poetry slams at the local, regional, and national level. Her goal is to use poetry as a tool to revolutionize the way we think and interact with the world around us.

Jennifer Balachandran lives in Cincinnati with her two daughters, where she works with tax accountants, at a church, and as a freelance editor of scientific manuscripts. She has had work published in *Terminus, Gabby Journal,* and *Flycatcher.*

Carol Barrett teaches for the Humanities and Culture major at Union Institute & University, and the Creativity Studies program at Saybrook University. The recipient of an NEA fellowship in poetry, she holds doctorates in both Creative Writing and Clinical Psychology. Her books include the prize-winning *Calling In The Bones* from Ashland Poetry Press. Over 200 of her poems appear in such diverse magazines as JAMA, Poetry International, Nimrod, Christian Century, The Celibate Woman Journal, Poetry Northwest, The Beekeepers Journal and Climbing Magazine.

Anjana Basu is a writer based in Calcutta, India. She has 5 novels, a book of short stories and two anthologies of poetry to her credit. Her byline has appeared in *Vogue India, Conde Nast Traveller India,* and *India Today Travel Plus.*

A three-time Pushcart Prize nominee, **Lana Bella** is an author of three chapbooks, *Under My Dark* (Crisis Chronicles Press, 2016), *Adagio* (Finishing Line Press, 2016), and *Dear Suki: Letters* (Platypus 2412 Mini Chapbook Series, 2016), has had poetry and fiction featured with over 320 journals, *2River, California Quarterly, Chiron Review, Columbia Journal, Otoliths, Poetry Salzburg Review, San Pedro River Review, The Ilanot Review, Third Wednesday,* and *Tipton Poetry Journal,* among others. She resides in the US and the coastal town of Nha Trang, Vietnam, where she is a mom of two far-too-clever-frolicsome imps. https://www.facebook.com/Lana-Bella-789916711141831/

C. Wade Bentley lives, teaches, and writes in Salt Lake City. For a good time, he enjoys wandering the Wasatch Mountains and playing with his grandchildren. His poems have appeared or are forthcoming in *Green Mountains Review, Cimarron Review, Best New Poets, New Ohio Review, Western Humanities Review, Rattle, Chicago Quarterly Review, Raleigh Review, Reunion: The Dallas Review, Pembroke Magazine*, and *New Orleans Review*, among others. A full-length collection of his poems, *What Is Mine*, was published by Aldrich Press in January of 2015.

Larry Blazek was born in Northern Indiana, but moved to the southern part because the climate is more suited to cycling and the land is cheap. Blazek has been publishing the magazine-format collage "OPOSSUM HOLLER TAROT" since 1983. He could use some submissions. He has been published in the *The Bat Shat, Vox Poetica, Leveler Poetry, Five Fishes, Front* and *Mountain Focus Art*, among others.

Annette C. Boehm is author of *The Knowledge Weapon* (2016) and the chapbook *The Five Parts of Love - Confabulating Sappho* (2012). She serves as a poetry reader for *Memorious - A Journal of New Verse and Fiction* and is a graduate of the Center for Writers at the University of Southern Mississippi.

Heather Bourbeau's fiction and poetry have been published in 100 Word Story, *Alimentum, The Citron Review, Cleaver, Duende, Open City, The Stockholm Review of Literature*, and Tupelo Press. Her piece "Hopscotch" was nominated for a 2015 Pushcart Prize. She was a finalist for the Randall Jarrell Poetry Prize, a Tupelo Press 30/30 poet, and the winner of the Pisk! Poetry Slam. Her journalism has appeared in *The Economist, The Financial Times, Foreign Affairs, Foreign Policy* and *The New York Times*. She was a contributing writer to the *New York Times* bestseller, *Not On Our Watch: A Mission to End Genocide in Darfur and Beyond* with Don Cheadle and John Prendergast. She has worked with various United Nations agencies, including the UN peacekeeping mission in Liberia and UNICEF Somalia.

Jason Braun teaches English at Western Illinois University. He has published fiction, poetry, essays, reported or been featured in *Prime Number*, *ESPN*, *Squalorly*, *The Nashville City Paper*, *The Evergreen Review*, *Lowestoft Chronicle*, *The Riverfront Times*, *The Chronicle of Higher Education*, and many more. He also makes apps and music, which you can find out more about at: jasonandthebeast.com.

In August 2015 Alan Britt was invited by the Ecuadorian House of Culture Benjamín Carrión in Quito, Ecuador for the first cultural exchange of poets between Ecuador and the United States. During his visit he did TV, radio and newspaper interviews gave presentations and read poetry in Quito, Otavalo, Ambatto, Guayaquil and Guaranda, plus the international literary conference sponsored by *La hermandad de las palabras 2015* in Babahoyo. He served as judge for the *2013 The Bitter Oleander Press Library of Poetry Book Award*. He read poetry and presented the "Modern Trends in U.S. Poetry" at the *VII International Writers' Festival* in Val-David, Canada, May 2013. Recent readings include the *6x3 Exhibition* at the Jadite Gallery in Hell's Kitchen/ Manhattan in December 2014, the Fountain Street Fine Art Gallery in Framingham, MA in June 2014, and the Union City Museum of Art/William V. Musto Cultural Center in Union City, NJ sponsored by LaRuche Arts Contemporary Consortium (LRACC) in May, 2014. His interview at The Library of Congress for *The Poet and the Poem* aired on Pacifica Radio, January 2013. New interviews for *Lake City Lights* and *Schuylkill Valley Journal* are available at http://lakecitypoets.com/AlanBritt.html and www.svjlit.com/aninterviewwithalanbritt. His latest books include *Lost Among the Hours*: 2015, *Parabola Dreams* (with Silvia Scheibli): 2013 and *Alone with the Terrible Universe*: 2011. He teaches English/Creative Writing at Towson University.

Paul Brooke is the author of three full-length collections: *Light and Matter, Mediations on Egrets*, and *Sirens and Seriemas*. His work typically combines photography with poetry. He is a full professor of English at Grand View University in Des Moines, Iowa.

Heath Brougher is the new poetry editor of Five2One Magazine. He has published two books titled *A Drought of Ichor* and *2* (Green Panda Press). Brougher's work has appeared or is forthcoming in *Yellow Chair Review, Chiron Review, Mobius, Gold Dust Magazine, Main Street Rag, Gloom Cupboard, eFiction India, Dark Matter Journal, Third Wednesday*, and elsewhere.

Maureen Anne Browne is a member of Ards Writers and attends workshops at the Seamus Heaney Centre for Poetry, Queens University Belfast. She has read her poetry at The Festival of the Peninsula, Swaledale Festival, summer season at La Mon Hotel. She has had her work displayed in public places in Havant, won various prizes in competitions, been published in magazines *Writing Magazine, Orbis, Honest Ulsterman*, and is currently working towards her first collection.

Educator, lecturer, performance poet, eclectic thinker, mentor with staunch multi-cultural mindset and entrepreneurial attitude, **Anca Mihaela Bruma** considers herself a global citizen, having lived in four continents. Her eclecticism can be seen in her intertwined studies, she pursued: a Bachelor of Arts (Romania) and a Master of Business Administration (Australia).

Amy Brunvand is a librarian and part-time nature mystic in Salt Lake City, Utah where she writes regularly for "Catalyst" magazine, mostly about environmental issues and dancing. Her previous poems appear in *Canyon Country Zephyr, saltfront*, and *Dark Mountain*.

Dave Buracker is a Washington DC-area poet and visual artist. His work has appeared in various publications to include *The Amherst Review, William and Mary's The Gallery,* and most recently *Contraposition, Vox Poetica* and *Yellow Chair Review.* Dave also has released numerous dark electronic music albums under various monikers, such as Maduro and Darkened. His forthcoming book *The Upstairs Room* will be published by Shabda Press in 2017.

Don Kingfisher Campbell, MFA in Creative Writing from Antioch University Los Angeles, poetry editor of the *Angel City Review*, publisher of *Spectrum* and the *San Gabriel Valley Poetry Quarterly*, organizer of the San Gabriel Valley Poetry Festival, host of the Saturday Afternoon Poetry reading series in Pasadena, California. For awards, features, and publication credits, please go to: http://dkc1031.blogspot.com

Matthew David Campbell is the author of the poetry collection, Harmonious Anarchy; *Weasel Press 2016*, and the chapbook The House of Eros, *Red Ferret Press 2015*. His poems have appeared, among other places, in *Tight, Spires, Forklift Ohio*, and the anthology, *The Brink: Post Modern Poetry from 1965 to the Present*. He holds and MFA from Bennington College.

John Canaday's poems have appeared in *Poetry, The Paris Review, Slate, The Southern Review, Raritan, The Hudson Review, Poetry Daily, VQR*, and *The New Republic*, among other journals and anthologies. His first book of poems, *The Invisible World*, won the Walt Whitman Award from the Academy of American Poets. Canaday is also the author of a scholarly study, *The Nuclear Muse: Literature, Physics, and the First Atomic Bombs*.

Janet Cannon's poems have been published in the *Berkeley Poetry Review, G.W. Review, The Midwest Quarterly*, and *Texas Review*—among others. She is the author of two published chapbooks *The Last Night in New York* (Homeward Press), and *Percipience* (Cross Cut Saw Press, now CC. Marimbo). Janet has taught ESL at The New School in NYC, and community colleges in New York and New Mexico. She has been an editor at Scholastic Books, and a technical writer for several high-tech corporations. Janet is a graduate of the University of Iowa.

Fern G. Z. Carr is the President of Project Literacy, a lawyer, a teacher and past President of the Society for the Prevention of Cruelty to Animals. She is a Full Member of and former Poet-in-Residence for the League of Canadian Poets. Carr composes and translates poetry in six languages including Mandarin Chinese. A 2013 Pushcart Prize nominee, she has been published extensively world-wide from Finland to Mauritius. In addition to multiple prizes and awards, honours include being cited as a contributor to the Prakalpana Literary Movement in India; her poetry having been taught at West Virginia University and set to music by a Juno-nominated musician; an online feature in *The Globe and Mail,* Canada's national newspaper; and her poem, "I Am", chosen by the Parliamentary Poet Laureate as Poem of the Month for Canada. Carr is thrilled to have one of her poems presently orbiting the planet Mars aboard NASA'S MAVEN spacecraft. www.ferngzcarr.com

Yuan Changming, 8-time Pushcart nominee and author of five chapbooks, grew up in rural China, began to learn English at 19, and published monographs on translation before moving to Canada. Currently, Yuan edits *Poetry Pacific* with Allen Yuan in Vancouver, and has poetry appearing in *Best Canadian Poetry, BestNewPoemsOnline, Threepenny Review* and 1119 others across 37 countries.

Kelly Cherry is the author of 25 books, 10 chapbooks, and 2 translations of classical drama. Just published: *Quartet for J. Robert Oppenheimer: A Poem.* Richard Rhodes has said of this book, "No biography yet written comes even close to this elegant skein of poems in capturing his life and character." Her most recent fiction: *Twelve Women in a Country Called America: Stories.* Former PL of Virginia. Member, Poets Corner, Cathedral Church of St. John the Divine, NYC. NEA, USIA, Rockefeller, Bradley Lifetime Award, Weinstein Award, Phillabaum Award, others, and a residency at the Institute for Advanced Study in Princeton. Publication in prize anthologies. Eudora Welty Professor Emerita of English and Evjue-Bascom Professor Emerita in the Humanities, University of Wisconsin Madison. Eminent Scholar, UAH, 2001-2005. More info and details on Wikipedia / Kelly Cherry.

Teresa Mei Chuc was born in Saigon and immigrated to the U.S. under political asylum with her mother and brother shortly after the Vietnam War. Nominated for a Pushcart Prize in 2012, she is author of two full-length collections of poetry, *Red Thread* (Fithian Press, 2012) and *Keeper of the Winds* (FootHills Publishing, 2014), and her work is forthcoming in the anthology, *Inheriting* *the War: Poetry and Prose by Descendants of Vietnam Veterans and Refugees.* Her newest chapbook of poetry is *How One Loses Notes and Sounds* (Word Palace Press, 2016), and she is editor of the poetry anthology, *Nuclear Impact: Broken Atoms in Our Hands.* She is founder and Editor-in-Chief of Shabda Press, a member of Coast to Coast Poetry Press Collective. Teresa has a Masters in Fine Arts in Creative Writing from Goddard College and teaches literature and writing at a public high school in Los Angeles.

Margaret Chula has been writing, teaching, and publishing Japanese-genre poetry for thirty-five years. Her seven collections include, most recently, *Just This.* She's been a featured speaker and workshop leader at writers' conferences throughout the United States, as well as in Poland, Canada, and Japan. In 2010, she was appointed Poet Laureate for Friends of Chamber Music composing poems during concert performances. She also served as president of the Tanka Society of America from 2011-2015.

Jennifer Clark is the author of the full-length poetry collection, *Necessary Clearings* (Shabda Press). Her second poetry collection, *Johnny Appleseed: The Slice and Times of John Chapman*, is forthcoming from Shabda Press. Her work has been published in *Columbia Journal, Concho River Review, Flyway, Nimrod,* and *Ecotone*, among other places. She lives in Kalamazoo, Michigan.

Susan Deer Cloud, a mixed lineage Catskill Mountain Indian, was born not all that long after atom bombs were dropped on Hiroshima and Nagasaki. A pro-peace poet-activist, she has received many honors, including a National Endowment for the Arts Literature Fellowship, two New York State Foundation for the Arts Poetry Fellowships, and an Elizabeth George Foundation Grant. Published in numerous literary journals and anthologies, Deer Cloud's most recent books are *Before Language, Hunger Moon* and *Fox Mountain.*

Erin Rose Coffin is a Masters of Fine Arts candidate in poetry at North Carolina State University, and she lives in Raleigh, North Carolina with her fiancé.

Sharon Coleman is a fifth-generation Northern Californian with a penchant for learning languages and their entangled word roots. Her poetry and short fiction appears in *Ambush Review, Clade Song, Rivet, Tule Review, riverbabble, Berkeley Poetry Review*, and her chapbook is *Half Circle*. Her collection of blink fiction, *Paris Blinks*, will come out in February 2016 by Paper Press. She writes for *Poetry Flash* and teaches at Berkeley City College. She co-curates the reading series Lyrics & Dirges and co-directs the Berkeley Poetry Festival.

Esteban Colon is the author of *Things I Learned The Hard Way*, a full length collection of poetry by Plain View Press. His work has appeared in a variety of anthologies, journals, and chapbooks. He has been known to perform at live venues around the city of Chicago, and has become a huge fan of everyone who truly enjoys poetry.

Gonzalinho da Costa—a pen name—teaches at the Ateneo Graduate School of Business, Makati City, Philippines. He is a management research and communication consultant. A lover of world literature, he has completed three humanities degrees and writes poetry as a hobby.

Doren Damico is an artist, musician, educator and freelance writer based in Los Angeles, California. Her first book, *When You Can't Scream... Or 10 Reasons Why I Smoke*, includes poetry, photographs of women, and an intimate narrative that explores the complex journey of trauma, acceptance and healing. She has published poetry in several anthologies, the most recent: *Coiled Serpent: Poets Arising from the Cultural Quakes and Shifts of Los Angeles* (Tia Chuchas Press); and *2016 In The Words of Women International Anthology* (Yellow Chair Press). dorendamico.com

Ellie Danak is an Edinburgh based poet with a background in researching Swedish crime novels. Her poems have been published in a wide variety of anthologies and magazines. She is on the Scottish Book Trust's New Writers Awards 2016 shortlist.

Colin Dardis is a poet, editor and mental health advocate, based in Belfast, Northern Ireland. He is the founder of Poetry NI and an ACES (Artists Career Enhancement Scheme) '15-16 recipient from Arts Council Northern Ireland, supporting talented emerging artists in developing their careers. www.colindardispoet.co.uk

David Andre Davison has taught students in the USA, South Korea, China, and the Philippines. David has published children's stories and a poem in magazines located in Southeast Asia. He resides in the Philippines with his wife Amy, who is a chef.

Lucille Lang Day (http://lucillelangday.com) has published ten poetry collections and chapbooks, including most recently *Becoming an Ancestor* and *Dreaming of Sunflowers: Museum Poems,* which won the 2014 Blue Light Poetry Prize. She is also co-editor of the anthology *Red Indian Road West: Native American Poetry from California* as well as the author of a children's book, *Chain Letter,* and a memoir, *Married at Fourteen: A True Story,* which received a 2013 PEN Oakland Josephine Miles Literary Award and was a finalist for the Northern California Book Award in Creative Nonfiction. Her poems, short stories, and essays have received nine Pushcart Prize nominations and have appeared widely in magazines and anthologies. She lives in Oakland, California, with her husband, writer Richard Michael Levine.

Elizabeth DeBunce is a writer from Southern Oregon who is currently majoring in English and Classical Studies at Lewis & Clark College. She spends most of her free time sleeping in, listening to The Mountain Goats, and writing about eggs, whether metaphorically or not. Her work has previously appeared in *(parenthetical): the zine, The Gold Man Review,* and *The Timberline Review.*

Julian de Wette was born in South Africa, is a graduate of Sarah Lawrence College, Bronxville, NY, USA, worked for the United Nations in New York, London, Windhoek, Almaty, Geneva & Bonn. He has published poetry in various literary journals such as *Poetry Australia, New Coin (South Africa),* and *New Contrast, South Africa*. Penguin Random House, Cape Town, published his first novel, *A Case of Knives* (2010). He now divides his time between South Africa and France.

M. Iqbal Dhadhra grew up in a small village in the Punjab. His children's poems and songs have been published in a variety of international teaching newsletters. He teaches English, Life Skills and Social Entrepreneurship for Young People in a vocational institute working for poverty alleviation and rehabilitation of the poor in Narowal, Pakistan. He presents at national and international conferences.

Drew Dillhunt is author of *Leaf is All* (Bear Star Press), which won the 2015 Dorothy Brunsman Poetry Prize and was a finalist for the National Poetry Series. His writing has also appeared in *VOLT, Mudlark, Tarpaulin Sky,* and *Jacket2.* He's released two albums of songs, including one with the band Fighting Shy, and is currently a member of the Seattle-based band Answering Machines. He lives in the Beacon Hill neighborhood of Seattle, where he serves as the Associate Editor of Hummingbird Press.

Liz Dolan's first poetry collection, *They Abide,* was nominated for The Robert McGovern Prize, Ashland University. Her second, *A Secret of Long Life,* nominated for a Pushcart, has been published by Cave Moon Press. An eight-time Pushcart nominee and winner of Best of the Web, she was a finalist for Best of the Net 2014. She won The Nassau Prize for nonfiction and fiction.

Alex Dreppec (artist's name) - born 1968 close to Frankfurt as "Alexander Deppert," studied psychology and linguistics and went to Boulder/Colorado for his Ph.D. (finished 2001). German author with hundreds of publications (both poetry and science) in German journals and anthologies, both the most renowned ("Der große Conrady" - since 2008) and the best sold among them. "Wilhelm Busch" Prize 2004. Numerous English poems were accepted by *Borderlands Texas Poetry Review, Notre Dame Review, Parody on Impression, English Journal. National Council of Teachers of English* (USA), *Orbis, The Interpreter's House, The Journal* (UK) and others so far.

Alex Duensing, whose mother was one of the co-founder's of Vision of Peace, an organization that facilitated student art exchanges between the U.S. and the U.S.S.R in the 1980's, has been deeply concerned about nuclear weapons since childhood. They were his very real monsters under the bed. They were (and remain) the same for the rest of the world…if only we'd realize.

Leanne Dunic is a multidisciplinary artist and is the singer/guitarist for The Deep Cove. She is the author of a book of lyric-prose entitled *To Love the Coming End* (Chin Music Press).

R.G. Evans's books include *Overtipping the Ferryman* (2013 Aldrich Press Poetry Prize), *The Noise of Wings* (Red Dashboard, 2015) and *The Holy Both* (Main Street Rag Press, 2017). His original music has been featured in the poetry documentaries *All That Lies Between Us* and *Unburying Malcolm*. He teaches high school and college English and Creative Writing in southern New Jersey. www.rgevanswriter.com.

Beatriz Fitzgerald Fernandez's chapbook, *Shining from a Different Firmament* (Finishing Line Press, 2015), was featured at the Miami Book Fair International last year. She's a former grand prize winner of the Writer's Digest Poetry Award and had read her poetry on South Florida's NPR news station. Her work was chosen in a national competition for the *Arte Latino Now 2017* exhibit in Queens College, Charlotte.

Gretchen Fletcher was projected on the Jumbotron in Times Square as she read one of her poems that won the Poetry Society of America's Bright Lights/ Big Verse competition. She leads writing workshops for Florida Center for the Book, an affiliate of the Library of Congress. Her poetry is included in numerous journals and anthologies, and her chapbooks, *That Severed Cord* and *The Scent of Oranges* were published by Finishing Line Press.

Michael C. Ford has been publishing steadily, since 1970, and credited with over 28 volumes of print documents.. He's recorded approx. 60 spoken word tracks which include 4 solo documents, since 1983. His debut vinyl received a Grammy nomination in 1986 and his Selected Poems earned a Pulitzer nomination on the 1st ballot in 1998. Hen House Studios has been promoting and marketing his CD project *Look Each Other in the Ears [2014]*. That document in both vinyl and CD formats features a stellar band of musicians, not the least of which were surviving members of a 1960s theatre rock quartet most of you will remember as The Doors.

Trina Gaynon is a literacy tutor. Her poems appear *The Great Gatsby Anthology, The San Diego Poetry Annual, Saint Peter's B-list: Contemporary Poems Inspired by the Saints, Obsession: Sestinas for the 21st Century, A Ritual to Read Together: Poems in Conversation with William Stafford, Phoenix Rising from the Ashes: Anthology of Sonnets of the Early Third Millennium, Bombshells: War Stories and Poems by Women on the Homefront, Knocking at the Door: Poems about Approaching the Other*, and several WriteGirl anthologies, as well as numerous journals including *Natural Bridge, Reed* and the final issue of *Runes*. Her chapbook *An Alphabet of Romance* is available from Finishing Line Press.

Lind Grant-oyeye has work published in several literary magazines worldwide and recently won the UHRSN human rights poetry award.

Born in Philadelphia, **Mary Gilliland** resides in Ithaca, NY, where she has taught writing at Cornell University and at Namgyal Monastery Institute of Buddhist Studies, the Dalai Lama's seat in North America. Her poetry has appeared in numerous journals and been awarded prizes nationally and internationally, and she has been a featured poet at Al Jazeera's International Film Festival in Doha. Poems included here in *Nuclear Impact* are pages from Gilliland's book-length poem INTELLIGENCE OF THE WATER. More of her work can be found in such magazines as *AGNI, Hotel Amerika, Notre Dame Review, Poetry, Stand*, and *Tampa Review*.

Benjamin Goluboff teaches English at Lake Forest College. Aside from a modest list of scholarly publications, he has placed imaginative work – poetry, fiction, and essays – in numerous small-press journals, most recently

Four Ties Literary Review, Stoneboat, and *War Literature and the Arts.* Some of his work can be read at www.lakeforest.edu/academics/faculty/goluboff/

Howie Good's latest poetry collections are *Bad for the Heart* (Prolific Press) and *Dark Specks in a Blue Sky* (Another New Calligraphy). He is recipient of the 2015 Press Americana Prize for Poetry for his forthcoming collection *Dangerous Acts Starring Unstable Elements.*

Norbert Gora is a twenty-six-year-old poet and writer from Poland. Many of his horror, SF and romance short stories have been published in his home country. He is author of many poems in English-language poetry anthologies around the world.

Miriam Bird Greenberg is the recipient of fellowships from the NEA, the Poetry Foundation, and the Provincetown Fine Arts Work Center, and the author of In the Volcano's Mouth, which won the 2015 Agnes Lynch Starrett Prize from the University of Pittsburgh Press. A former Wallace Stegner Fellow, she lives in the San Francisco Bay Area, where for many years she collaboratively developed site-specific performances for very small audiences. She teaches creative writing and ESL, though she's also crossed the continent aboard freight trains, as a hitchhiker, and by bicycle. The daughter of a New York Jew and a goat-raising anthropologist involved in the back-to-the-land movement, she grew up on an organic farm in rural Texas. She's currently at work on a manuscript of ethnographically derived poetry about economic migrants and asylum seekers living in Hong Kong's Chungking Mansions.

Nels Hanson grew up on a small farm in the San Joaquin Valley of California and has worked as a farmer, teacher and contract writer/editor. His fiction received the San Francisco Foundation's James D. Phelan Award and Pushcart nominations in 2010, 12, and 2014. Poems appeared in Word Riot, Oklahoma Review, Pacific Review and other magazines and received a 2014 Pushcart nomination, Sharkpack Review's 2014 Prospero Prize, and 2015 and 2016 Best of the Net nominations.

Jared Harel was awarded the 2015 'Stanley Kunitz Memorial Prize' from the *American Poetry Review*. Additionally, his poems have appeared or are forthcoming in *Tin House, The Threepenny Review, The Southern Review, Poetry Ireland Review, Shenandoah and Ecotone*. A graduate of Cornell's MFA program, he lives in Queens, NY and plays drums for the twang-rock band, The Dust Engineers.

Gwendolyn Hart teaches writing at Buena Vista University in Storm Lake, Iowa. Her second poetry collection, *The Empress of Kisses*, won the 2015 X.J. Kennedy Award from Texas Review Press. Her first collection, *Lost and Found*, is available from David Robert Books.

Poet, educator and former journalist, **Kathleen Hellen** is the author of the award-winning collection *Umberto's Night* published by Washington Writers' Publishing House and two chapbooks, *The Girl Who Loved Mothra* and *Pentimento*. Her poems are widely published and have appeared or are forthcoming in the *Massachusetts Review, The Nation, North American Review, Poetry Northwest, Poetry Daily*, the *Sewanee Review, Southern Poetry Review*, and elsewhere. She has served as senior poetry editor for the *Baltimore Review* and now sits on the editorial board of Washington Writers' Publishing House and judges its annual poetry contest. Her book reviews have been published in several journals, including the *Baltimore Review* and *Oyster Boy Review*. A graduate of Carnegie Mellon University, she teaches creative writing in Baltimore.

Joseph Hess received his MA in Poetry from Miami University and his MFA from Ashland University. You can find his work in *Marathon Literary Review, The Ekphrastic Review and Lime Hawk Literary Arts Collective*. His personal website has access to more of his publications at: *jmhess.ink*.

Jennifer Highland's poems have appeared in *Cider Press Review, Heron Tree, Josephine Quarterly Quiddity, Atlanta Review*, and other magazines and anthologies. She practices osteopathy in a solar-powered office in central New Hampshire.

Elizabyth A. Hiscox is the author of the chapbook *Inventory from a One-Hour Room* (Finishing Line Press) and her poetry has appeared in journals such as *Asylum Lake, The Fiddlehead, Gargoyle, Gulf Coast,* and *Hayden's Ferry Review.* She holds an MFA from Arizona State University and a PhD from Western Michigan University where she has served as Managing Editor for *Third Coast* and Layout Editor at *New Issues Poetry & Prose Press.* She teaches creative writing at Western State Colorado University.

Trish Hopkinson has always loved words—in fact, her mother tells everyone she was born with a pen in her hand. She has two chapbooks *Emissions* and *Pieced Into Treetops* and has been published in several anthologies and literary magazines, including *The Found Poetry Review, Chagrin River Review,* and *The Fem.* Trish is co-founder of a local poetry group, Rock Canyon Poets. She is a project manager by profession and resides in Utah with her handsome husband and their two outstanding children. You can follow her poetry adventures at http://trishhopkinson.com/.

Juleigh Howard-Hobson's writing has appeared in many places, including *Fine Linen, Trinacria, Newtown Literary, The Raintown Review, Caduceus: The Poets at Art Place Vol 8* (Yale University), *Sweet Lemons 2: International Writings With A Sicilian Accent; Legas Sicilian Series Vol XIX* (Legas), *Poem, Revised: 54 Poems, Revisions, Discussions* (Marion Street Press), *Poets' Guide To New Hampshire* (NH State Poetry Society), and *Mandragora* (Scarlett Imprint), along with many other venues—both in print and in pixel.

Among various awards, Howard-Hobson is a Million Writers Award "Notable Story" writer, a *Predators and Editor's* top ten finisher (single poem), she was shortlisted for both the Morton Marr and the Angels and Devils Poetry Prize (Holland Park Press), and has been nominated for the Best of the Net and the Pushcart Prize. She served as assistant poetry editor at *Able Muse,* as well as moderator at *Mamaphonic.* Her fourth and most recent formal poetry collection is *Remind Me* (Ancient Cypress Press). She is currently a staff contributor (literary reviewer) for *Heathen Harvest*. Her writings are forthcoming in *The Absinthe Anthology* (Hyacinth Girls Press), a yet to be titled book of modern riddle poems edited by Kate Light, *Think Journal, GAMBAzine, Anima, The Raintown Review* and *War Literature and the Arts*.

Elizabeth Hoover's poetry has appeared in *Pank, The Pinch*, and *The Los Angeles Review*, among others. She recently received the Difficult Fruit Poetry Prize from *IthacaLit*. Her creative nonfiction has been published in *Lunch Ticket* and *StoryQuarterly*, as the winner of their 2015 essay prize. She is an independent writer living in Pittsburgh.

Marc Hudson wrote "An Anniversary Noted" in August 2015 while he was living in Santa Fe and thinking much about the 70th anniversaries of Hiroshima and Nagasaki, and the Manhattan Project. He is recently retired from Wabash College where he taught medieval studies and creative writing. His books of poetry are *Afterlight* (U. of Mass. Press, 1983), *Journal for an Injured Son* (Lockhart Press, 1985, 1992), and *The Disappearing Poet Blues* (Bucknell UP, 2002). His translation of *Beowulf* was published by Wordsworth Editions, Ltd. of the U.K. in 2007. His poems have recently appeared in *The Sewanee Review, The Silk Road Review, Poet Lore*, and *Christianity and Literature*. His new book of poems, *East of Sorrow*, was published early in 2017 by Red Mountain Press.

Mark Hudson is a poet and a short story writer who publishes poetry and short stories often. He has been published internationally in England, Canada, and India, to name a few. He also has had many publications in print ad on-line. You can find his poem on-line at illinoispoets.org.

Donald Illich has published poetry in *The Iowa Review, Fourteen Hills*, and *Cold Mountain Review*. He won Honorable Mention in the *Washington Prize* book contest and was a "Discovery"/*Boston Review* 2008 Poetry Contest semifinalist.

Lowell Jaeger is founding editor of Many Voices Press and editor of *New Poets of the American West*, an anthology of poets from western states. Lowell has taught writing classes at numerous conferences and workshops and is currently Professor of English/Creative Writing at Flathead Valley Community College (Kalispell, Montana), where he also serves as Humanities Division Chair. He is a graduate of the Iowa Writer's Workshop, winner of the Grolier Poetry Peace Prize, and recipient of fellowships from the National Endowment for the Arts and the Montana Arts Council. Lowell was awarded the Montana Governor's Humanities Award for his work in promoting civil civic discourse. He is the author of seven collections of poems, the most recent of which is *Or Maybe I Drift Off Alone* (Shabda Press 2016).

Richard Jarrette is the author of *Beso the Donkey* (MSU Press, 2010), Gold Medal Poetry Midwest Independent Publishers Association 2011, which has been translated into Chinese by Yun Wang, and *A Hundred Million Years of Nectar Dances* (Green Writers Press, 2015). He is also the author of *The Pond and The Beatitudes of Ekaterina* (Green Writers Press Fall 2017).

Hershman R. John is Navajo—born for the Deer Spring People and the Bitter Water People. He received his BA in English and MFA in Creative Writing, both from Arizona State University. He is a full time faculty member at Phoenix College. His works have been widely published: *Arizona Highways*, *Arizona Republic*, *Flyway-A Literary Review*, *Hayden's Ferry Review*, *Journal of Navajo Education*, *Puerto del Sol*, *Water-Stone Review*… The University of Arizona Press published his first collection of poems entitled, *I Swallow Turquoise for Courage*.

Hershman R. John: "From a tribal perspective, many Navajos and Hopis died working the uranium mines, without protective gear, without caution that uranium is dangerous, and those mines still affect the same indigenous people today."

Jen Karetnick is the author of three full-length books of poetry, including the forthcoming books *American Sentencing* (Winter Goose Publishing, May 2016) and *The Treasures That Prevail* (Whitepoint Press, September 2016), as well as four poetry chapbooks. She is the winner of the 2015 Anna Davidson Rosenberg Prize for Poetry. Her work has been published widely in journals including *Barrow Street, Cimarron Review, december, North American Review, Poet's Market 2013, Seneca Review, SLAB, Spillway, Spoon River Poetry Review* and *Valparaiso Poetry Review.* She works as the Creative Writing Director for Miami Arts Charter School and as an award-winning freelance dining critic, lifestyle journalist and cookbook author.

Sharon Kennedy-Nolle holds several M.F.A. degrees as well as a Ph.D. in Nineteenth-century American literature. Her poems have appeared in *The Dickinson Review, Arsenic Lobster, The Round, Juked,* and *The Lindenwood Review,* among others. She lives and teaches in New York.

Mariko Kitakubo has published five books of tanka including two bilingual ones, *On This Same Star* and *Cicada Forest.* She has also produced a CD of her tanka titled «Messages.» Her most recent book of tanka poetry is *Indigo* (Shabda Press, 2016). Mariko is an experienced performer who has presented her poetry on at least 130 occasions, 80 of them overseas (Nov. 2015). She hopes to encourage more poetry lovers worldwide to appreciate and practice tanka.

Abigail Carl-Klassen's work has appeared or is forthcoming in *Cimarron Review, Guernica: A Magazine of Art and Politics, Post Road* and *Huizache,* among others and is anthologized in *New Border Voices* (Texas A&M University Press), *Goodbye Mexico: Poems of Remembrance* (Texas Review Press) and *Outrage: A Protest Anthology for Injustice in a 9/11 World* (Slough Press). She won the Manitoba Magazine Publishers Association Award for Best Suite of Poems and was nominated for a Pushcart Prize and Best New Poets 2015. She earned an MFA from the University of Texas El Paso's Bilingual Creative Writing Program and taught at El Paso Community College and the University of Texas at El Paso.

Deborah P Kolodji moderates the Southern California Haiku Study Group and is the California Regional Coordinator for the Haiku Society of America. Former president of the Science Fiction Poetry Association, she has a degree in mathematics from the University of Southern California and was recently named to the Board of Directors of Haiku North America. With over 900 published poems to her name, and four chapbooks of poetry, *Seaside Moon* (2005), *Red Planet Dust* (2006), *unfinished book* (2006), and *Symphony of the Universe* (2006), she finds inspiration in the beaches, mountains, deserts, and urban life of LA County.

Cecele Allen Kraus's family moved to Richland, Washington in 1943. Her father worked at the Hanford Site, where uranium was processed to plutonium. Kraus published three chapbooks: *Dreaming Barranquilla* (Troy Bookmakers 2009), *Tuscaloosa Bypass* (Finishing Line Press 2012), and *Harmonica* (Liquid Light Press 2014). Her poems have appeared in *Naugatuck River Review, Up the River, Windfall, Chronogram, Literary Gazette, Backstreet,* and *riverbabble,* and in two chapbook anthologies, *Zephyrs* and *Java Wednesdays.*

Mark Labbe is a graduate from Stonehill College, where he received a BA in English Literature. He currently works for The Pilot, a newspaper in Boston, and has published a poem in *From the Depths,* a literary magazine put out by Haunted Water Press.

Tiffany Rose Naputi Lacsado is a daughter of Guam, a futurist, a graduate student entrepreneur at Meridian University in the Integral Master of Business Administration program and Certified Lactation Educator with the Marin County Women, Infants and Children's Program. Her writings have been published in the *Yellow Medicine Review, the Oakland Tribune* and the *Marin County Insider.* She resides with her loving partner and two small children, Buhay and Shola-Rita in Oakland, California.

Aaron Lee is a pilgrim poet, writing mentor, community organizer and regulatory/ethics lawyer based in Singapore. He is acknowledged to have played a key part in the late 1990s renaissance of Singapore poetry. His three books of poetry, including *Coastlands* published in 2014, are critically acclaimed and he has won many awards for his writing. He also edited several books, including the best-selling anthology *No Other City: the Ethos Anthology of Urban Poetry*. Lee's work is studied at schools and universities, and he is regularly invited to literary festivals all over the world. In 2014, he co-founded the Laniakea Culture Collective with his wife, the national artist Namiko Chan.

Nina Lewis is a poet based in Worcestershire. Her poetry is published in a range of anthologies and magazines, including Abridged, Under the Radar and Here Comes Everyone and online. Nina's Haiku poetry was used in an Art Installation at the MAC Arts Centre and her poetry was displayed on the Wenlock Poetry Trail. She was commissioned to write and perform at Birmingham Literature Festival in her first year of writing poetry. She is currently working on her first collection and in her spare time works with young writers for Writing West Midlands. https://awritersfountain. wordpress.com

M.S. Lyle hails from NJ and currently writes from Roswell, GA, a revived mill-town hugging her beloved Chattahoochee River north of Atlanta. She earned an M.F.A. in Creative Writing from Lesley University. You can find some of her work in *Iron Horse Literary Review, Lunch Ticket, Postcard Poems and Prose, Fried Chicken and Coffee* and *The Write Room*. She's currently furiously editing her first full-length poetry manuscript and working on a collection of travel essays. Oh, and daydreaming. Above all else, daydreaming – a skill she gives high regard to not only as a poet, but as a sentient being in general.

Shahé Mankerian's most recent manuscript, *History of Forgetfulness*, has been a finalist at four prestigious competitions: the 2013 Crab Orchard Series in Poetry Open Competition, the 2013 Bibby First Book Competition, the Quercus Review Press, Fall Poetry Book Award, 2013, and the 2014 White Pine Press Poetry Prize. His poems have appeared in *Mizna*.

Des Mannay has performed at 'Unity', 'Maindee', & 'Hub' Festivals, 'Stoke Newington Literature Festival',KAYA Festival of World Music & Arts, and Walls:Muriau - Welsh mental health arts festival. Supported 'Attila the Stockbroker' on the 'Arguments Yard' tour. Convener of 'Poets on The Picket Line - South Wales Chapter'.

"Focused on hard-hitting social issues… poems which made a statement" (Sabotage Reviews) Winner of 'Rethinkyourmind' poetry competition (2015). 2nd and highly commended in Disability Arts Cymru poetry Competition (2015). 'Gold Award' winner in Creative Futures Literary Awards (2015), shortlisted for erbacce-prize for poetry (2015, and 2016), Welsh Poetry Competition (2015), John Tripp and Idris Davies poetry competition 2016, and Disability Arts Cymru poetry Competition (2016).

Des' poems are published in 'I Am Not A Silent Poet' online journal, 'The Angry Manifesto', 'Proletarian Poetry', 'Yellow Chair Review', 'Indiana Voice Journal', 'Stand Up And Spit', 'Red Poets'.

Peter Marcus' first book *Dark Square* was published by Pleasure Boat Studio: A Literary Press (2012). His poems have appeared in *The Antioch Review, Boulevard, Crab Orchard Review, Nimrod, Poetry Ploughshares, RATTLE, The Southern Review Spillway, UPSTREET, Witness* and others. He has upcoming poems in *The Green Linden Review* and *Miramar*. He has been a recipient of a state of Connecticut Arts Grant and residency fellowships at Vermont Studio Center and at Marble House Project. He is the academic program coordinator at Elms College (Chicopee, MA) Accelerated Bachelor's Degree in Psychology Programs at Holyoke Community College and Mount Wachusetts Community College.

Four of **Alwyn Marriage's** nine published books are poetry collections and she is widely represented in magazines, anthologies and on-line. Her latest poetry collections are *'Touching earth', 'festo'* and *'Notes from a Camper van';* and her first novel, *Rapeseed*, was published in 2017 by Stairwell. Alwyn has been a university philosophy lecturer, Director of two international

NGOs, an international Rockefeller Scholar and Editor of a journal. She is currently Managing Editor of Oversteps Books and a research fellow at Surrey University, England.

Nate Maxson is the author of several collections of poetry including *The Age Of Jive* and *The Whisper Gallery*. He lives in Albuquerque, New Mexico.

Michael McLane runs literary programming for Utah Humanities and is the director of the Utah Humanities Book Festival. He holds an MFA in Creative Writing from Colorado State University and an MS in Environmental Humanities from the University of Utah. His chapbook, *Trace Elements*, was published by Elik Press in 2015. His poems, reviews, and essays have appeared, or are forthcoming, in numerous journals including *Western Humanities Review, High Country News, The Dark Mountain Project, Terrain.org, Denver Quarterly, Interim, Colorado Review*, and *Laurel Review*. He is an editor with *Sugar House Review* and is one of the founding editors of *saltfront*.

A resident of NY, **Stephen Mead** is a published artist, writer, maker of short-collage films and sound-collage downloads. If you are at all interested and get the time, Google Stephen Mead and the genres of either writing, art, or both, for links to his multi-media work.

Britt Melewski's poems have appeared in *Puerto del Sol, Sporkpress*, and *Prairie Schooner* among others. He curates the New York City-based reading series FREE WATER. Melewski received his MFA at Rutgers-Newark in 2012. He lives in Brooklyn.

Andrew Merton's poetry has appeared in *Bellevue Literary Review, Alaska Quarterly Review, The Rialto (U.K.), Comstock Review, Asheville Poetry Review, Louisville Review, The American Journal of Nursing*, and elsewhere. His first book of poetry, *Evidence that We Are Descended from Chairs*, with a foreword by Charles Simic (Accents Publishing, 2012) was named Outstanding Book of Poetry for 2013-2014 by the New Hampshire

Writers' Project. Accents Publishing released his second book, *Lost and Found*, in 2016. He is a professor emeritus of English at the University of New Hampshire.

Jennifer Met lives in a small town in North Idaho with her husband and children. Her poetry and hybrid nonfiction have appeared or are forthcoming in *Gulf Stream, Zone 3, Nimrod, Kestrel, Harpur Palate, Tinderbox Poetry Journal, Moon City Review, Juked, Sleet Magazine, pacificREVIEW, the Lake, Haibun Today*, and elsewhere. Her first chapbook is forthcoming from Glass Poetry Press. Nominated for a Pushcart Prize, a finalist for Nimrod's Pablo Neruda Prize for Poetry, and winner of the Jovanovich Award, she serves as Poetry Editor for the *Indianola Review*.

Brittany Mishra was born and raised in the Pacific Northwest in the shadow of Mt. Hood and Mt. St. Helens. She attended Portland State University and received a BA in English. She now lives in Connecticut with her husband.

Nilesh Mondal, 22, is an undergraduate in engineering and a poet by night. He works at Terribly Tiny Tales, an online storytelling platform.

Darren Morris has published poems at *The American Poetry Review, The Southern Review, New England Review, The Missouri Review, Best New Poets*, and many others. He lives in Richmond, Virginia.

Shelley Marie Motz writes about identity, social justice and the arts. Her work has been published most recently in *The Globe and Mail* and *The Timberline Review*. She lives on Canada's west coast on the unceded territory of the Songhees and Esquimalt First Nations.

Margaret S. Mullins lives in Baltimore, Maryland. She is the author of *Family Constellation* (Finishing Line Press), editor of *Manorborn 2009: The Water Issue* (Abecedarian Press) and a Pushcart Prize nominee. Her work has appeared in *Alehouse, Creekwalker, New Verse News, Loch Raven*

Review, Borderlands: Texas Poetry Review, The Sun, and *Writer's Almanac,* among others, and been read by Garrison Keillor on NPR.

Madhumitha Murali is an MBA Finance from Bangalore India. She has her Facebook blog- "Poems of Inspiration" on her recent poems. Apart from poetry and writing she likes traveling and pencil sketching.

Don Narkevic, Weston, WV, has an MFA from National University. His recent poetry has appeared in *Blue Collar Review, Off the Coast,* and *Kentucky Review.* His poetry chapbooks include *Laundry,* published in 2005 by Main Street Rag. Narkevic's plays have received readings in Chicago, New York, and Virginia. FutureCycle Press published *Admissions,* a book of poems, in 2013.

Aimee Noel is an educator and activist from Dayton. She is a proud coordinator for the VIDA's 2015 Count, working to highlight gender disparity in the literary landscape. Her essays and poems, infused with the lake water and steel of a childhood near Buffalo, have been published in journals such as *Great Lakes Review, The Greening Review,* and *Slippery Elm* and have been featured on WYSO, a local NPR affiliate. She earned her MFA from Lesley University, won Ohio Poetry Association's 2014 William Redding Poetry Prize, and has a serious crush on letterpress.

Jules Nyquist lives in Albuquerque, NM and is the founder of Jules' Poetry Playhouse, LLC. She leads creative writing classes and invites visiting poets to share their work. She took her MFA from Bennington College, VT and her second poetry collection, *Behind the Volcanoes,* was a finalist for the 2014 NM/AZ Book Awards. Her website is www.julesnyquist.com

Richard O'Connell lives in Deerfield Beach, Florida. Collections of his poetry include *RetroWorlds, Simulations, Voyages* and *The Bright Tower* (University of Salzburg). His poems have appeared in *The New Yorker, The Atlantic Monthly, National Review, The Paris Review, Acumen,* etc. His most recent collections are *Dawn Crossing* and *Waiting for the Terrorists.*

David Morgan O'Connor is from a small village on Lake Huron. After many nomadic years, he is based in Albuquerque, where a short story collection progresses. He contributors monthly to; *The Review Review* and New Pages. His writing has appeared in; *Barcelona Metropolitan, Collective Exiles, Across the Margin, Headland, Cecile's Writers, The Great American Lit Mag, Bohemia, Beechwood, Fiction Magazine, After the Pause, The Great American Lit Mag* (Pushcart nomination), *The New Quarterly* and *The Guardian*. Tweeting @dmoconnorwrites

Emmet O'Cuana is a freelance writer based in Melbourne Australia, originally from Ireland. O'cuana writes for *Hopscotch Friday*, a website and digital magazine covering all areas of pop culture. He has also written about cinema for *Filmink* magazine, *Crosslight* magazine and *Film International*. O'cuana previously had short fiction published in *Aurealis* magazine, short comics published in *Decay, Outré* (http://outrepress.com/?p=2102), and wrote the script for Dan Gilmore's creator-owned *Kunghur #1* (http://kunghur.com/). Samples of his writing can also be found here - http://tiny.cc/rc297x

Antony Owen was born in Coventry. He is the author of four poetry collections by *Heaventree, Pighog* and *Hesterglock Press*. His poems have been published worldwide in several literary journals including translated work in war poetry anthologies by *Poetry International* (Europe) and *Coal Sack Magazine* (Japan). His fifth collection will focus on the atomic bombings and will be published by V.Press.

Paul Lobo Portugés—reared in Merkel, West Texas, until saved by UCLA, the American Film Institute, and UC Berkeley. Teaches creative writing at UCSB. Taught creative writing at UC Berkeley, USC, SBCC, and the University of Provence. Proud father of two sons. Books include *The Visionary Poetics of Allen Ginsberg, Saving Grace, Hands Across the Earth, The Flower Vendor, Paper Song, Aztec Birth, The Body Electric Journal, The Silent Spring of Rachel Carson,* and *Mao*. Poems are scattered in small magazines across America. Received awards from the National Endowment, the Ford Foundation, the American Film Institute, The Rockefeller Foundation, and the Fulbright Commission.

Vivian Faith Prescott is a fifth generation Alaskan of Sámi heritage. She was born and raised in Wrangell, Alaska and lives in Wrangell at her family's fishcamp. She has an MFA from the University of Alaska and a Ph.D. in Cross Cultural Studies. Her poetry has appeared in *Drunken Boat*, *North American Review*, *Poecology* and elsewhere. She is the author of a full-length poetry collection, *The Hide of My Tongue*, and two poetry chapbooks.

Kara Provost has published two chapbooks, *Topless* (Main Street Rag 2011) and *Nests* (Finishing Line Press, 2006), in addition to six microchapbooks with the Origami Poems project (origamipoems.com). Her poems have appeared in the *Connecticut Review*, *Main Street Rag*, *The Newport Review*, *Ibbetson Street*, *Tar Wolf Review*, and other journals. Poetry by Kara can also be found in a number of anthologies, including *Shifts: An Anthology of Women's Growth through Change*; the Wickford Art Association 2013 exhibit catalog, *Poetry and Art*; *Lay Bare the Canvas: New England Poets on Art*; and *In Praise of Pedagogy: Poetry, Flash Fiction, and Essays on Composing*, edited by David Starkey and Wendy Bishop. Kara teaches writing and directs the Writing Center at Curry College in addition to conducting community creative writing workshops for elementary students through adults. Currently, she is working on a full-length poetry manuscript. Although she grew up in Florida, she now lives near Providence, RI with her husband and two daughters. You can reach her at kara.provost@curry.edu.

Phoebe Reeves earned her MFA at Sarah Lawrence College, and now teaches English at the University of Cincinnati's Clermont College in rural southern Ohio, where she advises *East Fork: An Online Journal of the Arts*. Her chapbook *The Lobes and Petals of the Inanimate* was published by Pecan Grove Press in 2009. Her poems have recently appeared in *The Gettysburg Review*, *Hayden's Ferry Review*, *Drunken Boat*, *failbetter*, and *Memorious*.

Thomas Gordon Reynolds is a Canadian writer who has been marginally published in journals (and one novella) and a chapbook. Retired, disabled, recently married late in life and, also recently, a human to three rescue dogs.

He lives a border city, formerly industrial, now on hard times. He writes as necessary, when possible, and to little noticeable effect.

William Pitt Root's recent collections are *Strange Angels: New Poems* and *Sublime Blue: Early Odes of Pablo Neruda.* C.K. Williams has said "Root's poems contain a kind of natural truth sorely lacking not only in contemporary poetry but in our lives." Naomi Shihab Nye has declared "Root's voice is sinew, blood, and bone—the well-muscled body carrying light—a gift of passion containing whole landscapes and legacies." Appearing in more than 100 anthologies and 300 literary magazines (*New Yorker, Atlantic Monthly, Poetry*), his work has received grants from the Guggenheim and Rockefeller foundations, National Endowment for the Arts, a Stegner Fellowship at Stanford, three Pushcarts, and so on. Translated into 20 languages, his poems also have been broadcast on *BBC* and *Voice of America.* Currently he is poetry editor of *CutThroat, a Journal of the Arts.*

K. D. Rose is a poet and author. K. D.'s book, Inside Sorrow, won Readers Favorite Silver Medal for Poetry. Her poetry, essays, and short stories have been published in *Word Riot, Chicago Literati, Poetry Breakfast, BlazeVOX Journal, Ink in Thirds, Stray Branch Magazine* and others. Publication is forthcoming in *Literary Orphans, Eastern Iowa Review, Santa Fe Literary Magazine, Northern Virginia Review, The 2016 Paragram Press Anthology,* and *The Nuclear Impact Anthology.* She also won an Honorable Mention in the *2016 New Millennium Writings Poetry Contest.* Her latest release is *Brevity of Twit.* She has a B.S. in Psychology and a Master's Degree in Social Work.

Phil Saint Denis Sanchez is originally from New Orleans. His work has appeared in *Voicemail Poems, Alien Mouth Journal, Origins Literary Journal, Reality Beach,* and *Sonic Boom Journal. It is forthcoming on Tinderbox Poetry Journal, Button Poetry,* and *Shabda Press.* He studied music theory and composition at The City College of New York. In addition to writing poetry, he produces and composes music that blends electronic forms, soul, turn-of-the-century classical, the samba rhythms he studied in Bahia, and the brass and marching band traditions of his hometown. He records under the name SaintDenisSanchez and currently resides in Brooklyn, NY.

Born in Pennsylvania, **David Anthony Sam** has written poetry for over 40 years. He lives in Virginia with his wife and life partner, Linda. Sam has three collections and was the featured poet in the Spring 2016 issue of *The Hurricane Review* and the inaugural issue of *Light: A Journal of Photography & Poetry*. His poetry has appeared in over 60 journals and publications. His chapbook *Finite to Fail: Poems after Dickinson* was the 2016 Grand Prize winner of GFT Press Chapbook Contest and his collection *All Night over Bones* received an Honorable Mention for the 2016 Homebound Poetry Prize. www.davidanthonysam.com

Credits:
In 2016, David's poems were accepted by *50 Haikus; Aji Magazine; Arlington Literary Journal; Dark Matter Journal; December; Dual Coast Magazine; Folia; GFT Press: Gravel; Heart & Mind Zine; Heron Tree; Hurricane Review; Inwood Indiana Magazine; Into the Void: Into the Void: Luminous Echoes: A Poetry Anthology; Jazz Cigarette; Light: A Journal of Photography and Poetry; Literature Today; Meat for Tea: The Valley Review; Poetry Quarterly; Red Earth Review; Red Savina Review; Route 7 Review; Rust + Moth; Shabda Press; Smoky Blue Literary and Arts Magazine; The Summerset Review; Tanka Journal; Touch: The Journal of Healing; Three Line Poetry; The Write Place at the Write Time; The Yellow Chair Review.*

Bonnie Shiffler-Olsen is co-founder of Rock Canyon Poets. Her work is featured in *Dialogue: A Journal of Mormon Thought, Outlet, new bourgeois, Touchstones Journal,* and elsewhere.

Michael Shorb was a poet, fiction writer, editor, and children's book author. As an international poet, his poetry has been published in more than 100 magazines and anthologies, including *Michigan Quarterly, The Nation, The Sun, Salzburg Poetry Review,* and *Kyoto Journal.* He was the recipient of a PEN AWARD, won a Merit Award for the Franklin-Christoph Poetry

Contest, and was nominated for a Pushcart Prize. He lived in and loved San Francisco. Michael succumbed to GIST, a rare form of cancer in 2012.

Michael Skau is an emeritus professor of English at the University of Nebraska at Omaha. He has published poems in *Carolina Quarterly, Northwest Review, Paintbrush, Kansas Quarterly, Laurel Review, Passaic Review, South Carolina Review, Hawai'i Review,* and *Texas Review,* among many others. He was named Winner of the 2013 William Kloefkorn Award for Excellence in Poetry, and his collection of poems, *Me & God,* was published by Wayne State College Press in 2014.

Martha Silano's most recent books are *Reckless Lovely, What the Truth Tastes Like,* and with Kelli Russell Agodon, *The Daily Poet: Day-By-Day Prompts For Your Writing Practice.* Martha edits *Crab Creek Review* and teaches at Bellevue College.

Born in Bridgeport, Connecticut, in 1944, **Claude Clayton Smith** grew up in nearby Stratford, where he graduated from Frank Scott Bunnell High School. He holds a BA from Wesleyan, an MAT from Yale, an MFA from the Writers' Workshop at the University of Iowa, and a DA from Carnegie-Mellon. He is the author of eight books, co-editor/translator of two others, plus a variety of short fiction, poetry, essays, and plays. In 2009 he moved to Madison, Wisconsin, with his wife Elaine, who has been his first reader and editor since their marriage in 1976. They have two adult sons. Besides reading and writing, his hobbies include fishing, golf, and softball. He was a licensed professional boxing judge in Ohio.

John Sokol writes and paints in Akron, OH. His paintings and drawings are included in many public and private collections. His poems have appeared in *The Berkeley Poetry Review, Georgetown Review, Literal Latte', Poet Lore,* and *Quarterly West,* among others. His short stories have appeared in *Akros, Descant, Mindscapes, The Pittsburgh Quarterly* and other journals. "In the Summer of Cancer" (poems), and "The Problem with Relativity" (short stories) are his latest books.

J. R. Solonche has been publishing in magazines, journals, and anthologies since the early 70s. He is the author of *Beautiful Day* (Deerbrook Editions), *Heart's Content* (Five Oaks Press), and co-author of *Peach Girl: Poems for a Chinese Daughter* (Grayson Books).

Harvey Preston Soss lives and works in Brownstone Brooklyn where he's been writing for three years now, having won Writer's Digest Writing Competition poetry awards in both 2015 and 2016. Two of his poems have been selected to be published in conjunction with the University of Canberra's Vice-chancellor's 2016 International Poetry Contest. Several others are presently awaiting publication here and abroad. This past January, he abandoned his law practice, primarily devoted to criminal defense of indigents, to write full-time.

Aline Soules' poetry has appeared in such publications as *100 Words, Literature of the Expanding Frontier, Kenyon Review, Houston Literary Review, Poetry Midwest, Long Story Short, Newport Review, Kaleidowhirl, Reed Magazine, Tattoo Highway,* and *Shaking Like a Mountain.* Her poetry chapbook, *Evening Sun: A Widow's Journey* (Andrew Benzie Books), and her full-length work of prose poetry and flash fiction, *Meditation on Woman* (Anaphora Literary Press), are available through Amazon. Follow her on Twitter (@aline_elisabeth) or visit her website/blog (http://alinesoules.com).

Steven Stam is an English Teacher, Writer, and Runner from Jacksonville, Florida where he lives with his wife Adriana and two small children. Steven tends to focus on his home of Florida and the oddities therein. In doing so, he writes primarily flash fiction, believing the model fits modern society's desire for instant gratification. His work can be found in *Fiction Southeast, Kudzu House Quarterly,* and *the Rappahannock Review,* among others.

Scott T. Starbuck's books are *Industrial Oz: Ecopoems* (Fomite, 2015), *Lost Salmon* (MoonPath, 2016), and the forthcoming *Hawk on Wire: Ecopoems* (Fomite, 2017) which is mainly about climate change. He was a Friends of William Stafford Scholar at the "Speak Truth to Power"

Fellowship of Reconciliation Seabeck Conference, an Artsmith Fellow on Orcas Island, writer-in-residence at the Sitka Center for Art and Ecology, and 2016 PLAYA climate change resident in poetry. His eco-blog, *Trees, Fish, and Dreams*, with audio poems is at riverseek.blogspot.com

Bekah Steimel is a poet aspiring to be a better poet. She lives in St. Louis, MO (USA) and can be found online at bekahsteimel.com and followed @ BekahSteimel.

Lisa Stice received a BA in English literature from Mesa State College (now Colorado Mesa University) and an MFA in creative writing and literary arts from the University of Alaska Anchorage. She taught high school for ten years and is now a military wife who lives in North Carolina with her husband, daughter and dog. She is the author of *Uniform* (Aldrich Press). You can find out more about her and her publications at lisastice.wordpress.com or facebook.com/LisaSticePoet.

Cheryl Stiles' poems and essays have appeared in *Poet Lore*, *Atlanta Review*, *Slant*, *32 Poems*, *Pilgrimage*, *Gargoyle*, *Southern Women's Review*, and other journals. Stiles works as a university librarian in the Atlanta area.

Marc Swan lives in Portland, Maine; poems recently published in *Poet Lore*, *Sheepshead Review*, *Gargoyle*, *Poetry NZ*, *Toad Suck Review*, *Westerly* (Aus), among others. Tall-lighthouse Press in London, England published his last two poetry collections: *In a Distinct Minor Key* (2007) and *Simple Distraction* (2009).

Laura Sweeney recently graduated from Iowa State University with a double master's degree in interdisciplinary social science and public administration, minors in English and Women's Studies, as well as certificates in Community Leadership and Social Justice.

Sweeney's ethnographic research and writing experience includes analyzing communication and decision-making strategies as the Rocky Flats

Environmental Technology Site (nuclear plutonium plant) moved towards its historic closure in 2005. To highlight the divergent perspectives of the sixty-one workers she interviewed, she excavated and juxtaposed narrative vignettes emerging from the abundant data. Her paper, 'The Rocky Flats Closure Project – Lessons Learned in Worker Stakeholder Engagement,' was presented at the 15th ICEM 2013 Conference in Brussels, Belgium.

Currently, Sweeney facilitates Writers for Life, which offers grant-funded creative writing workshops throughout central Iowa. She represented the Iowa Arts Council as a delegate to the First International Teaching Artist's Conference, in Oslo, Norway. Her publications include poems in *The Daily Palette, Poetica, Pilgrimage, Broad!, Appalachia, Evening Street Review, Negative Capability, Main Street Rag, Lyrical Iowa,* and the *Journal of Poetry Therapy.* Her essays have appeared in *The Good Men Project* and the anthology *Farmscape: The changing rural environment.*

Carl Wade Thompson is a poet and the graduate programs writing tutor at Texas Wesleyan University. His work has appeared in *The Concho River Review, The Mayo Review, The Enigmatist, The Blue Collar Review, Cenizo, Sheepshead Review, Anak Sastra,* and *Labor: Studies in Working-Class History of the Americas.*

J. C. Todd is a 2014 Pew Fellow in the Arts, a 2015 Alliance of Artists Residencies Fellow to Ucross, and a finalist for both the 2015 Robert H. Winner Award and the 2006 Lucille Medwick Memorial Award, from the Poetry Society of America. Publications include *FUBAR* (Lucia Press, March 2016), *What Space This Body* (Wind Publications, 2008) and two chapbooks, with poems and translations in *The Paris Review, American Poetry Review, Cleaver, Crab Orchard Review, Referential,* and others, and in anthologies, including *New European Poets* and *50 Over 50.* Fellowships and awards include those from the Pennsylvania Council on the Arts, Leeway Foundation, Hambidge Center, Virginia Center for the Creative Arts, Ragdale Foundation, Baltic Centre for Writers and Translators in Sweden and VCCA's international artist exchange to the Artists' House at Schloss Wiepersdorf in Germany.

She is on the faculty of the Creative Writing Program at Bryn Mawr College and the MFA Program at Rosemont, near Philadelphia, Pennsylvania.

Rodney Torreson served from 2007-2010 as poet laureate of Grand Rapids, Michigan. He is the author of four books, his most recent being *The Secrets of Fieldwork*, a chapbook of poems published by Finishing Line Press in 2010. His two full-length books are *A Breathable Light* (New Issues Press) and *The Ripening of Pinstripes: Called Shots on the New York Yankees* (Story Line Press). His poems have also appeared in such places as *The Seattle Review*, *Poet Lore*, *Spillway* and Ted Kooser's national newspaper column, *American Life in Poetry*.

Tom Tracey (b.1980) holds a DPhil in English from St. John's College, Oxford, where he was a Prendergast Scholar and twice won the Mapleton-Bree Prize for Creative Arts. He has published a number of scholarly essays on the work of David Foster Wallace and has also conducted social policy research on behalf of *Seanad Éireann* (the Irish Senate). His poems have appeared in several international publications including *Agenda's* online Broadsheet 23 (2014) and *Oxford Poetry* (2008). In 2016, his work featured in the *GFT Press*, *Cardiff Review*, *The Menteur*, *The Ofi Press*, and the *Rat's Ass Review*. He lives and teaches in his hometown, Dublin, where he occasionally writes for the *Dublin Review of Books*.

Jonathan Travelstead served in the Air Force National Guard for six years as a firefighter and currently works as a full-time firefighter for the city of Murphysboro. Having finished his MFA at Southern Illinois University of Carbondale, he now works on an old dirt-bike he hopes will one day get him to the salt flats of Bolivia. He has published work in *The Iowa Review*, on Poetrydaily.com, and has work forthcoming in *The Crab Orchard Review*, among others. His first collection *How We Bury Our Dead* (Cobalt/Thumbnail Press) was released in March, 2015.

Mark J. Tully is a community organizer and playback theatre guy.

Julie Thi Underhill is an interdisciplinary artist, scholar, and activist based in Berkeley, California. Her creative work includes photography, film/video, performance, painting, poetry, and memoir essay. Her scholarship centers the Chăm population as she investigates how historical memories of genocide, colonialism, and war continue to impact this little-known community native to Việt Nam. As a delegate, Julie has spoken twice at the United Nations Human Rights Council in Geneva, Switzerland, on behalf of women's rights, religious freedom, and continued survival for the Chăm in Việt Nam. She also campaigns against nuclear power plant construction near Chăm populations in Việt Nam. Julie holds interdisciplinary degrees from The Evergreen State College (B.A., Liberal Arts) and UC Berkeley (M.A., Ethnic Studies). She has published in *Troubling Borders: An Anthology of Art and Literature by Southeast Asian Women in the Diaspora*; *Completely Mixed Up: Mixed Heritage Asian North American Writing and Art*; *TrenchArt Monographs: hurry up please its time*; *Veterans of War, Veterans of Peace*; *Embodying Asian/American Sexualities*; *Takin' It to the Streets: A Sixties Reader*; *ColorLines*; and *Hayden's Ferry Review*. She lectures at California College of the Arts and San Francisco State University. Her website is jthiunderhill.com.

Political activist and wilderness advocate, **Pam Uschuk** has howled out six books of poems, including *Crazy Love*, winner of a 2010 American Book Award, *Finding Peaches in the Desert* (Tucson/Pima Literature Award), and *Wild in the Plaza of Memory* (2012). A new collection of poems, *Blood Flower*, appeared in 2015. Translated into more than a dozen languages, her work appears in over three hundred journals and anthologies worldwide, including *Poetry, Ploughshares, Agni Review, Parnassus Review, etc.* Uschuk has been awarded the 2011 War Poetry Prize from *WINNING WRITERS*, 2010 *New Millennium* Poetry Prize, 2010 Best of the Web, the Struga International Poetry Prize (for a theme poem), the Dorothy Daniels Writing Award from the National League of American PEN Women, the King's English Poetry Prize and prizes from *Ascent, Iris,* and AMNESTY INTERNATIONAL.

Associate Professor of Creative Writing and Editor-In-Chief of *CUTTHROAT, A JOURNAL OF THE ARTS*, Uschuk lives in Bayfield, Colorado and in

Tucson, Arizona. Uschuk is often a featured writer at the Prague Summer Programs, teaches workshops at the University of Arizona Poetry Center and was the 2011 John C. Hodges Visiting Writer at University of Tennessee, Knoxville. She's finishing work on a multi-genre book called *The Book of Healers Healing: An Odyssey Through Ovarian Cancer* as well as editing the anthology, *Truth To Power: Writers Respond to the Rhetoric of Hate and Fear.*

Amy Uyematsu is a Japanese-American poet and teacher from Los Angeles. She has five published collections: *Basic Vocabulary* (Red Hen Press, 2016), *The Yellow Door* (Red Hen, 2015), *Stone Bow Prayer* (Copper Canyon Press, 2005), *Nights of Fire, Nights of Rain* (Story Line Press, 1998), and *30 Miles from J-Town* (Story Line, 1992). Amy was co-editor of the widely used anthology, *Roots: An Asian American Reader* (UCLA, 1971). Now retired, she was a Los Angeles Unified Schools high school math instructor for 32 years. She currently teaches a writing workshop in Little Tokyo.

Richard Vargas was born in Compton, CA, attended schools in Compton, Lynwood, and Paramount. He earned his B.A. at Cal State University, Long Beach, where he studied under Gerald Locklin and Richard Lee. He edited/ published five issues of *The Tequila Review*, 1978-1980. His first book, *McLife*, was featured on Garrison Keillor's Writer's Almanac, in February, 2006. A second book, *American Jesus*, was published by Tia Chucha Press, 2007. His third book, *Guernica, revisited*, was published April 2014, by Press 53. (Once again, a poem from the book was featured on Writer's Almanac, to kick off National Poetry Month.) Vargas received his MFA from the University of New Mexico, 2010. He was recipient of the 2011 Taos Summer Writers' Conference's Hispanic Writer Award, was on the faculty of the 2012 10th National Latino Writers Conference and facilitated a workshop at the 2015 Taos Summer Writers' Conference. He has read his poetry to audiences in Los Angeles, Chicago, Madison, Albuquerque/ Santa Fe, Indianapolis, and Boulder. Currently, he resides in Rockford, IL, where he edits/publishes *The Más Tequila Review.*

Emily Walling's visual and written work can be found in journals such as *Apeiron Review, The Caribbean Writer, Cactus Heart, The MacGuffin,* and upcoming in *Riding Light Review* and *Eureka Literary Magazine*. Her creative work is about the physical, emotional, and psychological connections people have with nature. Emily is working on a master's degree in rhetoric and writing.

Poet and cosmologist **Yun Wang** grew up in rural southwest China. She began writing poetry when she was 12, and majored in Physics at Tsinghua University when she was 16. She came to the U.S. for graduate school in Physics in 1985. She is the author of two poetry books, *The Book of Totality* (Salmon Poetry Press, 2015) and *The Book of Jade* (Story Line Press, 2002), Winner of the 15th Nicholas Roerich Poetry Prize. Her two poetry chapbooks are *Horse by the Mountain Stream* (Word Palace Press, 2016) and *The Carp* (Bull Thistle Press, 1994). Wang's book of poetry translations is *Dreaming of Fallen Blossoms: Tune Poems of Su Dong-Po* (White Pine Press, 2018). Wang's poems have been published in numerous literary journals, including *The Kenyon Review, Cimarron Review, Salamander Magazine, Green Mountains Review,* and *International Quarterly*. Her translations of classical Chinese poetry have been published in *Poetry Canada Review, Willow Springs, Connotation Press,* and elsewhere. Wang is a Senior Research Scientist at California Institute of Technology. She is the author of the cosmology graduate textbook, *Dark Energy* (Wiley/VCH, 2010). She was elected a Fellow of the American Physical Society in 2012.

Karen Warinsky was a finalist in the 2013 Montreal International Poetry Contest and a semi-finalist in 2011. The top 50 poems were published in an anthology by Véhicule Press. Two of her poems appear in the book *Joy Interrupted*, an anthology on motherhood, and most recently a memoir about her grandmother was published in the book *Dear Nana*, (both books available through Amazon). Ms. Warinsky teaches high school English in Massachusetts.

Michael Waterson grew up in Pittsburgh, PA and has lived in Northern California for more than 40 years. He is a retired journalist and poet laureate emeritus of the Napa Valley. He holds a BA from San Francisco State University and an MFA from Mills College, both in Creative Writing.

Laura Madeline Wiseman's recent books are *An Apparently Impossible Adventure* (BlazeVOX Books), *Wake* (Aldrich Press), and *Leaves of Absence* (Red Dashboard). She teaches in Nebraska. Her collaborative book *Intimates and Fools* (Les Femmes Folles) with artist Sally Brown Deskins, is an Honor Book for the 2015 Nebraska Book Award. Her essay on long distance cycling "Seven Cities of Good" is an honorable mention for the *Pacifica Literary Review*'s 2015 Creative Nonfiction Award.

Miriam Weinstein's poems appear in numerous journals including *Evening Street Review, Snow Jewel, The Quotable*, an anthology by Holy! Cow Press, and in a forthcoming anthology by Red Bird Press. Her chapbook *Twenty Ways of Looking* by Finishing Line Press will be released in Summer 2017. She completed a two year apprenticeship program in poetry at the Loft Literary Center in Minneapolis. Growing up in during the Cold War deeply impacted Weinstein's life.

Sarah Brown Weitzman, a Pushcart Prize nominee, has been widely published in hundreds of journals and anthologies including *The North American Review, Miramar, New Ohio Review, Thema, Rattle, Mid-American Review, Poet Lore, The Bellingham Review, Ekphrasis, Spillway*, etc. Sarah received a Fellowship from the National Endowment for the Arts. A departure from poetry, her fourth book *Herman and the Ice Witch*, is a children's novel published by Main Street Rag.

Rae Wick currently has a humor blog being optioned by ABC Studios, has been published in *Chicken Soup For The Soul* and many poetry/ non-fiction mags. She is a longtime advocate for the appreciation of diversity and civic engagement, and is finishing her Master's Degree in clinical mental health counseling.

Daryll Michael Williams is a twenty-one-year-old communications student born and raised in Cape Town, South Africa. His poem "the dead tree gives no shelter" references T.S Eliot's 'The Waste Land' in the title and body.

Karl Williams has published two books with leaders in the self-advocacy movement (the civil rights work of people with intellectual disabilities); his prose and lyrics and poems have been published in magazines and journals and books; his recordings have been used in videos, on websites, and on the stage. Songs from Williams' six CDs have aired on NBC, Fox, cable, public television, and on German TV, as well as on SIRIUS and on earth-bound radio stations around the world.

Kath Abela Wilson travels to math and music conferences with her mathematician-historical flute player husband Rick Wilson who accompanies her performances. Her *Poets on Site* write, perform and workshop in gardens, galleries, and home salons near Caltech in Pasadena. She hosts *Poetry Corner* for *ColoradoBlvd.net* and is secretary of *Tanka Society of America*. She loves playing percussion, tambura, dancing, singing, Asian poetry, free verse, making books, and publishing in international anthologies and journals.

Mantz Yorke lives in Manchester, England. His poems have appeared in a number of print magazines, anthologies and e-magazines in the UK, Ireland, Israel, Canada, the US and Hong Kong.

Peggy Zabicki is a published author of many nature themed poems. She lives and works in Chicago and is inspired by sunrises over Lake Michigan and people at play in the parks, which are scattered through the city.

Sally Zakariya's poems have appeared in 50-some print and online journals. She is the author, most recently, of *When You Escape* (Five Oaks Press, 2016), as well as *Insectomania* (2013) and *Arithmetic and other verses* (2011), and the editor of a poetry anthology, *Joys of the Table* (2015). Zakariya blogs at www.butdoesitrhyme.com.

Acknowledgments

"The Pedestal" by Elizabyth A. Hiscox : *Gulf Coast: A Journal of Literature and Fine Art*

"Across the Mountain" by Alwyn Marriage: *Touching earth* by Alwyn Marriage (Oversteps Books, 2007)

"After the Bomb I," "After the Bomb XIV," "After the Bomb XXIV" by Michael Skau: "After the Bomb XXIV," was published in *Sequoia 33.1* (Summer 1989)

"Atomic Agatha" by Alex Dreppec: Holly Harwood (ed.): *Words Fly Away - Poems for Fukushima* (Green Wind Press, 2014)

"Critical Mass" by Jennifer Highland: *Critical Mass* (2015)

"Ernesto de Fiori's 'Soldier'" by Lowell Jaeger: Grolier Poetry Peace Prize – selected by Denise Levertov, 1987

"Fifth Grade Air Raid Drill, 1955" by Andrew Merton: *Lost and Found*

"David Nicodemus" by John Canaday: *The Bulletin of the Atomic Scientists*

"Edith Warner" by John Canaday: *At Length Magazine* and *Filling the Hole in the Nuclear Future: Art and Popular Culture in Response to the Atomic Bomb in the US and Japan*, ed. by Robert Jacobs (Hiroshima Peace Institute and Rowman & Littlefield, 2010)

"Future Tense" by Aaron Lee: *Five Right Angles* (Ethos Books, Singapore 2007)

"Genesis Revisited: The Chernobyl Buffalo" by Pamela Uschuk: *Poems & Plays: Last Call* and *Blood Flower* (Wings Press 2015)

"Of Simple Intent" by Pamela Uschuk: *Without Birds, Without Flowers, Without Trees* (Flume Press Chapbook Prize, 1990)

"Rafting the River of Death" by Pamela Uschuk: from *Crazy Love* (Wings Press, 2010)

"hail to the jellyfish" by Janet Cannon: *Rochester Peace and Justice Education Center Publication*, No. 154

"Hiroshima is a Name We Don't Know Yet" by Sarah Brown Weitzman: *Transnational Magazine*, Vol. 3, 2015

"'Hiroshima!' I Cried" by Joel Allegretti: *Nerve Lantern: Axon of Performance Literature*

"Imagining Peace, August 1945" by J.C. Todd: *Paterson Literary Review*

"Inundation," by Margaret Chula: Friends of Chamber Music Concert Program, 2013.

"Untitled," by Margaret Chula: Third Place Winner Yuki Teikei Haiku Contest, 2012

"scintigraphy" by Kath Abela Wilson: *The Atomic Era* online Special Feature, Atlas Poetica, ed Don Miller

"Hiroshima Day" by Kath Abela Wilson: *Fire in the Treetops: Celebrating Twenty-Five Years of Haiku North America*, ed Michael Dylan Welch

"nuclear family" by Kath Abela Wilson: *but for their voices* ed . Carolyn Hall, Two Autumns Press, Haiku Posts of Northern CA, 2015 "precipice" by Kath Abela Wilson: *Books and Coffee* on the Art of Susan Dobay, Poets on Site, 2010

"Inside the Atomic Clock" by Kath Abela Wilson: *Totem* Caltech Literary Journal 2013

"Recollection" by Kath Abela Wilson: *On Expressions and Interpretations of Manzanar,* Poets on Site, 2008

"Curtis LeMay Plans to Strike First" by Benjamin Goluboff: *Kentucky Review*

"Lightning in a Bottle" by C. Wade Bentley: *New Orleans Review*

"Litany" by Michael McLane: from *Trace Elements: Mapping the Great Basin & its Peripheries* (Elik Press)

"Lucky Ones" by Alan Britt: *Levure Littéraire #10*, France-USA-Germany

"Lullaby" by Michael McLane: *Otis Nebula*

"The Globe in Nuclear Claws" by M. Iqbal Dhadhra: *Newsletter of Global Issues Special Interest Group*, (January 2008, Issue 22)

"Emma Goldman Falls in Love (with Tolstoy) at the End of the World" by Abigail Carl-Klassen: Matter (2016)

"Fallout" by Jennifer Met: *Moon City Review*

"No-Go-Zone" by Jennifer Met: *pacificREVIEW,* 2015

"Cold Angels" by Sharon Coleman: *riverbabble*

"first snow after the end of the world" by Sharon Coleman: *Silences*

"Three Haiku/Senryu" by Fay Aoyagi: *In Borrowed Shoes* (Blue Willow Press, 2006), *The Heron's Nest*, (Volume X, Number 4, December 2008), *Beyond The Reach of My Chopsticks* (Blue Willow Press, 2011)

"Shock and Awe" by Abigail Carl-Klassen: *491 Magazine* (2012)

"Beso's Dust" by Richard Jarrette: from *Beso the Donkey* (MSU PRESS, 2010)

"The Sea Duck" by Richard Jarrette: from *A Hundred Million Years of Nectar Dances* (Green Writers Press, 2015), previously published *Water Stone Review #15* (Jane Kenyon Prize finalist)

"To a Sacred Statue" by Richard Jarrette: from *A Hundred Million Years of Nectar Dances* (Green Writers Press, 2015)

"Trees with No Branches/Flowers with No Names" by Kathleen Hellen: *Sunrise from Blue Thunder*, a Pirene's Fountain Anthology

"Pictures in Bufano's Garden" by Kathleen Hellen: *Sycamore Review*

"Bonsai" by Kathleen Hellen: *Sunrise from Blue Thunder*, a Pirene's Fountain Anthology

"Chernobyl Undone" by Fern G. Z. Carr: *new contrast*, 2009, Cape Town, South Africa

"In the Beginning" by Fern G. Z. Carr: *Poetry USA*, 2005, San Francisco, California

"Wild Asparagus" by Cecele Allen Kraus: *Windfall*, 2008 (a different version of poem)

"Hanford Works" by Cecele Allen Kraus: *Liquid Light Press* (2014): *"Hanford Works"* as part of a poem entitled "Pinetucky Baptist Singing School," in the chapbook, *Harmonica* by Cecele Allen Kraus

"The Homemaker's Rain Dance", "This Outdated Future" and "Greater Noctule" by Annette C. Boehm are taken from *The Knowledge Weapon* (Bare Fiction Press, 2016)

"The Product is Safe" by Lucille Lang Day: from *The Curvature of Blue: Poems* (Červená Barva Press, 2009) by Lucille Lang Day. First published in *New Zoo Poetry Review*

"Where the Radiation Goes" by Lucille Lang Day: *Canary*

"Fear of Science" by Lucille Lang Day: from *Infinities: Poems* (Cedar Hill Publications, 2002) by Lucille Lang Day. First Prize, Janice Farrell Poetry Contest, 2007.

"October '62" by Rodney Torreson: *The Windless Orchard*

"Party Boy" by Jules Nyquist: New Mexico Humanities Council "now See Hear" project

"Planet Called Earth" by Alan Britt: *Levure Littéraire #10*, France-USA-Germany

"Preemptive Strike" by Nate Maxson: *Empty Mirror*, 2015 and *The Whisper Gallery*, LitFest Press

"Rocket Science" by Nate Maxson: *Empty Mirror*, 2015 and *The Whisper Gallery*, LitFest Press

"Godzilla" by Richard Vargas: *McLife* (Main Street Rag Press, 2005)

"Digger Troll" by Laura Madeline Wiseman: *Gingerbread House*, 2016

"portrait of a nuclear family" by Janet Cannon: *Peace or Perish: A Crisis Anthology, Poets for Peace*

"Prisoners of War, 1956" by John Sokol: *SLANT, XIII*, 1999, Conway, Arkansas

"Thoughts Near the Close of Millennium" by John Sokol: *Quarterly West, #41*

"Tonight I believe" by Bekah Steimel: *Subterranean Quarterly*, 2013

"The Homeless Hires of Fukushima" by Heather Bourbeau: *A Quiet Courage*, December 2015

"The Next State" by Trish Hopkinson: *The Day After by Art Access & Utah Campaign to Abolish Nuclear Weapons*, August 2015

"Denial" by Trish Hopkinson: a found poem from *A Chorus of Stones* by Susan Griffin, chapter 1, pgs. 3-17. Originally published by *The Fem*. June 25, 2015. Online.

"The Bright Side of Nuclear Winter" by Jared Harel: *Prairie Fire Magazine*

"The Committee for the Restoration and Display of the Enola Gay" by Don Narkevic: *Rain Dog Review*, 1995

"The Point of No Return" by Beatriz Fitzgerald Fernandez: *Spark: A Creative Anthology*

"the price of nuclear energy" by Alwyn Marriage: *Sunrise from Blue Thunder* (Pirene's Fountain, 2011)

"Theory of Light" by Hershman R. John: *I Swallow Turquoise for Courage* (Tucson: The University of Arizona Press, 2007)

"Trinity" by Richard O'Connell: *National Review*

"Fifties Blues" by Roger Aplon: *TULE Review*, Fall 2013

"Desert Landscape: Roots Clouds & Water" by Roger Aplon: *By Dawn's Early Light At 120 Miles per Hour* (Dryad Press – 198)

"Chernobyl Necklace" by Teresa Mei Chuc : *Poet Lore*, Volume 111 Number ¾

"Love After Fukushima" by Teresa Mei Chuc was published in *La Bloga: Floricanto for Fukushima*, in *Spectrum 3: LoveLoveLove*, in *Truth to Power (Cutthroat: A Journal of the Arts)* and in *Keeper of the Winds* (FootHills Publishing).

"Baking Uranium" by Aimee Noel: *Great Lakes Review*, Issue 4, 2014

"Calculating Exposure" by Aimee Noel: *Great Lakes Review*, Issue 4, 2014

"Nagasaki" by Maureen Anne Browne: *Baskalier Publishing*, 2010

"Elegy to a Shrine" by Bonnie Shiffler-Olsen: *The Day After*

"Chernobyl Spring" by Michael Shorb: *Whale Walker's Morning* (Shabda Press, 2013)

"The Anti-Tyger" by J.R. Solonche: *Dark Matter: A Journal of Speculative Writing*

"Tonight I Believe" by Bekah Steimel: *Subterranean Quarterly, 2013*

"the statisticians keep on counting" by Colin Dardis: *The Spleen*, issue one, Dec '10

"We Knew Nothing Then" by Miriam Bird Greenberg was published online at *Killing the Buddha* for the week of May 28, 2009. "After All This" and

"Utopia" by Miriam Bird Greenberg appeared in the chapbook *All night in the new country*, published by Sixteen Rivers Press in September 2013

"Variations on a Theme by Shinoe Shōda" by Darren Morris: Collaborators and co-translators - Ami Hagiwara, Department of Global and International Studies, University of Northern British Columbia and Jeremy D. Schmidt.

Darren Morris: "The poems included in "Variations on a Theme by Shinoe Shōda" are not pure translations of Shinoe Shōda's work, with which I take great liberties. They are interpretations, or response poems written "after" the original subject, setting, and sense. In rewriting them, I wanted to call attention to her self-published book of tanka form, *Sange*, from which they were taken, written and distributed in 1947, secretly, under U.S. occupation and strict censorship after the war. Shōda lived through the atomic bombing of Hiroshima, which the poems describe. A second remaining copy of *Sange* was recently discovered and donated to the Hiroshima Peace Memorial Museum."

"Dreamscape" by Yun Wang: from *The Book of Totality* (Salmon Poetry Press, 2015) by Yun Wang, first published in *FutureCycle Poetry*

"Futurescape" by Yun Wang: from *The Book of Totality* (Salmon Poetry Press, 2015) by Yun Wang, first published in *FutureCycle Poetry*

"Mad Princes" by Michael Waterson: *Soundings Review*, a publication of Northwest Institute of Literary Arts.

"'Hiroshima!' I Cried" by Joel Allegretti, first published in *Nerve Lantern: Axon of Performance Literature*

"Attempt" by Elizabeth Hoover: *Rattle*

"My Last Journey" by Des Mannay is based on a line drawing, which bears the caption "Two feet of a victim whose body vanished in a single puff; they stood upright, stuck to the concrete road", in Kenzaburo Oe's Hiroshima Notes (Tokyo, YMCA press, 1981). He used both the picture and caption as a prompt.

"Dead Dolphins" by Des Mannay is based on a news story of Dolphin's bodies being washed up on the beach near Fukushima; found with radiation on their lungs.

"The Ruination" by Des Mannay is based loosely on the concept S A J Bradley's translation of the Anglo-Saxon poem "The Ruin" from 'The Exeter Book' in Anglo-Saxon Poetry (London, J M Dent & Sons Ltd 1991 edn). Mannay's is based on the hypothetical discovery of post-apocalyptic ruins.

"After Fukushima" (a tanka sequence) by Mariko Kitakubo: Some parts of the sequence first appeared in *Rattle*, assisted by Kath Abela Wilson.

Excerpt from "Basic Vocabulary" by Amy Uyematsu: This is a long 35-part anti-war poem in Uyematsu's latest book, *Basic Vocabulary* (Red Hen Press, 2016).

"Standing on This Flat Earth" by Esteban Colon first appeared in Issue 3 of Siren.

"After Us" by Esteban Colon first appeared in the chap book "Between Two Lines" from Exact Change Press.

"On Facing Miro's "Tete" by Lowell Jaeger appeared in *Poetry Northwest*

"Nothing Lasts Forever" by Lowell Jaeger appeared in *Trestle Creek Review*

"Ants" by Lowell Jaeger appeared in *Canary*

"Troll Ashes" by Laura Madeline Wiseman: The Crawl Space, Issue 1, May 2016

"In the Wake of Nuclear Testing in India and Pakistan 1998" by Matthew David Campbell: From Harmonious Anarchy (Weasel Press, 2016).

"Living At The End Of Time" by Karl Williams (Greene Street Records, 1985 & 1999) from the album of the same name available at http://www.cdbaby.com/cd/karlwilliams3

"Napali" by Scott T. Starbuck: *Particles on the Wall* website and *Antinuclear Shows*

"At the Nevada Nuclear Test Site" by Scott T. Starbuck: *Green Fuse,* the chapbook *The Eyes of Those Who Broke Free* (Pudding House Publications, 2000), and in *Industrial Oz: Ecopoems* (Fomite, 2015)

"Plutonium Fish" by Scott T. Starbuck: *Cement Squeeze,* the chapbook *The Eyes of Those Who Broke Free* (Pudding House Publications, 2000), *Industrial Oz: Ecopoems* (Fomite, 2015), and *Fresh Water: Poems from the Rivers, Lakes, and Streams* (Pudding House Publications, 2002)

"Here — for the moment" and "Twenty ways of looking at my life" were first published by Finishing Line Press in Miriam Weinstein's chapbook *Twenty Ways of Looking.*

"Plastic #7 [Teflon]" by Drew Dillhunt first appeared in *Leaf is All* (Bear Star, 2015)

"Helen of Bikini" by Phoebe Reeves, *Eureka Literary Magazine,* Summer 2015.

Index

555

CPSIA information can be obtained
at www.ICGtesting.com
Printed in the USA
FFOW02n2316230417
34868FF